Constructing the Nation

SUNY series, Philosophy and Race

Robert Bernasconi and T. Denean Sharpley-Whiting, editors

Constructing the Nation

A Race and Nationalism Reader

Edited by
Mariana Ortega
and
Linda Martín Alcoff

Cover art: painting entitled Virgen de las Calles, pastel on paper, © Ester Hernandez; collection of Sandra Cisneros

Published by State University of New York Press, Albany

Printed in the United States of America

For information, contact State University of New York Press, Albany, NY
www.sunypress.edu

Production by Diane Ganeles
Marketing by Anne M. Valentine

Library of Congress Cataloging-in-Publication Data

Constructing the nation : a race and nationalism reader / edited by Mariana Ortega and Linda Martín Alcoff.
p. cm. — (SUNY series, Philosophy and race)
Includes bibliographical references and index.
ISBN 978-1-4384-2847-5 (hardcover : alk. paper) — ISBN 978-1-4384-2848-2 (pbk. : alk. paper)
1. Nationalism—United States—History. 2. Race relations—United States—History. 3. Group identity—United States—History. I. Ortega, Mariana. II. Alcoff, Linda.
E169.1.C7154 2009
305.800973—dc22

2008055626

10 9 8 7 6 5 4 3 2 1

To our parents

Contents

Acknowledgments

We would like to thank Nicolás Leon Ruiz for editorial assistance and Sarah McGrath for preparing the index.

INTRODUCTION
The Race of Nationalism

Mariana Ortega and Linda Martín Alcoff

> In a world of nation-states, nationalism cannot be confined to the peripheries. That might be conceded, but still it might be objected that nationalism only strikes the established nation-states on special occasions. Crises, such as the Falklands or Gulf Wars, infect a sore spot, causing bodily fevers: the symptoms are an inflamed rhetoric and an outbreak of ensigns. But the irruption soon dies down; the temperature passes; the flags are rolled up; and, then, it is business as usual.
>
> —Michael Billig, *Banal Nationalism*

THE MOMENTOUS EVENT that we have come to identify simply as "9/11" is still a "sore spot" that has not healed in the body-politic of the United States. It manifests itself in a variety of symptoms, such as delights in (and demands for) regular and excessive patriotic displays, a persisting paranoia about the "other" lurking within our midst, unceasing military violence against the enemy abroad, and acceptance of the "necessity" of torture—all for the sake of freedom, unity, and the homeland. Nationalism is, as Billig put it, "banal"; it is an everyday habit and the nation's "endemic condition."[1] But it also swells at moments of crisis and is politically exploited by varied political actors. Recall Joan Didion's comment that 9/11 "had been seized—even as the less nimble among us were still trying to assimilate it—to stake new ground in old domestic wars."[2] Not to mention the foreign wars that have already claimed the lives of untold numbers.

In the aftermath of 9/11, even after the flags have been rolled up, as Hurricane Katrina challenged the myth of racial equality in the nation, and as the election of President Obama opened new political possibilities, the United States continues to be in a color-coded alert, at war with an amorphously defined global "terror," and still pushing its version of democracy abroad. Less overt is the project of self-rejuvenation it pursues simultaneously—however quixotic and desperate—in the hope of attaining again the moral vanguard it achieved after World War II. The United States wants once again to feel morally righteous so that it can unite the population against the new evil—this time the evil of the "axis of terror." The evil outside cannot be vanquished by a divided, demoralized, and dissipated nation. Indeed, as Samuel P. Huntington argued in his role as consultant to the Trilateral Commission, the real threat to the survival of Western culture comes from within, from a politicized, increasingly diverse electorate full of ungrateful immigrants who reject assimilation and deny the unity of American identity, the homogeneity of Western culture, and the moral superiority of the United States.[3] For many who think like Huntington, 9/11 was a wake-up call that the internal threat to national unity can no longer be tolerated; thus the agitation over "illegals" has increased, no matter what part of the world they come from.

It is clearly a mistake to overplay the events of 9/11 or regard them as vicious attacks against a free, exceptional, benign nation. Far from new to U.S. soil, terrorism was the ordinary condition of life endured by African Americans who grew up under Jim Crow, and attacks on this scale are hardly unfamiliar in the world at large.[4] Still, whether it is seen as a sign of an autoimmune disorder, as Derrida has claimed,[5] or as an unbelievable, unforeseen, undeserved assault against an innocent nation, 9/11 remains a watershed moment in shifting the imaginary of U.S. nationhood, profoundly affecting countless individual lives as well as the social and political status of various ethnic groups for years to come. It thus remains a rich, discursive text that can be read as a complex and contradictory document about the cultural terrain from which U.S. nationalism constructs itself.

As Mindy Peden reminds us in her chapter in this volume, nations are not constructed ex nihilo but out of a preexisting cultural terrain. Nation-states sometimes have the earmarks of voluntary associations, and their laws of inclusion and exclusion—especially where there is a version of representative democracy—mimic the idea of a collective, intentional act of self-creation. In this way, nations are often contrasted with ethnic groups on the basis of their foundation in voluntary, intentional, and rule-governed practices, as against ethnic groups that are imagined to grow more organically and that develop their associated cultural practices in more arbitrary and less rational ways.[6] Yet voluntariness and intentionality are neither exhaustive nor particularly descriptive of the truth about how contemporary nations have been constructed, or how their boundaries are in reality managed. Applying for the famous "green card" in the United States, for example, which is a key instance of border control marking the boundaries of the nation, is a Kafkaesque process in which the criteria are never fully explained and the end point can keep receding in the distance for decades. Rather than rational or deliberate, the process is influenced by ideological distortions of one's country of origin and tribal prejudices against one's race or ethnicity. Individual applicants find themselves arbitrarily interpellated as insiders or outsiders, as credentialed professionals or unskilled workers, as safe bets to become loyal and hardworking or as more likely to become a burden or a threat. Stigmatized groups—such as those from countries marked as "evil" or just viewed as "backward"—find it nearly impossible to alter their ideological representation or, as a result, their political status.

When an event like 9/11 occurs, the social hierarchy of marginalized groups gets quickly shifted about with profound effects on individual lives. Aaron McGruder, writer of the comic strip *Boondocks*, famously celebrated this shift for African Americans with his Huey character chanting gleefully "We're number 2!" Muslims, Arabs, and South Asians looking like Arabs quickly became the most vilified minorities in the United States, this in a country whose majority population has such a scant knowledge of world geography that a dangerously large and loose category of potential hate-crime victims was quickly created. In upstate New York, for example, a Sikh temple was burned to the ground by teenagers who mistook turban-wearing Sikhs for Muslims and assumed that the name of the Temple, Gobind Sadan, was a pro-Bin Laden slogan. Hate crimes as well as the practices of Homeland Security are less a rational response to real threats than a prompt, and alibi, for preexisting cultural chauvinisms and varied racisms. Stephen Sondheim's succinct claim is still correct that "it's okay to be in America if you're a white in America," but there have been shifting configurations of who is acceptable and who is not among the nonwhites in America.

Whether from misinformed teenagers or the federal government, responses to 9/11 reveal that the dividing line between "nation," "ethnic group," "race," and "culture" begin to disappear when we look at the reality, as opposed to the idealization, of nationalism. In light of this fact, we set out in the turbulent period after 9/11 to collect a volume of theoretical analyses about the intersection between race and nationalism that would critique this culture's conflation of race and national identity, a conflation that became increasingly overt as the number of victims increased, the lost were not found, and the pain, the anger, and the flags multiplied. In particular, we wanted contributors to address the following questions: What does it mean today to be an "American" when one does not represent or embody the norm of "Americanness" because of one's race, ethnicity, culture of origin, religion, or some combination of these? What is the norm of "Americanness" today, how has it changed, and how pluralistic is it in reality? We offer this volume of chapters not as a reading of 9/11 or a cultural study of the United States, but as a theoretical response and rumination on the political and cultural context of the nationalism we have all experienced since that time—from the pro-war students in our classrooms who mistake good citizenship with the refusal to consider critiques of the nation, to the daily barrage of a xenophobic media that encourages American exceptionalism and its false protestations of innocence in a sea of global corruption.

It is our view that philosophers and social theorists need a better understanding of the shifting terrain of the national political imaginary. The discourses of philosophy and social theory need to consider the real-world conditions of normative concepts and categories such as "rights," "freedom," "citizenship," "unity," and, as Monique Roelofs's chapter included in this volume shows, "aesthetic value." These topics should no longer be broached in abstract or ahistorical terms, as if unmediated by racial identity or culture or unmarked by their moment in history. This collection of chapters is meant to be a contribution toward a corrective of the tendencies toward unreflective abstractions about concepts of the nation, showcasing theoretical work that does not erase or pretend to transcend its context. If we want to analyze nationalism as a norm governing individual practices, assessing its meaning as well as its political effects, we must analyze it in the discrete and specific particularity of its (ever-shifting) context. This approach will show in particular, we believe, that in order to understand the cultural conditions of nationalism in the context of the United States today, the conditions that have forged the specific form of nationalism that we are experiencing as well as the variety of forms it can take, we must address the constitutive role played by race and ethnicity as well as other vectors of social identity (e.g., and especially, religion) in the construction of the imaginary community of the United States. As Peden puts it, riffing Stuart Hall, race is "the idiom through which the nation is subjectively experienced."

Importantly, it is no coincidence that both of the editors of this volume are from Central America (Nicaragua and Panama)—a region that has suffered more from U.S. military interventions than anywhere else in the world with the exception of Southeast Asia. Both of us are in the United States today in part because of a confluence of transnational relations that evolved from these military actions, including covert operations, neocolonial dependence, and full-scale invasions. Although we have indeed found shelter here, it remains difficult as Central Americans by birth to adopt without ambivalence the embrace of the "colossus of the North," no matter how welcoming. The different analyses of the intertwining of race/culture/ethnicity and U.S. nationalism provided in this volume are contributions by various theorists and scholars who, like us, are culturally marginal within the United States and who thus might notice more than others—if one follows standpoint theory—the cultural imprint that affects the political debates about immigration, about rights, about security, and about whether torture is truly "American." Coming from Lebanon, India, Colombia, the Netherlands, Argentina, Iran, and numerous minoritized communities within the United States, the authors here offer critical yet nuanced analyses of the intersections of race and nationalism that are rarely visible in the mainstream.

We now turn to the three central areas by which the chapters in this volume have been organized: freedom, unity, and homeland. These are surely three of the most powerful tropes deployed to construct, revitalize, and maintain U.S. national identity and nationalistic practices in a period of heightened alert and fear of terror. The chapters here provide pointed critical analyses of these ideas as tropes but also as sets of practices, as normative ideals, and as embedded within political theories and institutions. They also make pointed but constructive suggestions about how to improve our national culture.

Freedom

> History has not revealed a deeper irony than the destruction of the spirit of democratic liberty in the name of devotion to it, which we have witnessed in this nation in the past five years.
>
> —Reinhold Niebuhr, *The Irony of American History*

In the first chapter, "Cultural Affirmation, Power, and Dissent: Two Mid-century U.S. Debates," Elizabeth Kassab explores the concept of freedom as manifested in U.S. cultural self-understanding and national identity during the 1947 Inter-American Congress of Philosophy and the 1952 *Partisan Review* symposium "Our Country and Our Culture." Kassab's historical exploration into the philosophical reflections on the relationship between nation and culture at two important moments—after the war and at the onset of McCarthyism—reveal the growing pains of a nation that was still insecure about its global position, but that had nonetheless adopted the task of becoming the new world leader with the responsibility to guard democracy from the threat of internal and external communism after the collapse of Europe. Through her analysis of an earlier period of nationalist self-consciousness, Kassab reveals a striking similarity between these discussions regarding freedom, power, leadership, nationalism, and dissent, and discussions in the aftermath of 9/11—thus she begins her chapter with Niebuhr's quote, as his comment is as relevant today as it was in 1952.

Yet this striking repetition underscores how diminished our current climate of dissent and critique has become while the sense of amnesia and a belief in the fundamental innocence of the nation lives on. In the earlier period, there was a surprising reflexivity by philosophers of that generation about the relationship of nation to culture; they seemed to recognize that the United States' new postwar status in the world would inevitably affect its humanistic disciplines. Following through on this idea, Kassab presses us to consider how North American philosophy itself is affected by its context, not just as a global leader, but as the leading *imperial* nation. Her chapter thus invites us to wonder, if nationalism is built out of a preexisting cultural terrain, what of philosophy? Surely it is plausible, and not a vulgarity of reductionism, to argue that the United States' changing position in the global political economy since World War II has affected its growing disallegiance from European philosophy, and has enhanced its ability to overcome its previous cultural insecurity vis-à-vis the superiority of "old" Europe. If this seems clear enough, what other internal movements within philosophy as it is done in the United States are also affected by the shifts of cultural position? To paraphrase from one of the United States' more influential "epistemologists" (Donald Rumsfeld), what else do we not know that we do not know?

It is precisely the notion of a contrived innocence—innocence in the sense of infantilization and an inability to engage in judgment, reflection, and critique—that is explored by Kyoo Lee in chapter 2, "When Fear Interferes with Freedom: Infantilization of the American Public Seen through the Lens of Post–9/11 Literature for Children." Lee provides a critique of post–9/11 U.S. culture by way of an examination of children's post–9/11 literature as an allegorical mirror that reflects the nationalistic re-*bildung*, the ideological and homogenizing project of educating U.S. youth not to ask questions and thus remain innocent. Lee shows that when fear interferes with the process of growth and maturation—the process of becoming a self-reflective being—the necessity for comfort and protection from those dark "others" inside and outside our borders whose motives remain opaque to us begins to dominate other impulses. Thus, the national project of bildung spills into a "color education" that, while pretending to offer a multicultural approach and a respect for all colors, neatly divides the nation into a simplistic black and white binary of "'they' who terrorize versus 'we' who are terrified." Lee's chapter recalls Susan Sontag's declaration regarding the suffering of others: "No one after a certain age has the right to this kind of innocence, of superficiality, to this degree of ignorance, or amnesia."[7]

In "Muslim Women and the Rhetoric of Freedom" (chapter 3), Alia Al-Saji explores how the binary logic of "us and them" works through constructions of "oppressed" and "liberated" women. Al-Saji's chapter exposes the gendered and racialized dimensions of a national discourse that calls for the freedom of the oppressed veiled Muslim woman. The appeal for the liberation of the oppressed feminine other is part and parcel of a discourse that requires a representation of a fundamentalist and oppressed other in order to forge a representation of a politically enlightened, culturally unified United States. The liberation of the veiled Muslim woman thus symbolizes not only the liberation of women from oppressive masculinist forces but also serves to reinforce the idea that Islam is intrinsically and irrevocably fundamentalist. Al-Saji further shows how the veiled woman suffers from a double othering as she becomes other both to enlightened Western men and to liberated Western women; she is the other as a Muslim and also she is the other as an oppressed woman without the "freedom" (or coercion) to bare her body in public. Her veil itself becomes racialized, essentialized, and ultimately reduced to a metonym for Islam and the oppression of women. In revealing the structures that sustain the Western representations of the veiled Muslim woman, Al-Saji exposes how Western feminist discourses can fall into the trap of "cultural racism" and neocolonialism, paradoxically in the name of freedom. The discourse of feminism itself can all too easily be recuperated by both American exceptionalism and U.S. imperialism when it assumes decontextualized concepts of freedom and of embodiment.

Unity

> "United We Stand" brings me no comfort. . . . "United" since when? For what cause? Under whose terms? I feel a moral obligation to grieve the tragic loss of human life at the same time that I denounce the multifaceted political reality leading up to this horrible (inter)national tragedy. In doing so, I am brought back to one elemental truth about cultural memory: it can become what we need it to be in times of incomprehensible suffering—part reality and part fiction, depending on memory's most familiar tropes of race, gender, and nationhood.
>
> —Chana Kai Lee, "Memories in the Making and Other National Fictions"

This section starts with María Lugones's and Joshua M. Price's "Faith in Unity: The Nationalist Erasure of Multiplicity" (chapter 4) a moving reflection on patriotic unity prompted by 9/11, Hurricane Katrina, and the May 1, 2006, immigrant marches, three key events that manifest the intertwining of race and nationalism. Lugones and Price make a connection between post–9/11 practices to achieve patriotic unity—such as "the war on terror," militarization of the border, the USA PATRIOT Act, and new forms of racial profiling—and "cognitive practices" of what they term "structural monoculturalism" that call for certainty, simplicity, unity, and compromise and that privilege Eurocentric knowledge and languages. Lugones and Price are particularly interested in the recent shift in structural monoculturalism from (supposedly) rational negotiations that aim for compromise to the establishment of dogmatic claims by way of faith, which they see as signaling a shift toward a process of conversion in which American unity is achieved through the identification with a politicized conservative Christianity. This new monoculturalism, according to Lugones and Price, further strengthens certainty and simplicity through faith while construing alternative accounts of the world as invalid and unimportant, and even dangerous and antagonistic. From the perspective of this new, simplified version of monoculturalism, structural multiculturalism begins to appear to be "nonsensical, impossible, chaotic, politically suspicious, and divisive" and the hard-won cultural support for multiculturalism is eroded.

Multiculturalism itself in its various U.S. incarnations looks woefully inadequate from the perspective of the rich debates currently going on by postcolonial theorists in Latin America, who are introducing the idea of *interculturalidad*: an ongoing counterhegemonic process in which, in Catherine Walsh's words, as quoted by Lugones and Price, there is a "reciprocal translation of knowledges in the plural." Against the "juxtaposed silos" imagery of multiculturalism, this idea foregrounds the mutual exchange *and change* that occurs when cultural variety is actually valued. In light of this, Lugones and Price call for an epistemological shift toward a multivoiced solidarity in place of a univocal simplicity, a solidarity exemplified by the heterogeneity of the participants in the May 1, 2006, pro-immigrant marches. They also call for a non-ornamental multiculturalism and *interculturalidad* that will be respectful of plural epistemologies and the epistemic privilege of those whose knowledge has been subordinated.

While Lugones and Price concentrate on the cognitive practices of structural monoculturalism that foster patriotic unity, in "Muslim Immigrants in Post–9/11 American Politics: The 'Exception' Population as an Intrinsic Element of American Liberalism" (chapter 5), Falguni A. Sheth emphasizes the role played by the American political ideology of liberalism in maintaining unity. Liberal, democratic societies create unity, Sheth argues, by creating an exception population that is subject to the law but not legally entitled to its protections and rights. She shows how in the aftermath of 9/11 Muslims have become this exception population. According to Sheth, the process of outcasting a particular population is dependent on a dual (ontological and normative) interpretation of the term "person," which in turn leads to a vacillating interpretation of constitutional protections of human rights. In an analysis of American immigration law, Sheth shows how a "legal person" is understood not just as a human but as a "human-like-us," and how constitutional rights are selectively interpreted as natural or inalienable rights only for members of the group. Since Muslims are not deemed "human-like-us," they are consequently not worthy of constitutional rights. According to Sheth, liberalism's appeal to universal rights and equal protection paradoxically works to legally and politically segregate particular populations that threaten the cultural homogeneity and political unity of the United States. In this way, liberalism's pluralist ideal of equality has managed to coexist with a long practice of very divergent treatment for "exception populations."

Sheth wonders productively if we can anticipate the warning signs of U.S. liberalism's tendency to create exceptions to the rule of equality under the law and fair treatment. But she plausibly maintains that the material problems of exclusion and abjection cannot be solved at a metalevel or simply by tweaking the terms of liberal political theory. The construction of exception populations is not ultimately caused by an inadequate theory, and therefore it cannot be decisively avoided by a theoretical maneuver. Sheth's analysis suggests that there is no avoidance of contextual analysis and public debate over specifics, such as the specifics of the political implications of Islam, of Christianity, or of fundamentalism in any form.

Mindy Peden revisits this tendency of the United States to claim unity while at the same time being exclusionary when she recalls Frederick Douglass's words: "Fellow citizens, above your national, tumultuous joy, I hear the mournful wail of millions! . . . What, to the American slave, is your 4th of July?" In "Situating Race and Nation in the U.S. Context: Methodology, Interdisciplinarity, and the Unresolved Role of Comparative Inquiry" (chapter 6), Peden takes up the question of the intersection between U.S. national identity and race as this is manifested within the disciplines of philosophy and political science. While there have been various attempts within these disciplines to address nationalism and the concept of the nation, Peden questions why race itself ("the idiom through which the nation is objectively experienced") has not been foregrounded as an object of study itself rather than merely as a variable that helps explain nationalism. She explains this failure as the effect of two problematic trends in the literature: the trend toward viewing the United States as so essentially specific and exceptional that structural critiques don't apply, and the trend toward mimicking scientific methods that overgeneralize cases, thus obscuring more literary and philosophical approaches that might reveal the context and particularities of the construction of U.S. nationhood. These trends may seem to be at cross-purposes—the one emphasizing particularism and the other downplaying it—yet they both have the effect of sidestepping race. To illustrate the problems with these trends Peden analyzes the work of Anthony Marx and Karl Deutsch. From this analysis she suggests that, if we are to provide rich, contextual analyses of the relationship between U.S. nationalism and race and thus avoid the pitfalls of previous scholars, we need to use an interdisciplinary approach. Interdisciplinarity will counteract the tendency to nationhood as a transhistorical category, and it will also make possible the incorporation of writings by those from the margins, such as Frederick Douglass, Ida B. Wells, Alain Locke, and

W. E. B. Du Bois, that will "subvert assumptions of homogeneity and [show] how racial construction and exclusion have accompanied the U.S. national project since its inception."

Peden also calls for a national discussion about "the various cultural conditions . . . that allow ordinary people to experience the nation as such." Eduardo Mendieta's "Citizenship and Political Friendship: Two Hearts, One Passport" (chapter 7) takes up precisely this discussion in a personal and reflexive analysis of what it means for him to be an American in light of the racial exclusion and racial injustice perpetrated in the very midst of the mythology of a "united America." In describing his "two hearts," Mendieta explores his ambivalence toward the United States, a country where he is both welcomed and also shamed because of his race. He develops a complex account of the relationship between citizenship and public affect, what he calls "public somatology," arguing that citizenship is not merely a collection of rights and duties but also includes affects—particularly the loyalty and trust that makes possible political friendship and solidarity. To make his case about the importance of affect in the production of law, Mendieta discusses Ogletree's and Bell's analyses of *Brown v. Board of Education*, and to clarify his notion of political friendship, he examines the work of Aristotle, Kant, and Cicero. He ultimately appeals to a notion of political friendship that involves both freedom of judgment and trust in our co-citizens in order to produce conditions without which it would be impossible to have national pride or self-respect. To Chana Kai Lee's question posed earlier—"'United' since when? For what cause? Under whose terms?"[8]—Mendieta provides the following answer: unity is achieved through the conditions of political friendship but this will be possible only when the United States becomes a nation that does not shame and humiliate its citizens. As he states, "A nation that labors intently on humiliating many of its most 'faithful citizens' —in Bell's words—calls forth not just their skepticism, but their disloyalty. And a society in which neither self-respect nor national pride are possible can neither improve itself or imagine itself as a country whose moral character is yet to be forged." Remaining hopeful, however, Mendieta prompts us to imagine U.S. citizenship as a postnational American identity that recognizes its history of racial injustice and commands our loyalty without requiring humiliation and dishonor.

Homeland

O, let my land be a land where Liberty
Is crowned with no false patriotic wreath,
But opportunity is real, and life is free,
Equality is in the air we breathe.

(There's never been equality for me,
Nor freedom in this "homeland of the free.") . . .

O, I'm the man who sailed those early seas
In search of what I meant to be my home—
For I'm the one who left dark Ireland's shore,
And Poland's plain, and England's grassy lea,
And torn from Black Africa's strand I came
To build a "homeland of the free."

—Langston Hughes, "Let America Be America Again"

This section problematizes the notion of the cherished "homeland" by showing how an imperial nationalism makes its presence felt even in those spaces we might deem most progressive or, at least politically neutral and unfettered by ideology: the arena of resistant scholarship (in this case, postcolonial scholarship) and the area of aesthetics.

In chapter 8, "On the Limits of Postcolonial Identity Politics," Namita Goswami sounds a warning note about the ways in which counter-hegemonic theoretical projects can be recuperated to serve American exceptionalism once again. She analyzes the pitfalls of postcolonialism as practiced by Indian American postcolonial scholars who, in trying to achieve the "American" Dream by way of class advancement, reinforce U.S. nationalism and foreign policy premised on exceptionalism. Goswami argues that postcolonialism naturalizes both the dominance and the innocence of the United States and obscures its own colonial practices. She suggests that, while claiming to be victims of racism and on the side of the U.S. underclass, this new Indian American "model minority" promotes the Anglocentrism and Eurocentrism of the U.S. academy at the expense of U.S. African American, Native American, and Latin American scholarship in ethnic studies departments. Goswami also claims that this group becomes "native informants" of their original homeland for U.S. neocolonialist practices. Paradoxically, Goswami's analysis summons a picture of postcolonialism as a passage into neocolonialism. Following Spivak, Goswami asks postcolonial theorists to think about the condition of possibility for their migrant history, which should allow them to see how they themselves can be agents of domination. She also encourages them to see themselves as Americans that make up part of the American homeland, not in the sense of being "Anglo-clones," but as first world hyphenated Americans, since "America *is* hyphenated."

The volume concludes with Monique Roelofs's "Theorizing the Aesthetic Homeland: Racialized Aesthetic Nationalism in Daily Life and the Art World," in which she alerts us to the ways in which taste, race, and nationalism merge to form a sense of an aesthetic homeland. This racialized aesthetic nationalism constructs a homeland by disowning and abjecting spaces that are racially other. Roelofs argues that the relationship between aesthetics and racialized nationalism is not new; rather, it has its roots in the history of aesthetic theory, specifically the work of Shaftesbury, Hume, Kant, and Addison. She points to the ways in which racialized aesthetic nationalism creates a proprietary conception of visual culture at the level of everyday experience and thus gives rise to a sense of being at home in one's "own" cultural environment, an environment that needs to be constantly affirmed and protected. She provides examples of racialized aesthetic nationalism at the level of the everyday in the aftermath of 9/11: the U.S government's means of cultural surveillance and its injunction to go shopping as well as the *New York Times'* commemorative vignettes about victims of the 9/11 attacks. Roelofs further connects the workings of racialized aesthetic nationalism at the level of the everyday to the level of the art world by providing an analysis of the critiques of the work of Colombian artist Fernando Botero by Rosalind Krauss and Arthur C. Danto. She argues that Danto's interpretation of Botero's *Abu Ghraib* series is particularly suffused by assumptions about race and nation that inhibit his ability to read the work as what it is, a powerful, political indictment of U.S. military policies and practices.

Roelofs's analysis brings us back to the question of what we do not know that we do not know about our own national culture. If the assessment of Fernando Botero's art by our leading philosopher-critics is so disabled by a racialized and nationalist blindness, then where is there cause for hope? If race is truly the idiom through which the nation is subjectively experienced, how can nationalism itself be made nonexclusionary? As we hope this volume reveals, the answers to these questions do not lie in further abstractions from race and identity, in which theorists try to downplay and ignore the color and cultural origin of citizens, but rather, precisely through a mobilization of the experiences, perspectives, and theoretical insights of the true diversity that makes up this nation.

Notes

1. Michael Billig, *Banal Nationalism* (London: Sage, 1995), 6.

2. Joan Didion, *Fixed Ideas* (New York: New York Review of Books, 2003), 12.

3. For an interesting assessment of Huntington's argument, see David Palumbo-Liu, "Multiculturalism Now: Civilization, National Identity, and Difference Before and After September 11," in *Identity Politics Reconsidered*, ed. Linda Martín Alcoff, Michael Hames-García, Satya P. Mohanty, and Paula Moya (New York: Palgrave Macmillan, 2006), 126–141.

4. Susan Neiman, *Evil in Modern Thought: An Alternative History of Philosophy* (Melbourne, Australia: Scribe, 2002).

5. Giovana Borradori, *Philosophy in a Time of Terror, Dialogues with Jürgen Habermas and Jacques Derrida* (Chicago: University of Chicago Press, 2003).

6. See, for example, Jorge J. E. Gracia, *Surviving Race, Ethnicity and Nationality: A Challenge for the Twenty-First Century* (Lanham, MD.: Rowman and Littlefield, 2005).

7. Susan Sontag, *Regarding the Pain of Others* (New York: Farrar, Straus and Giroux, 2003), 114.

8. Chana Kai Lee, "Memories in the Making and Other National Fictions," *Signs* 28, no. 1 (2002): 439.

Part 1

Freedom

1

Cultural Affirmation, Power, and Dissent

Two Midcentury U.S. Debates

Elizabeth Suzanne Kassab

> We are engaged in such a perpetual liturgy of self-congratulations about the vaunted virtues and achievements of the "American way of life" that we not only make ourselves odious to the world, but also rob ourselves of the political wisdom required to wield power in a world which refuses to be made over into the image of America. Furthermore our frustrations and our hatred of the foe have created an hysteria through which public discussion of foreign policy has practically ceased, the foreign policy has been frozen into inflexible rigidity, and our cherished liberties are being engulfed. History has not revealed a deeper irony than the destruction of the spirit of democratic liberty in the name of devotion to it, which we have witnessed in this nation in the past five years.
>
> —Reinhold Niebuhr, *The Irony of American History* (1952)

The terrorist attacks of 9/11 provoked a sense of shock, insecurity, and defensiveness among Americans. They mobilized a spontaneous movement of solidarity and unity in the face of a dangerous enemy and in a situation of open conflict. The U.S. government reacted by declaring "war on terrorism" and by passing the USA PATRIOT Acts to legalize what it regarded to be special defense measures of surveillance and protection. It invaded Afghanistan and Iraq in "preemptive" strikes against alleged bases of threat in order to eradicate terrorism and establish democracy. This chapter is not about the motivations, circumstances, and results of these reactions, nor about their moral and political dimensions. Rather, it is about the interpretation of events that was voiced in the public debates across the country. Some people showed concern about the curbing of civil rights and liberties for the sake of security and expressed distress at the growing repression of dissent and critique in the name of unity and patriotism. Others saw the need to reexamine U.S. foreign policy of the recent decades, especially regarding the Middle East. Many more perceived the terrorist attacks as acts of aggression against Western civilization, against the "American way of life," and against democracy. Interestingly, this was not the first time that Americans were raising issues of cultural identity, democracy, unity, and critique in connection with war and peace. Half a century earlier another war and another threat had given rise to similar discussions and similar concerns, namely, World War II and the Soviet communist threat. This chapter recalls two major intellectual debates that took place in 1947 and in 1952 and sheds light on the issues that were discussed then.

The first one was at an inter-American philosophy conference right after the war and the second one was in a literary journal at the onset of McCarthyism. Still under the shock of war, the first debate is dominated by the concern with peace, democracy, and world understanding, and by the role of culture and philosophy in securing them. It is also centered on the question of cultural leadership after the demise of Europe, whether the Americas had the capacity and maturity to take over the responsibility of such a leadership, whether they had come into their own by developing a thought of their own and a philosophy of their own. Attempts are made to clarify the meaning of such a specificity and at the same time to underline the importance of true universality, based on dialogue, not hegemony. On the U.S. American side there is, on the one hand, a sense of insecurity, a certain awe in the face of the responsibility, and a willingness to open up to and learn from other cultures, and on the other hand, there is a sense of self-confidence, self-referentiality, and even self-congratulation.

Five years later, these attitudes are more pronounced. There seems to be a greater sense of righteousness and a greater awareness of power and success and, at the same time, a perception of threat and insecurity that brings to prominence the question of loyalty and dissent. It is these same issues of cultural affirmation, power assertion, defense of democracy, solidarity, patriotism, and critique that emerge in the aftermath of the 9/11 attacks. It is thus interesting to revisit the earlier discussions of these issues.

The Second Inter-American Congress of Philosophy

In 1947 the second Inter-American Congress of Philosophy was held at Columbia University in New York City, jointly with the annual meeting of the Eastern Division of the American Philosophical Association (APA). The first one had taken place in Port-au-Prince, Haiti, in 1944.[1] The proceedings of the 1947 meeting were published in 1949 in the ninth issue of *Philosophy and Phenomenological Research*. They listed papers, both by North American philosophers and Latin American philosophers, on the usual philosophical topics such as the theory of knowledge, the philosophy of religion, metaphysics, aesthetics, ethics, logic, philosophical anthropology, and philosophy of history. But the opening papers asked the rather unusual questions: Is there an Ibero-American philosophy? (Risieri Frondizi) and Is there a North American philosophy? (Ralph Barton Perry). These set the particular tone of the conference. What was meant by such philosophies and how had such queries become the focus of an inter-American philosophy meeting?

The President of the Eastern Division of the APA and Chairman of the organizing committee of the congress, Cornelius Krusé, then Professor of Philosophy at Wesleyan University, elaborates on these questions in his Presidential Address, published first in 1948 in *The Philosophical Review* and entitled "What contribution can philosophy make to world understanding?" "[T]houghts of an Inter-American Congress of Philosophy," he says, "were war-born," and not only out of a "Good Neighbor policy," nor simply because of the difficulty of holding large International Congresses under war conditions, but out of a need to face the grave challenges to peace and culture caused by the war and the collapse of Europe, and the fall of France in particular. The need for a post-European cultural responsibility and leadership had emerged and the Americas were called upon to fulfill it. For this task, he adds, the two Americas needed to work together and therefore to get to know one another.[2]

The idea of the congress was also, he thought, in response to UNESCO's call on philosophers to contribute to world peace through facilitating world understanding.[3] In its 1948 meeting in Mexico City, UNESCO had put the comparative study of cultures as a top priority in its program with the view of promoting a sympathetic understanding between cultures.[4] Philosophers from North and South America, he adds, needed to come together to explore the best ways of carrying out this mission. Sadly, he observes, the two parts of America had developed closer cultural ties with Europe than with one another, in spite of their comparable colonial pasts.[5] Indeed, this continues to be the case across the postcolonial world. Its different regions remain focused on the West and isolated from one another. Rarely do their thinkers meet and share with one another their comparable concerns and struggles, and rarely are their debates examined in connection with one another.[6]

Having explained the circumstances and purposes of the congress, Krusé moves on to addressing the main difficulties of the task at hand: (1) Being up to the needed task, that is, that of being able to produce the necessary philosophical work; (2) determining the nature of that work; and (3) agreeing on the very definition of a philosophical activity. He formulates the first difficulty in the following terms:

> We raised the question—following a popular trend in recent Ibero-American discussions: Is there an Ibero-American—is there a North American philosophy? . . . When the question is raised, the real issue is not the restriction of a particular philosophy to regional uses, but rather whether we have come of age after centuries of European tutelage. Have we become philosophically mature enough to initiate ourselves a philosophical tradition? Can we do more than simply appropriate the history of philosophy? Can we also help make it? Are we learners only, or also discoverers and teachers of new philosophical insights, hitherto neglected and unnoticed?[7]

He explains how not to understand those regional philosophies when he states:

> It is true that even if the questions of the titles were answered in the affirmative, no one would contend that Ibero-American philosophy had validity for Ibero-Americans only, or that North American philosophy was restricted for North American use.[8]

According to him, the particularity would have to be understood in the same way that one speaks of British empiricism, Continental rationalism, Platonism, Aristotelianism, and so on, namely, some original way of raising and answering philosophical questions. But then what is philosophy? Different schools of philosophy, he says, seem to have different views of the very nature of their discipline. But these differences notwithstanding, philosophy is to be sharply distinguished from propaganda, which employs force and manipulation in spreading ideas. Philosophy, on the contrary, operates through rational persuasion and education. One of its main tasks, he says, is the examination of values and value judgments; and one of its main important contributions to world understanding is the defense of the possibility of an objective grounding of values and the rejection of subjectivism. The central value that needs such grounding, he affirms, is democracy, itself based on reason. This alone could ensure the peaceful life of a world community.[9] This does not imply uniformity for him. On the contrary, its plurality is to be valued and protected and one of the tasks of philosophy in realizing this ideal is the exploration of the plural meanings that basic concepts such as "the rights of man," "liberty," "life," "law," and "democracy" have in the various communities of the world. This is another mission that UNESCO's 1948 program had invited philosophers to undertake. The perennial task of philosophy since Socrates, he recalls, has been the clarification of meanings of common terms such as "justice," "peity," and "friendship." For this task, Krusé states that philosophers "should be ready to listen and to learn, as well as to inquire what possible meaning varying peoples may give to one and the same term. Irascibility and a gift for picturesque invective would seem to have little place in such an enterprise."[10] Moreover, Krusé finds it extremely important for philosophers to get closely acquainted with cultures other than their own and to learn to make philosophy together with philosophers from cultures other than their own. He thinks that North Americans can find inspiration in the multicultural life of their southern neighbors in Latin America.[11]

It is the same plural nature of Latin American identity and its impact on culture and politics that F. S. C. Northrop, philosophy professor at Yale at the time, opposes to North American monoculture. Contrary to the case in the United States, dominated by a single Anglo-Saxon culture, Mexico, he says, includes a number of cultures that compete over the determination of political, economic, and cultural policies: a pre-Spanish Indian culture, a Spanish Roman Catholic culture, a Lockean and Voltairean democratic culture, a French and British positivistic culture, as well as a democratic political culture combined with an economic communist one.[12] The United States on the other hand, says Northrop, has been dominated by one constant ideology derived from British culture and thus philosophically unchallenged by competing ideologies and worldviews.[13]

Northrop does not ask why the United States has not nurtured a multiplicity of cultures like Mexico has done. He just states the fact and moves on to explaining the relevance of the philosophy of culture in such culturally plural settings as that of Mexico. In these settings, he says, the evaluation of proposed policies leads ultimately to an examination of the fundamental cultural beliefs and values on which they are based. This is how the philosophical discussion of beliefs and values comes to occupy a central place in Mexican public life and in its press and the relevance of the philosophy of culture becomes manifest. This is why he suggests that, "Philosophers of the United States should read the newspapers of Mexico City. Such an experience would demonstrate the crucial importance of the philosophy of culture in the contemporary world."[14] The Latin American experience of dealing with diverse cultural doctrines can serve as a valuable source of inspiration for the post–World War II world that is marked, according to Northrop, much more than the post–World War I world by ideological conflicts.[15] This experience shows that doctrines in the various domains of life, be it in economy, politics, or culture, are interconnected in a given culture and that the adequate understanding of these doctrines cannot be achieved without an exploration of the fundamental beliefs of that given culture. Northrop advocates here a holistic view of cultures. According to him, different cultural beliefs are different answers to common human questions and are to be appreciated according to their own rationales rather than be put on an evolutionary scale with the West as its yardstick. A proper philosophy of culture cannot support an evolutionary and ethnocentric view of history. In his 1946 book, *The Meeting of East and West*, Northrop offers a comparative philosophy of culture based on an examination of the basic beliefs and values of a number of Western and Eastern cultures.

In a paper entitled "The Philosophy of Democracy as a Philosophy of History," New York University professor Sidney Hook warns strongly against holistic views of culture that reduce cultures to a few metaphysical premises. He also strongly attacks monocausal theories of history that explain complex historical phenomena through single factors in a deterministic way. For Hook, theories that view cultures and history to be metaphysically determined are not only false but also dangerous for world peace and unity, because they put forth false, unbridgeable metaphysical differences. Democracy, instead, is a philosophy that facilitates the peaceful dealing with differences. Like Krusé, Hook sees the defense of democracy as one of the important tasks of philosophy. He understands democracy as the uncoerced consent of a community and its ability to check and control power through operating institutions and basic liberties, such as the freedom of speech, of assembly, and of press. He sees it involving the political as well as the economic and the cultural aspects of communal and individual life. Hook stresses the pragmatic, operational understanding of peace and democracy, based both within nations and between nations, on consequences in experiences rather than on presuppositions of theory and metaphysics:

> to make the justification for democracy rest upon any metaphysical or theological premise is an invitation to disaster. . . . The philosophy of democracy can best function as a philosophy of history today not by excogitating formulae of salvation or equations of doom for our society but by finding the operational equivalent of ideals, by suggesting specific institutional devices, specific mechanisms and instrumentalities governmental and nongovernmental for increasing the area of uncoerced agreement

> among men . . . we cannot make absolutes of doctrines, tastes, or principles as *preconditions* of the democratic process without unloosing the furies of fanaticism. The only thing we can be fanatical about are the processes of democratic consensus within nations and among nations.[16]

For the Mexican philosopher Leopoldo Zea, the most urgent task in world understanding is inter-American understanding. Understanding each other's ideas and values is for him the genuine meaning of universality rather than the imposition of one's beliefs on others. The human basis of commonality among various peoples and cultures is what makes that genuine universality and understanding possible, while at the same time preserving the distinct personality of those communities. The outstanding feature of this congress, according to him, is that of having gathered thinkers who are interested in, and well acquainted with, one another's cultures. He examines the kind of awareness that each of the Americas has had of the other and hopes that such conferences would help correct and complement it. Zea reviews the various images that Latin Americans have had of the United States over time. On the one hand, Latin Americans have seen the United States as a model of liberation, of democracy, of inventiveness, and of material progress. On the other hand, they have seen it as a genocidal, racist, and imperialist power, driven by ruthless greed, institutionalizing slavery at home, and ready to support dictatorships abroad, and in South American countries in particular, for its own profit. Moreover, while the United States has occupied a central, if complex, place in the minds of Latin Americans, Latin America has only had an instrumental relevance for the United States, either as a market for its products, or a source for raw materials and/or fields of speculation.[17] This asymmetry in perception and power has engendered a distorted self-image of the Americas, especially of Latin America, that needs to be corrected by such encounters:

> Ibero-America, feeling herself impotent in the field of the material, sublimated her impotence by considering herself the maximum expression of spirit in America, while assigning to North America a purely material role. For her part, North America saw in Ibero-America nothing but a group of half-savage tumultuous peoples, worthy only of despotic government. Mutually, the two Americas denied one another's spiritual capacity, and absolute misunderstanding came to rule their necessary relations.[18]

Zea hopes that conferences such as the 1947 Inter-American Congress may promote another, more genuine and cultural, interest in one another's cultures. At the end of his paper, he comes back to the notion of universality in philosophy. For him, universality should, on the one hand, be the result of the abstractions with which any philosophy needs to operate and, on the other hand, should be rooted in the reality from which the abstractions are made. The reality that he would like to see defined and reflected on is America as a whole, rather than Ibero- or North America. As Zea states:

> The universal, to which all philosophy should aspire, must be achieved starting, as does all authentic philosophy, from our reality. For this reason, it is urgent that we define, clarify, make explicit, just what that reality is. It is necessary to abstract from that reality what we can call the idea of America, i.e., that which is common to our two Americas, of the North and of the South. In this Congress we have already asked ourselves if there exists an Ibero-American philosophy or a North American philosophy. Why not go on to question ourselves about the possibilities of an American philosophy? That is, why not question ourselves about the possibilities of a philosophy which respects what is private to each one of the Americas and can at the same time be valid for both?[19]

In his long philosophical career, Zea will not tire from advocating such an inter-American philosophical dialogue and from defending the idea of a philosophy true to its abstract nature and at the same time connected to the lived realities of concrete communities. But his hopes to achieve such a dialogue do not seem to have been realized in the years following this congress. Some forty years later the eleventh Inter-American Congress of Philosophy held in Guadalajara, Mexico, in 1985, was devoted precisely to "America and its philosophical expression." The problem of cultural imperialism and that of its impact on philosophy seemed to have grown in acuteness and the two Americas did not appear to have grown closer.

In his keynote address to this 1985 congress, U.S. philosopher Richard Rorty ignored the problem of cultural imperialism and focused his presentation on the connections between analytic and continental philosophy. He claims that philosophy could only emerge in enclaves of freedom and prosperity. This gave rise to a number of protests that were published in the APA *Proceedings and Addresses* of 1986 (59) and 1987 (60). In an article entitled "The Debate over Cultural Imperialism" Canadian philosopher Thomas Auxter criticized the way Euro-American philosophy presented itself as the universal philosophy, while excluding the African, Asian, and Latin American philosophies. Moreover, he criticized the evasion of the issue of cultural imperialism during the meeting, as for instance in Rorty's speech, but also its evasion in the previous meeting held in Florida. He saw philosophy as a major force in this cultural warfare and in the rationale for domination.

Ofelia Schutte, the Cuban feminist philosopher based in the United States, saw the meeting as a great "dis-encounter" and called for an end to cultural imperialism in philosophy. She attacked the implicit and explicit assumption made in the field that Anglo-Eurocentric conscience was the measure of all things. She noted the absence of invited women speakers of Hispanic participants from the United States and raised the question of the recognition of Spanish as an international language of philosophy. Leopoldo Zea, in his turn, contested the idea that philosophy had emerged throughout history in circumstances of affluence and freedom and gave examples from ancient and modern philosophy, saying on the contrary, that it was often oppression and the need to satisfy social and political wants that gave rise to important philosophical thoughts. He demanded for Latin American philosophers what European and U.S. philosophers had offered themselves, namely, the opportunity to address their needs philosophically—philosophy here understood as systematic and rigorous thinking rather than an institutionalized traditional profession. Virginia Black from the United States argued that cultural imperialism was a consequence of choices that certain societies made for their economies; their failure to adopt free trade and their inability to renounce statism and corruption were what made their societies weak and dependent. For her, a stronger economy was what led to a stronger recognition of one's culture. In another piece,[20] Zea again addressed the logicism upheld by U.S. philosophers in the Guadalajara meeting and proposed "*diálogos*" instead of "*logos*" as an instrument for genuine inter-American understanding. Only in "diálogos" he said, could there be room for the plurality of human expressions and concerns.

In spite of this widening imperialistic gap between the two Americas, philosophers from both parts raised similar questions back in 1947: Is there an Ibero-American philosophy? and Is there a North American philosophy? These questions were, as indicated, the titles of the opening papers of the congress. In answering the first question, Argentinian philosopher Risieri Frondizi reviews the successive stages of the development of Latin American philosophy, but starts first with a definition of philosophy. He insists on the importance of viewing philosophy as an independent and well-defined discipline, consisting mainly in the critical and systematic examination of concepts and ideas. These may relate to concrete life issues, but their philosophical examination cannot be subordinated to those issues. This is not to reduce philosophy to a narrow academic activity, he adds, or to disengage it from life concerns altogether, but to ensure for it a recognizable and independent status that is indispensable for its proper functioning. All too often, he says, philosophy in Latin America has been confused with politics and with aesthetic, social, educational, and economic policies. As a critical, analytic discipline it is not to be equated with Weltanschauungen, or world-views, as has often been the case.

Examining the history of philosophy in Latin America, Frondizi recognizes five stages: the Weltanschauung of the native cultures; the Christian scholastic philosophy brought in by the Spanish colonizers; the critique of this scholasticism with the modern ideas of Descartes, Gassendi, Locke, and the like; the positivism of Comte and Spencer (turned into politics in the Diaz dictatorship); and the last stage, which is the present and the future. This history, he notes, has been dominated by the often passive reception of European philosophy:

> Up to the present, Ibero-American philosophy is simply the rethinking of the European problems that have reached our shores. It is certain that European philosophic currents acquire, in this soil, characteristics of our own, and perhaps in this way there will be arrived at in the future a conception purely Ibero-American, but up to now the process of digestion necessary for the rise of such a conception of our own, has not been completed. . . . We wish to refer, nevertheless, to this stage, because no doing permits us to point out what is lacking in present-day thought which would enable us to speak of an Ibero-American philosophy, in the same way as we speak of German, English, or French philosophy.[21]

But Frondizi cautions against the obsession with a truly "Latin American" philosophy that can turn itself into an impediment to the development of such a philosophy. Too much attention has been devoted to that "Latin Americanness" and not enough to philosophy itself. He states that, "In order that an Ibero-American philosophy may arise, one has to 'make' philosophy, and nothing else; the Ibero-American character will come as an addition. . . . If we are truly Americans, all our activities and creations, insofar as they are authentic, will reflect our quality of Americanism."[22] Finally, he adds that even as an abstract discipline, philosophy cannot but remain connected to the concrete life problems from which it stems. It is this connection that explains Latin American philosophers' preoccupation with certain issues more than others, namely, cultural philosophy, philosophic anthropology, and ethics.

The question concerning North American philosophy is also addressed by Harvard professor of philosophy Ralph Barton Perry. Like the rest of his colleagues, Perry starts his answer with a discussion of the meaning of universality and particularity in philosophy. On the one hand, he insists on the universality of any genuine philosophical work,[23] and, on the other hand, recognizes the specific focus on certain topics and certain approaches that different philosophies may have. This specificity may be the result of certain linguistic, ethnic, geographical, national, or epochal influences. Based on this understanding of particularity in philosophy, Perry presents the specificities of North American philosophy as a reflection of the specificities of what he calls the "American mind."[24] He lists among them buoyancy, zestfulness, resourcefulness, and self-reliance. Indeed, in a "buoyant" presentation of this American mind, Perry sees individualism as its most characteristic feature. Curiously, it is quite a conformist social and intellectual individualism. He defines American individualism as the "intercourse and cooperation of many" and "confidence in achievement through organization and combined effort" rather than the isolation of a human being.[25] Thus, according to Perry, American individualism

> is less likely to promote that creative originality in art or fundamental discovery in pure science which is the fruit of solitary genius, than the technical devices by which organized effort—even in art and science themselves—can produce results. The individual who holds himself apart, who will not "join," who does not "belong," who does not "play the game," who does not "get together," who does not "row his weight in the boat," is viewed with suspicion.[26]

Unlike Frondizi, Perry is not critical of this lack of originality and daring in U.S. American intellectual and artistic production. He sees in it an absence of fanaticism and doctrinaire rigidity and a general tendency toward moderation. For him this is the result of the hospitality and eclecticism of American life as well as the result of the intellectual's involvement in the economic activity of the country. As he states:

> This moderation is connected with the tendency to hospitality and eclecticism which has already been remarked; and it may account for America's comparative lack of intellectual daring and originality—its producing many busy and efficient thinkers, scattered through a thousand colleges and universities, rather than a few sages, prophets, and revolutionaries. The American mind does not live on mountain tops or in ivory towers but in union railway stations; or in skyscrapers which accommodate a throng of occupants, engaged in diverse enterprises, and whose offices are connected by elevators, telephones, and public address systems.[27]

Many factors, including economic, ethnic, and cultural, contribute, according to Perry, to the making of this individualism. In a word, it is, as he calls it, the "circumstances of the settlement of the country and the varied composition of its population" that have given rise to this characteristic.[28] He adds, "[t]he self-confidence of Americans is due to many causes, including the bounty of nature, the temperate climate, the Protestant emphasis on personal responsibility, and the adventurous character and happy mixture of racial stocks."[29] In this "happy mixture" there is no mention of African slaves or of annihilated and/or colonized natives. The "circumstances of the settlement of the country" do not rouse any further questioning for him. At the beginning of his paper, while trying to define the terms "North American" and "American," Perry says that "[i]n the United States the only people known as 'North Americans' are the North American Indians, and presumably the title does not refer to them: at any rate I know nothing about their philosophy."[30] In this chilling brief statement he does not see the need to ask why those "North American Indians" would not be involved in answering the title question Is there a North American philosophy? nor does he show concern about his not knowing anything about their philosophy.

In pursuing the characterization of his "American mind," Perry enumerates a number of aspects that are in fact the leitmotifs of the postindependence U.S. debates on culture and identity: the pursuit of wealth and the seizing of opportunities, the development of industry and the production of mass culture, the belief in success, the purchasing power on the world culture market, and faith in happy endings. Regarding the concern as to whether industrial wealth can be beneficial to culture he claims that "the pursuit of wealth affords the most notable or notorious manifestation: not the drowning of culture by the hum of industry, but the idea of making culture hum."[31] As to the phenomenon of buying culture, it should not, according to him, cause any embarrassment, "If they do not make it they can buy it. This does not offend their pride, for they feel that they buy it with what they *have* made."[32] As to the disillusionment and self-critique that may have grown in the last half century, he thinks that they are characteristic of a "sophisticated élite" rather than representative of the "American mind" he describes. All of these issues, including that of the place of criticism and dissidence in the United States, are, as we will see shortly, the main themes of the symposium organized a few years later, in 1952, by the *Partisan Review* and called "Our Country and Our Culture."

Like Frondizi, Perry presents a periodization of U.S. American philosophy from the Puritan-Protestant thought of the seventeenth and early eighteenth centuries, to the philosophy of the Enlightenment of the eighteenth century culminating in the ideology of the American Revolution, to the Scottish or Common Sense School, the romantic-transcendentalist philosophy and Post-Kantian idealism, reaching finally the pragmatic and realistic movements. It is in these last movements that he sees a truly "American" philosophy emerge, a philosophy that corresponds to the distinctive profile of the American mind he described. Although Perry ends his chapter by calling on the two branches of the "American family," North and South, to search for a common understanding between them and between them and the world, his paper remains largely self-referential. Contrary Krusé, Northrop, and Hook, he does not discuss "North America" in relation to the rest of the world. His view of North American culture remains entirely Eurocentric.

Before moving to the discussion of our second midcentury debate on culture and identity, also occasioned by the collapse of Europe during World War II, it is interesting to contrast this "buoyant" view of Perry with that of some of his contemporaries. In *The World and Africa*, published in 1947, W. E. B. Du Bois addressed explicitly the problem of the collapse of Europe in the first two chapters entitled, respectively, "The Collapse of Europe" and "The White Masters of the World." He began with the following opening paragraph:

> We are face to face with the greatest tragedy that has ever overtaken the world. The collapse of Europe is to us the more astounding because of the boundless faith which we have had in European civilization. We have long believed without argument or reflection that the cultural status of the people of Europe and of North America represented not only the best civilization which the world had ever known, but also a goal of human effort destined to go on from triumph to triumph until the perfect accomplishment was reached. Our present nervous breakdown, nameless fear, and often despair, comes from the sudden facing of this faith with calamity. In such a case, what we need above all is calm appraisal of the situation, the application of cold common sense. What in reality is the nature of the catastrophe? To what pattern of human culture does it apply? And, finally, why did it happen?[33]

In the two chapters mentioned, Du Bois traced the causes of this collapse back to the moral contradictions inherent to European civilization: the cultivation, on the one hand, of the Christian values of brotherhood and love, of progress and prosperity, of the fine arts and the sciences and, on the other hand, the ruthless pursuit of wealth and power, even at the cost of dehumanizing others and ultimately of dehumanizing themselves: "There was the assumption of the absolute necessity of poverty for the majority of men in order to save civilization for the minority, for that aristocracy of mankind which was at the same time the chief beneficiary of culture."[34] Then he added, "When a culture consents to any economic result, no matter how monstrous its cause, rather than demand the facts concerning work, wages, and the conditions of life whose result make the life of the consumer comfortable, pleasant, and even luxurious, it is an indication of a collapsing civilization."[35] Without demonizing European culture, Du Bois deplored in it the weakness, if not the absence, of a forceful self-criticism:

> The dawn of the twentieth century found white Europe master of the world and the white peoples almost universally recognized as the rulers for whose benefit the rest of the world existed. Never before in the history of civilization had self-worship of a people's accomplishment attained the heights that the worship of white Europe by Europeans reached.[36]

Reviewing the colonial history of this self-congratulating Europe, Du Bois recognized in its history a consistent violence that reached ultimately its own soil in World War II. For those who do not know or have chosen not to know that colonial past, violence might seem to come from nowhere and might seem to burst suddenly in the middle of a "fine" civilization. But those who have been at the receiving end of that colonial history know that the refinement of that civilization was to a great extent at the expense of their lives and their own humanity. In a passage reminiscent of Aimé Césaire's *Discourse on Colonialism*,[37] Du Bois wrote,

> There was no Nazi atrocity—concentration camps, wholesale maiming and murder, defilement of women or ghastly blasphemy of childhood—which the Christian civilization of Europe had not long been practicing against colored folk in all parts of the world in the name of and for the defense of a Superior Race born to rule the world. Together with the idea of a Superior Race there grew up in Europe and America an astonishing ideal of wealth and luxury.[38]

Du Bois went on to recall all the scientific and cultural rationalizations that were given in European culture for this racist exploitation of non-Europeans. It is, according to him, this dehumanization of others that led to the collapse of human culture in Europe and North America. Like his Latin American counterparts mentioned by Zea, Du Bois seemed to have become acquainted with that other side of the innocent and buoyant Euro-America. It must have been also James Baldwin's experience who described in the mid-1950s his perception of the cathedral at Chartres in comparison to that of his contemporaries in a European village:

> The cathedral at Chartres, I have said, says something to the people of this village which it cannot say to me; but it is important to understand that this cathedral says something to me which it

> cannot say to them. Perhaps they are struck by the power of the spires, the glory of the windows; but they have known God, after all, longer than I have known him, and in a different way, and I am terrified by the slippery bottomless well to be found in the crypt, down which heretics were hurled to death, and by the obscene, inescapable gargoyles jutting out of the stone and seeming to say that God and the devil can never be divorced. I doubt that the villagers think of the devil when they face a cathedral because they have never been identified with the devil. But I must accept the status which myth, if nothing else, gives me in the West before I can hope to change the myth.[39]

The voices of people of color will grow louder in the second half of the twentieth century and will present their own views of an Euro-American definition of U.S. culture; they will deconstruct it, demystify it, and reject its status in the United States and in the world.

The 1952 *Partisan Review* Symposium "Our Country and Our Culture"

A few years after the 1947 philosophy congress, the *Partisan Review*, then one of the leading literary journals in the country, convened thinkers, writers, and artists to a symposium entitled "Our Country and Our Culture."[40] It invited them to reflect on the impact that the political, economic, and cultural transformations of the first half of the century had had on the cultural and intellectual life of the country. Among these transformations was the emergence of the United States as an economic and political super power from World War II, together with a rival super power governed by a communist regime. This rival superpower was presented by the U.S. government as a threat to the security and to the value system of the country. This government set up an investigation committee, namely, the American Committee of Un-American Activities, led by Senator Joseph McCarthy. It was already in full action by 1952. This defensive atmosphere and the actions taken by McCarthyism had blurred the line between patriotic loyalty and total conformism, hence the question of the place of critique and dissidence under such circumstances. Other transformations were the expansion of industry, the growth of the mass media, the widening of mass culture, and the commodification of culture. Here, too, the collapse of Europe as the unchallenged reference for culture and thought was a most significant phenomenon.[41] The *Partisan Review* solicited thoughts on the changing attitude of intellectuals toward the United States after this collapse and those transformations. The editorial statement presented the theme of the symposium in the following way:

> For more than a hundred years, America was culturally dependent on Europe; now Europe is economically dependent upon America. And America is no longer the raw and unformed land of promise from which men of superior gifts like James, Santayana, and Eliot departed, seeking in Europe what they found lacking in America. Europe is no longer regarded as a sanctuary; it no longer assures that rich experience of culture which inspired and justified a criticism of American life. The wheel has come full circle, and now America has become the protector of Western civilization, at least in a military and economic sense.[42]

The four questions it put to the participants were (1) To what extent have American intellectuals actually changed their attitude toward America and its institutions? (2) Must the American intellectual and writer adapt himself to mass culture? If he must, what forms can his adaptation take? Or, do you believe that a democratic society necessarily leads to a leveling of culture, to a mass culture which will overrun intellectual and aesthetic values traditional to Western civilization? (3) Where in American life can artists and intellectuals find the basis of strength, renewal, recognition, now that they can no longer depend fully on Europe as a cultural example and a source of vitality? and (4) If a reaffirmation and rediscovery of America is under way, can the tradition of critical nonconformism (going back to Thoreau and Melville and embracing some of the major expressions of American intellectual history) be maintained as strongly as ever?[43] The contributions of the participants were published in the 1952 issues of the *Partisan Review* (3, 4, and 5), and then as a book entitled *America and the Intellectuals*.[44] There were twenty-three participants, only one of whom was a woman. None of them was of any racial minority.[45]

Most of the participants agreed that a change had indeed occurred over the last two decades, both in the attitude of the American intellectual toward his or her country and in the country itself. Intellectuals tended now to identify more with their country and to have less difficulties being productive in it. The country in general had become less provincial and somewhat less anti-intellectual. However, the participants pointed out many ambiguities and pitfalls in these changes.

Among the most significant changes that had occurred in the recent years was, for the majority of the participants, the rise of the United States as a political and economic world power. Politically, it stood out as the democratic system par excellence that succeeded to guarantee individual liberties and a free society. After the rise of fascism in Europe and the exposure of Stalinism in the Soviet Union, U.S. democracy couldn't but win the approval and adherence of intellectuals who saw the importance of such a democracy for their very existence and creativity. This democracy was now perceived to be challenged and threatened by communism. It was in need of protection. But for many the obsession with this threat as well as the hysterical measures taken for this protection constituted themselves a danger to freedom and democracy. Some participants underlined the centrality of the confrontational politics of the country, of the war economy and of the weapon industry that were behind its growing economic and political power. Norman Mailer saw in this politics a direct threat to democratic liberties.[46]

Along the same lines, Reinhold Niebuhr acknowledged the threat of the Soviet Union but expressed concern about the paradoxical approach taken to protect the U.S. democratic system from it:

> We are forced, moreover, to face a ruthless and intransigent foe, whose calumnies against us are so shockingly beside the point, that even the most critical and sophisticated patriot is tempted to become an uncritical one. But this temptation must be resisted. For we are almost in greater peril from the foes within than from the foe without. The foes within are the spirits of hysteria, hatred, mistrust, and pride. We are engaged in such a perpetual liturgy of self-congratulations about the vaunted virtues and achievements of the "American way of life" that we not only make ourselves odious to the world, but also rob ourselves of the political wisdom required to wield power in a world which refuses to be made over into the image of America. Furthermore our frustrations and our hatred of the foe have created an hysteria through which public discussion of foreign policy has practically ceased, the foreign policy has been frozen into inflexible rigidity, and our cherished liberties are being engulfed. History has not revealed a deeper irony than the destruction of the spirit of democratic liberty in the name of devotion to it, which we have witnessed in this nation in the past five years.[47]

This "irony" will be one of the central themes of Niebuhr's work.[48] A related theme will be that of the challenges of coping with the power accumulated by the country. In the symposium he says,

> [t]he peril of American life is particularly great because we have, without apprenticeship, suddenly become the most powerful nation on earth, fated to wield hegemonic power, in a vast alliance of nations. We have been placed in this position in a tumultuous period of history in which no clear pathway from insecurity to security is discernible and in which the sense of frustration is therefore very great.[49]

For some others, this very same rise to power can itself create a problem of adherence to it. According to Daniel Riesman,

> it is hard to detach one's loyalties from a weak, threatened, or defeated nation; it is perhaps even harder to attach one's loyalties to a newly powerful one. It is hard for us not to feel we are selling out when our views (let us say, our discovery of the virtues of our bourgeois "capitalism") not only keep us out of trouble but open up jobs or audiences for us. Indeed, it is our bad luck as intellectuals that we had to recognize our country's growing intellectual and cultural differentiation and emancipation at the same moment that our world role has grown and Europe's lessened—especially as we have such a long tradition of mindless or defensive boasting to live down.[50]

For many, the intellectual's Socratic role of questioning and doubting is particularly important in this rise to power. For others, the reemergence of individualism is a much-needed antidote to the prevailing pressures of conformism and blind patriotism. For the majority, freethinking, some form of alienation and distance from society, as well as the possibility of dissidence remain to be fundamental necessities to any form of genuine intellectual life. Europe can still serve as a model in this respect. Political affirmation should not prevent cultural freedom and intellectual dissidence. It is to be distinguished from cultural acquiescence, especially from submission to mass culture. Political democracy should not be equated with majority rule in cultural matters.

On the other hand, mass culture is not to be seen in total negativity. Its vivacity, vigor, and potentials need to be recognized. Instead of antagonizing mass culture, intellectuals should find ways to influence it—engaging it without being contaminated by it. In the final analysis, art and ideas need to be relevant to the lived realities of their environment. Culture needs to relate to the national experience and avoid being an abstraction. Many of the participants recognize the integration of the intellectual in the administration of the country, in its governmental and educational agencies as a positive development. They see in this growing phenomenon one of the causes behind the more positive relation of the intellectual to the country and behind the decrease to some extent of its anti-intellectualism.[51] Among these is also the rise of the prestige of academia and the availability of moneymaking jobs for intellectuals. For many, World War II and the inflow of European intellectuals to the United States confirmed the value of American civilization. Still, for some the country remains culturally underdeveloped in spite of the many advances made in the various fields. In a provocative statement James Burnham says:[52]

> The cause of our changed judgment on America is evidently in us, not in any shift of our national stars. Culturally we remain what we have been: a "semi-barbarian superstate of the periphery," dependent still on the older spiritual soil in spite of new roots, with Rome and not Athens the potential form of the future. Let us not build a case out of counterfeit. The objective justification for the intellectuals' "reaffirmation and rediscovery of America" is in the first and sufficient instance political and military.[53]

Intellectuals, both European and American, thinks Burnham, have to serve as links between Europe and America and to use the potentials of this new world with the aid of the spiritual tools of what he calls the "traditional Western civilization." He sees a cultural continuity between Europe and America that needs to be acknowledged, and thus claims, "[w]e cannot affirm America without reaffirming Europe and the West. Humans are beings with a history, a past; Europe is our past; and even God cannot will the past not to have been."[54] But even if this continuity is acknowledged, the "indigenization" of American culture is seen by some to be important. Otherwise, for them, culture would remain an abstraction and American culture provincial. According to Lionel Trilling,

> [i]t is in a way wrong or merely academic to talk of the influence of European thought on American thought, since the latter is continuous with the former. But insofar as the American intellectual conceived of the continuity as being an influence, it no doubt was exactly that, and in being that it was useful and liberating. Yet now it seems to me that if the European influence, as a conscious thing, has come to an end, this is, at the moment, all to the good (except of course, as it implies the reason for its coming to an end, and as it may suggest a diminution of free intercourse, of which we can never have enough). The American intellectual never so fully expressed his provincialism as in the way he submitted to the influence of Europe. He was provincial in that he thought of culture as an abstraction and as an absolute.[55]

For those who agree with this need of connecting culture with local realities, the "indigenization" of culture does not mean the cultivation of a self-satisfied cultural nationalism. The importance of remaining open to world cultures for the growth of culture in general is emphasized. Springs of creative power are to be sought everywhere. They cannot be limited by geography or history. And Europe may be politically confused or even bankrupt, but culturally it remains a fertile stock from which the American intellectual can draw, as he or she can draw from his or her own national stock. For still others the continuity between Europe and the United States cannot be seen anymore in terms of subservience or colonial imitation, given the reality of the latter's power. According to Horace Gregory, what a European sees in the United States

> *is* Europe, with a few fragments of Asiatic and African culture, sprouting here and there, shifted geographically to the North American continent. Worst of all, this projection of European culture can no longer be patronized; it cannot be told that it is colonial and subservient to what Europe is today; it is too powerful. America is the European dream transformed into physical reality.[56]

Gregory adds that the American artist cannot but be aware of his country's power and of its being the center of the world, with Europe being its museum. American culture is for him a reshuffling of the European cultural elements by a society endowed with unparalleled means of power, together, as he put it, with some fragments of Asiatic and African culture and the "remains (which should not be exaggerated) of North American Indian culture."[57] Only in another contribution will a remark about race be made: Max Lerner will mention the plight of the "Negro population" and the problem of their civil rights that still awaits a solution. In no other passage is the issue of race raised in the whole symposium.

Finally, in the critical conception of U.S. American identity, some emphasize that this cannot be done in a holistic fashion, but that it needs to address particular aspects and particular figures. For example, Irving Howe asks, "Need we really lose ourselves in such immensities as 'America'? Must one hate or love such a grab-bag of abstractions as 'America'—or 'France' or 'Ethopia'? It seems more sensible to take America bit by bit, item by item, person by person."[58] David Riesman on the other hand will demand the right to confusion, vagueness, and openness in this search for self-identity:

> I am saying that an endless process of discovering ourselves, our burgeoning audiences, and our country may prove life-giving; it may also help us avoid the recurrent error, in a rapidly changing culture, of entrenching prejudices while still thinking of ourselves as heretics. Yet this is only possible if we are not too frantic in our search for originality, for sure conviction, and for good conscience. We will often find that our discovery has been made by others. We will often find that we need to take a stand against being forced to take a stand; that we have a right to be vague, confused, and indecisive.[59]

On the fiftieth anniversary of this symposium, the same journal organized a conference in May 2002 called "The Changing Role of Intellectuals, Artists, and Scientists in America, 1952–2002."[60] The conference had five major topics: Intellectuals and Writers Then and Now, The Ascendance of Science and Technology, The Media and Our Country's Agenda, What Happened to the Arts? and "European/American Relations: Who Leads?[61] In its overall apologetic tone the conference was a sad illustration of the worst fears of the 1952 critics: uncritical patriotism, conservative self-righteousness, and self-congratulation. In the aftermath of the 9/11 terrorist attacks, no genuine questioning of U.S. foreign policy is allowed, nor is an inquiry into the U.S. corporate expansionism welcomed.[62] France is seen to have replaced the Soviet Union in its anti-Americanism, and the European Union is regarded as a fragmentation of the democratic world and a dismantling of the nation-state.[63] European critiques of the United States and Israel are reduced to anti-Semitism.[64] Complaints are made about multiculturalism,[65] as well as about racial, political, and moral correctness. They are seen as threats to the Western canon and to the standards of excellence, leading to relativism. However, these complaints are made without delving into the arguments and the counterarguments related to these issues.[66]

Leitmotifs of a Powerful Postcolonial Country: American Issues of Culture, Power, and Critique

The issues raised in this critical evaluation of the country and its culture made by U.S. intellectuals are similar in many respects to those raised by Latin American, African, Indian, and Arab intellectuals around the same time in their debates on their own countries and cultures. But they also differ from them in some significant aspects.

What they have in common is this measuring up to European culture, this need to assess the maturity, value, and independent standing of one's culture with respect to those of the European. And in each case, this reflection is carried out with reference to Europe on a one-on-one basis, in isolation from other comparable postcolonial debates. The attempt made in the 1947 philosophy congress to conduct reflections on such questions in dialogue between North and South America has remained a rare instance with no real follow-up. Also common to these postcolonial debates is the need to link ideas to lived realities, to connect culture and philosophy to local lived experiences. The question that follows immediately from this concern is that of the meaning of particularity and universality in art, in literature and especially in philosophy. How to have a literature/a philosophy of one's own without falling into chauvinism and provincialism becomes an important challenge. The questions about the nature and identity of one's own culture call on questions about the identity of one's country or region: What is it to be North American, Latin American, African, Indian, or Arab? Who defines it? How? On what basis? Moreover, what room does the affirmation and demarcation of one's culture from that of Europe leave for critique and dissent? One is faced with the difficulty of affirming one's culture without giving in to self-glorification and/or total conformism (or to self-hatred, for that matter).

While in all other postcolonial debates one of the major obstacles in affirming cultural independence is the economic and political dependence vis-à-vis Europe (and later the "West" including Europe and the United States), in the U.S. debates a clear awareness of economic and political supremacy over Europe dominates, especially after World War II. This confidence in an unmatched wealth and power seems to lessen the awe toward Europe, even on the cultural level. The problem of U.S. intellectuals is to prove the compatibility of this wealth and power with the possibility of creating a valuable culture. For Latin Americans, Africans, Asians, and Arabs this wealth and power will, soon after World War II, become associated with, if not replace, European hegemony and constitute with it or in its stead "Western" hegemony. Moreover, the Europeanness, and more particularly the "Anglo-Saxonness," of U.S. culture do not seem to be an issue, at least in the dominant discourses. The only concern is about the need to adjust them to the American realities. The United States is understood to be a version of Europe. That the United States could have/should have been anything other than European, if in an Americanized way, is completely absent in these discourses. In all other debates, whether Latin American, African, Asian, or Arab, the European component is seen as one among others in shaping the region's culture, and a component introduced into it through the highly problematic circumstances of colonialism.

Some of the leitmotifs of these midcentury U.S. debates on culture have been recurring themes of intellectual discussions in the country since its independence, namely, the place of culture in a civilization dominated by commerce, industry, and technology; the relevance of culture to lived and changing realities; the challenges of wielding tremendous power; democracy, freedom, and pluralism; and the cultural definition of the country. Indeed, throughout the nineteenth and twentieth centuries, U.S. thinkers called for the creation of a spiritual and cultural wealth for the new country, in addition to the building of cities and railroads and banks and industries. They pleaded for the creation of an "American" culture that would represent their independent country without necessarily relinquishing their admiration and respect for the old and rich European culture, especially the French and the English.

What the revisiting of these midcentury debates reveals is the persistence of the central question of critique in a time of perceived danger. Whether in the face of a threatening communist Soviet Union or in the face of an aggressive and violent al-Qaeda organization, the fear for democracy is not only from the external aggressors but also from the internal measures taken to protect it. Reconciling dissidence and critique with defensive patriotism is in the beginning of this new century, as it was in the mid-twentieth century, a most challenging task. Reflecting on the economic and political foreign policy of this powerful and "innocent" nation remains as forbidding as ever.

Notes

1. The proceedings were published in *Travaux du Congrès international de philosophie consacré aux problèmes de la connaissance* (Port-au-Prince, Haiti: Imprimerie de l'état, 1947).
2. *Philosophy and Phenomenological Research* 9 (1949): 512. Hereafter cited as *PPR*.
3. Also the Rockefeller Foundation had apparently given a generous grant to enhance the role of philosophy in the life and education of the United States and of the world (*PPR*, 513).
4. See the program of the Third Philosophy Day organized by the UNESCO on November 18, 2004, in Paris. It is interesting to note that more than a century later the "dialogue of cultures" is still the major theme of the organization.
5. *PPR*, 512–513.
6. In this connection see Elizabeth Suzanne Kassab, "Integrating Modern Arab Thought in Postcolonial Philosophies of Culture," *American Philosophical Association Newsletter* (Fall 2004): 2–7.
7. *PPR*, 515–516.
8. Ibid., 515.
9. Ibid., 522–523.
10. Ibid., 529.
11. Ibid., 529–530. A similar understanding of democracy and a similar view of South America is defended by Waldo Frank in his *South American Journey* (New York: Duell, Sloan and Pearce, 1943), esp. 365, 369.
12. *PPR*, 568–569.
13. Ibid., 568.
14. Ibid.
15. See F. S. C. Northrop, *The Meeting of East and West* (New York: Macmillan, 1946), introduction.
16. *PPR*, 584–585.
17. On the United States side the writer Waldo Frank had presented similar analyses in 1943, in *South American Journey* (ibid., 359ff) and already in *The Rediscovery of America* (New York: Duell, Sloan and Pearce, 1929), 267ff.

18. *PPR*, 542.

19. Ibid., 543.

20. Leopoldo Zea, "Philosophy as an Instrument of Interamerican Understanding" *Social Epistemology* 1 (1987): 123–130.

21. *PPR*, 351.

22. Ibid., 352.

23. *PPR*, 356–357

24. It would be interesting to compare Perry's characterization of the North American mind with those of the Latin American mind done for instance by Samuel Ramos in *Profile of Man and Culture in Mexico* (Austin: University of Texas Press, 1962) and by Octavio Paz in *The Labyrinth of Solitude* (New York: Grove Press, 1985). For more on the American mind by Perry, see his *Characteristically American* (New York: Knopf, 1949) and his chapter entitled "World Culture and National Culture" in his book *One World in the Making* (New York: Current Books, 1945), 170–203.

25. *PPR*, 358.

26. Ibid., 366.

27. Ibid.

28. Ibid., 360.

29. Ibid., 358.

30. Ibid., 356.

31. Ibid., 358.

32. Ibid., 359; emphasis in original.

33. W. E. B. Du Bois, *The World and Africa* (New York: Viking Press, 1947), 1.

34. Ibid., 17.

35. Ibid., 41.

36. Ibid., 26.

37. Aimé Césaire, *Discourse on Colonialism* (New York: Monthly Review Press, 2000), 36.

38. Du Bois, *The World and Africa*, 23.

39. James Baldwin, "Stranger in the Village," *Harper's*, October 1953, reprinted in James Baldwin, *Notes of a Native Son* (1955; Boston, MA: Beacon Press, 1983), 174.

40. Following is a selection of literature about the journal and its intellectual context: William Phillips, *A Partisan View: Five Decades of the Literary Life* (New York: Stein and Day, 1983); Warren Susman, ed., *Culture and Commitment, 1929–1945* (New York: George Braziller, 1973); Warren Susman, *Culture as History: The Transformation of American Society in the Twentieth Century* (New York: Pantheon Books, 1984); Richard Hofstadter, *Anti-Intellectualism in American Life* (New York: Knopf, 1970), esp. the conclusion; Russell Jacoby, *The Last Intellectuals: American Culture in the Age of Academe* (New York: Basic Books, 1987),

esp. chap. 4; Thomas Bender, *New York Intellect: A History of Intellectual Life in New York City, From 1750 to the Beginnings of our Own Time* (Baltimore: Johns Hopkins University Press, 1987). Also relevant to the themes of the symposium is Horace M. Kallen's book *Culture and Democracy in the United Sates* (Piscataway, NJ: Transaction Publishers, 1998).

41. One of the editors of the journal, Philip Rahv, had edited a few years previous a set of essays written by major American writers on their experiences of Europe entitled *Discovery of Europe: The Story of American Experience in the Old World* (Boston, MA: Houghton Mifflin, 1947). Of direct relevance to our topic is his introduction, xi–xix.

42. *Partisan Review* (1952): 284. Hereafter cited as *PR*.

43. Ibid., 286.

44. *America and the Intellectuals: A Symposium* (New York: Partisan Review, 1953). I will be using the journal as a reference.

45. The names of the participants as they appear in the journal are Newton Arvin, James Burnham, Allan Dowling, Leslie A. Fiedler, Norman Mailer, Reinhold Niebuhr, Philip Rahv, David Riesman, Mark Shorer, Lionel Trilling, William Barrett, Jacques Barzun, Joseph Frank, Horace Gregory, Louis Kronenberger, C. Wright Mills, Louise Bogan, Richard Chase, Sidney Hook, Irving Howe, Max Lerner, William Phillips, Arthur Schlesinger Jr., and Delmore Schwartz.

46. *PR*, 300.

47. Ibid., 302.

48. See, for instance, Reinhold Niebuhr, *The Irony of American History* (New York: Scribner Library, 1949).

49. *PR*, 302. Waldo Frank calls this disease of power "Americanism," but he traces it back to European modernity. The latter, according to him, emptied medieval European culture of its spiritual dimensions and caused the downfall of this culture. It is this agonizing culture that has arrived in America. Only a revival of that great spiritual tradition with the help of the impulses of the new world can save that culture from the lethal temptations of greed and war. See Frank's *The Rediscovery of America* (New York: G. Braziller, 1929) and *Chart for Rough Water* (New York: Doubleday, 1940; reprint, New York: Duell, Sloan and Pearce, 1947).

50. *PR*, 313–314.

51. On the subject of U.S. anti-intellectualism see Hofstadter, *Anti-Intellectualism in American Life*; Jacoby, *The Last Intellectuals*.

52. In an article published a year later, in 1953, in the same journal, Herbert Marcuse presents a critical analysis of European anti-Americanism: "European Anti-Americanism," *Partisan Review* 20 no. 3 (1953): 314–320.

53. *PR*, 290.

54. Ibid., 291.

55. Ibid., 323.

56. Ibid., 437.

57. Ibid.

58. Ibid., 580.

59. Ibid., 313.

60. The proceedings were published in the fall 2002 issue of *Partisan Review* 69, no. 4 (2002): 500–669.

61. The speakers were Norman Podhoretz, Sanford Pinsker, John Patrick Diggins (an African American), Raymond Kurzweil, Gerald Weissmann, James Collins, Hilton Kramer, Michael Meyers, Edward Rothstein, Jules Olitski, Robert Brustein, Cynthia Ozick, David Pryce-Jones, Liah Greenfeld, and Walter Laqueur.

62. *Partisan Review* (2002): 532–541.

63. Ibid., 638, 643.

64. Ibid., 655–669.

65. Ibid., 620–621.

66. For more on the issue of multiculturalism see Allan Bloom, *The Closing of the America Mind* (New York: Touchstone Book, 1987); William Bennett, *The De-Valuing of America* (New York: Touchstone Book, 1992); John Arthur and Amy Shapiro, eds., *Campus Wars: Multiculturalism and the Politics of Difference* (Boulder, CO: Westview Press, 1995).

2

When Fear Interferes with Freedom

Infantilization of the American Public Seen through the Lens of Post–9/11 Literature for Children

Kyoo Lee

We crossed the ocean seeking opportunity,
seeking freedom,
seeking peace.
Surely it wasn't our fault
that we found our opportunity occupied
by those we named Indians,
Though they had never seen India;
redskins,
. . . A plane crashes into a tower.
Two planes.
Two towers.
Another into the heart
Of our ability to make war.
We are afraid.
We are afraid.
We are afraid.
What will they do next?
What will we do?
A plane crashes into a tower.

—Marion Dane Bauer, "A White American's Lament"

Urgent Needs

The above poem opens the "Reacting and Recovering" section of *911: the Book of Help.*[1] This anthology of essays, stories, poems, and artwork aims to offer "teachers and parents a vehicle for opening discussion with children and young adults about fear, heroism, hate, and healing."[2] This text seeks to "provide comfort in time of need," because

> [w]ritten words give power to the powerless, and hope to the hopeless. They bring light to darkness, courage to fear and companionship to loneliness. When tragedy struck our nation on September 11, 2001, teachers and parents struggled with what to say to the children. A year has passed, but the images of that horrible day are forever implanted in the minds, hearts, and souls of all Americans. Children, especially, need to reflect upon that day, and find ways to express their thoughts and feelings. What better way than through the writings of authors they already respect?[3]

Eight years on, I find myself echoing that urgency: "Children, especially, need to reflect upon that day." *Teacher's Guide for 911* amplifies the voice of the haunted poet: "Discuss what Marion Dane Bauer means when she writes that . . . fear 'diminishes our humanity.' How can fear interfere with freedom? Debate whether our nation's attempt to protect us is indeed creating more fear."[4] Indeed, "how can fear interfere with freedom?"

My plan is to offer some philosophical observations on the post–9/11 infantilization of the American public. And my thoughts are anchored on a case, a kind of literalized allegory, a sample of mainstream pedagogic literature for American children and young adults relating to the event "9/11,"[5] the aesthetically ontologized and selectively historicized spectacle that haunts the recent American memories that have been immediately packaged and globally exported. Focusing on the political logic and rhetoric of "home" or "homeland" that "protects us" from "them," I will show how the figures of the threatening other, media-theatrically contrasted with those of the united family and friends, become not simply antagonized but specifically racialized.

The current political context that our reading inhabits and at the same time problematizes is the aggressive delimitation and production of a national pronoun, "we," who wage a war after and within the extended war of 9/11, we who "bring the holy war *home*."[6] That is, the reflexive urgency of 9/11, still resonant today, sets the stage for interrogating the roles, places, and modes of patriotic discourse in American children's literature. The wake-up call has brought to the surface another cold war, a struggle between, this time, the United States of America and its other that causes un-united states of affairs.

Thus, the guiding premise of this chapter is that the urgent task, posed since *September 12th, 2001: (When) We Knew Everything Would be All Right* was written,[7] of "rebuilding the nation" through an ideological re-*bildung* or sociopsychical homogenization of future citizenship, calls for an equally urgent, critical examination of its mechanism, political and rhetorical. Here I am recalling the urgency with which Ellen Willis suggested, already in the winter of 2001, that we pay immediate attention to the powers and perils of cultural politics in the post–9/11 United States. Eight years on, what this chapter seeks to anatomize, in that same theoretical spirit, while using children's literature as an allegorical mirror, is the modes of coextensive interaction between the post–9/11 wars abroad and the ethnocultural "war at home." Such an interdisciplinary interrogation into the complex duality and duplicity of the political present, also undertaken as an attempt to interweave the conceptual resources of philosophical inquiry and the material richness of children's literature, is then a kind of "cultural criticism" that Theodor Adorno envisioned against the reified, "bewitched" reality of cultural capitalism fueled by "vulgar positivism and pragmatism."[8] In the end, I've come to agree with Adorno that "cultural criticism must become social physiognomy."[9]

An Allegory of *September 11, 2001: The Day That Changed America*

Why children and their books? Immediately apparent is their allegorical hook: the narrative simplicity, graphic directness, and pedagogic topicality of coated terror stories offer manageably analytic and even magnetic access to the otherwise elusive, multilayered "event." Saint-Exupéry, for instance, began composing *The Little Prince* during World War II. "A picture of a hat," with which the story begins, is x-rayed to reveal a picture, in it, of "a boa constrictor digesting an elephant." Immediately subtextualized here, with the graphic literalness, is an allegorical tension between the adult world of oblivious civilization and the children's world of unadulterated perceptions: the hat, in which the violence of the jungle is hidden, reveals the failure of moral imagination in the world of adults who seem to have lost the ability to see things as they are. Or take Dr. Seuss, of the 1960s, whose transgressive mobilization of domestic material such as butter, ham, and egg in many stories of minibattles brings close to home the polarized realities of the cold war, to which those indifferent to *New York Times* editorials or reports from the Soviet Academy of Sciences too can relate, the child or the childlike. Allegory then, as Walter Benjamin noticed when few did, is not simply a hermeneutical trick; it is an alchemist's lens through which the dis/order of social epistemology reveals itself. Allegorical narrative seeks to do justice to the historical ontology of the ambiguous.

The narrative ambiguity and parallelism of allegory creates inner distance. Allegory brings theatrical comfort, and to that extent it is socially therapeutic—especially in times of crisis, individual or collective.[10] Thus, a nation at a historical turning point will sublimate the aggregated traumas and confusions of such a moment through storytelling or dramatization. And predictably, the "countertransferentiality"[11] or counterfactuality of reactionary fables reveals the reflexively inscribed polarity of contradictory self-images emerging from the ruins of the traumatic event; the victim becomes the victor, and "community defensiveness"[12] will at times allow the victory to be permanent, at least momentarily. Such narrative consolation on a mass scale, taking the form of symbolic co-crying and cuddling, that is, literary reconciliation with each and every inner child, collectively contributes to the reduction of posttraumatic symptoms that one cannot and must not "ignore, deny, belittle, or tolerate"; one will have to live with and eventually overcome the inner child's "somatic complaints, sleep difficulties and nightmares, clingy and regressive behaviors, fears, inability to concentrate, avoidance of talking about the event, irritability, hypervigilance, acting-out behaviors, repetitive play,"[13] and so on. Eight years since, and eight years from now, we are and will not be surprised by the abundance of post–9/11 stories for children.

What kind of story and what sort of child reader, inner or outer, should one envision in the aftermath of globalized national shock such as "the" 9/11, a singularized event in the recursive calendar of the unified world? A vulnerable child made more vulnerable by the imaginary return of the original trauma? Something akin to a prehistoric crisis of the absent presence of the world, for example, the ultimately "horrible terrifying thoughts . . . what if both Mom and Dad hadn't come home?"[14] Now, does the same sensitive child ever ask the five-year-old question of metaphy sical origin "Where . . . from?" at least once, at least later on? Simply: *why* did that happen? Do we see or hear any questions of that kind? Oddly, no, although there are a couple of notable exceptions, one of which enabled this chapter to start. Here is what nine-year-olds and above are reading today:

1. In 1990, Iraq invaded Kuwait and the United States launched Operation Desert Storm.
2. Desert Storm helped push the Iraqi invaders out of Kuwait.
3. Following Desert Storm, the United States left soldiers in Saudi Arabia to help prevent future skirmishes.
4. Saudi Arabia also is a source of much of the oil upon which the United States depends.
5. Osama bin Laden was very upset about having U.S. soldiers in Saudi Arabia.

6. The nation is considered home of the two most holy places in the region of Islam.
7. He also hated the support the United States provided to Israel.
8. He began to talk with other people about driving these infidels out of the holy lands.
9. As time went on, it appeared his hatred of America grew. He declared a holy war against the US.
10. He began recruiting more people to help him.[15]

Let me propose a minireading experiment. Let us imagine and follow a thoughtful child reader, who is trying to absorb the information presented in the numbered list by putting it through some sort of reasoning process. This nine-year-old reader has limited but good vocabulary that is rapidly growing. So first, Osama was very upset (5). That's why he did it. But *why* was he upset? We helped Kuwait and Saudi Arabia (1–3) because they were invaded or were about to be by Iraq and we also helped Israel (7). So we help people when they need our protection[16]—but then what was Israel's problem (question 1)? Was Iraq trying to invade Israel too? That is unclear but what we know is that Osama did not like the fact that we helped Saudi Arabia and Israel when they were in trouble (5, 6). Then, why did he dislike it (question 2)? The book also says Saudi Arabia has oil that we need. Does it then mean that Osama does not like us using Saudi Arabia's oil? But then does that mean Israel and Kuwait too, both, have oil? Is that then *why* we helped Saudi Arabia? But we are helping people in need, not people we need (question 3). What is this IS-lahm, a religion? Osama hates US being in Saudi Arabia (5), but what has it got to do with Saudi Arabia being IS-lahm (6), and what has it go to do with US supporting Israel (7)? What are the connections? (question 4) And also, how can Osama think that Saudi Arabia is a holy land but also that people in it are unholy? And does "people" mean both Saudi Arabians and the American soldiers living with them? How can they be unholy when they are already in the holy land? *Why* are they unholy (question 5)? Is that because they have or need oil? Then does that make US, the United States, unholy too? Is that why Osama attacked US too? (9) But are we not supposed to be holy too, like Osama thinks he is (8) (question 6)? And more importantly, is Osama then going to attack anybody he thinks unholy? Are we then unholy (question 7)? If we really are actually holy, will he ask us to fight for and with him? Against whom (question 8)? Are we supposed to fight against him or fight with him against us? Who are we: fellow Americans, as we say (question 9)? How can we fight against and also for us? But Osama should not attack us because we are religious too; we go to church. So why are we fighting (question 10)?

The cited passage, which our imaginary child reader is trying to understand, illustrates, among other things, the extent to which publicly accessible reasoning has become scarce in a country rich in publicly accessible information. With the exception of *911: The Book of Help*, written in the tone and style of egalitarian dialogue, and another text that I will introduce later, nowhere in the texts I examined, not unlike what we examined here, is there present or implied a child thinker with original sensibility, analytical ability, and contextual awakening. Almost no one in those books asks meaningfully and logically ordered questions about causes or origins, and almost everyone in those books seems handheld or umbilicalized by an imaginary parental supervisor who would do the question and answer for the kids concerned, after doing a perfunctory thirty minutes of homework on their daily trip to the CNN newsroom that offers a 24/7 recursive diet of incredible stories that keep them bolted to their recliner.

Today, the United States of America, the hypermilitarized media-aesthetic state that exploits popular culture and entertainment as a weapon of mass distraction and inscription, seems to have reached a critical stage of compulsive self-hypnotism. Even a TV commercial for a local supermarket, "we're holding a spatula and salute you,"[17] cryptically reinscribes in the popular memory the much publicized scene of the wartime president soon-to-be holding up an American flag, emerging from the rubble of ground zero.[18] Given the paternalistic dominance and structural capitalization, since the culture war of the early 1990s, of quasi-theocratic right-wing politics in the United States today that significantly feeds into the concerted process of infantilization/domestication, anti-intellectualization, and media-production of public sensibilities, it is unsurprising that most post–9/11 "comfort"[19] books for children leave little room for creative self-reflection and critical self-examination: to wit, for the cultivation of the Emersonian faculty. After consuming those "here & now reproducible"[20] books with cookie-cutter drawings of recovered white heterosexual nuclear middle-class families plus occasional dogs and neighborly look-alikes, the target reader—or, shall we say, the targeted reader—in pajamas is supposed to feel secure in the bosom of "God who cried too" or inspired to emulate *New York's Bravest* that dates as far back as the 1840s. Or generally, they are to feel simply "a lot better,"[21] thus able to go out and play freely, happily forgetting all about what happened.

At times like this, trauma is unavoidable, and sensitivity is necessary. And precisely for that reason, the nation in mourning has a collective responsibility to articulate and express her future vision and hope; the national tragedy has united them and us, children and adults. Then the question for us is whether we are using the defenselessness of the child to reinforce our own childish defensiveness. Will they ever get to think about those fellow children sleeping around the U.S.–Mexico border, dreaming good dreams and bad dreams?[22] Will the children of the United States ever be arrested by a sudden grayness of the world, by the paradox that the parallel "rebuilding of a nation" at home and abroad leads to the simultaneous shrinking and spreading of the homeland? Will they ever discover this paradox that nation-building is an act that is at once supremely optimistic and supremely oppressive? Will they ever wonder, facing our leader facing a hate killer, whether we too are "defiant and evasive"?[23] Will they ever be touched by this terribly simple irony of might: strong and vulnerable?

The notable weakness of public reflection paralleling the military strength of social conditioning is hardly shocking, yet alarming nonetheless. In the same vein, we need to pay attention to the proliferation of age-diversified pedagogic books on the national political catastrophe, which contributes to the homogenization of public voices and views on it. We will not forget that we have been attacked, but we have forgotten that we have often been attackers, justly or not. We seem to want to forget pernicious and predictable side effects of the Rooseveltian doctrine of "Get action, do things,"[24] that is, "the domination of the world";[25] indeed, are not the American moments, guilt, and identities easily, if not entirely, definable by the military images of attacks and counterattacks? Foundational genocide; battle with colonial Britain; the Spanish-American War; Pearl Harbor;[26] Hiroshima—are we not walking into a memory hole yet again when escorted into the Philippine House of Representatives and away from thousands of local protesters who refuse to share our cheerleaders' ultimate goal? (An)aestheticized[27] "imperial amnesia"[28] it is; are we going to continue to ignore that the United States too has (been) playground bullies, and not a few (times)? But, "Why? Why? Why?"[29]

Although at least one of our books calls into question the nationalized drive toward world dominance as an explanatory background to what happened, the pattern of the other tragedy is clear enough. The reactive introversion and historical amnesia of the nation in mourning, locatable in the little corner of American literature today, quietly demonstrates the extent to which a strategic alliance between pedagogy and ideology, between mnemonic technology and media politics, is being forged in the name of national and international pride linked to the discourse of "moral values" that rests on the socio-Darwinian convertibility of mortal[30] threats to moral[31] threats: the simultaneous individuation and unification of Pan-American identity in the name of freedom has come at a sloganized price that one buys without realizing its worth, actual and virtual.

Color Un/Conscious: No/Black and White

Hit, panic; collapse, panic; terrified faces running away, eyeballs glued to TV; we blanked out, blacked out. Ground Zero has become something of a location for a horror film that harbors serialized memories of a collective panic attack. The nation watched, in "real time," over and over again, the safe house of identities and ideals turning into the graveyard of the undead, suddenly and completely. The site houses, and has become, a contemporary allegory of the national house in ruin.

Now, where does the United States turn? Where should the United States turn at this political "zero point" of the twenty-first century, performatively designated as such? Is she progressing or regressing? "It is my experience," says the performance artist Anna Deavere Smith, "that when things are upside down, there is an opening for a person like me. When things fall apart, you can see more and you can even be part of indicating new ways that things can be put together."[32] The compositional metaphor she is employing when envisioning a future that is a gift of rupture is inspirational. What new ways is the United States exploring? Or is she? How is the shattered public space to be reconfigured? How is American membership within the global community to be reidentified, regrouped, and reproduced in the aftermath of the catastrophic fall?

Ground Zero remains gray, and the White House under President Bush became whiter than ever. Scared and raced, we are scaring and racializing each other. We want "all in our control" and nothing beyond our control, since we are a nation believing in purely controlled peace.[33] The promise of American liberty and equality is being compromised by collective acts—for example, the USA PATRIOT Act—of profound evasion and amnesia. One pretends as if nothing had happened, or nothing that requires reasoned reflection, or else one proceeds as if no one should be protected from the invasive violence of imperial sovereignty. Unpleasant facts, whitewashed and airbrushed, are tossed into and are piling up in the repressed archive of national memories. While the ex-president focused on the hard work, the really hard work God made him do, the ex-vice president forged the "one percent doctrine": a theory of preemptive strike that justifies, on the basis of paradigmatic convertibility of statistical probability to selective liability, the military destruction of would-be enemies such as terrorists parading as tourists, which in turn justifies domestic policing actions such as the racial profiling and incarceration of U.S. citizens, residents, and visitors of Arab, Muslim, and South Asian origin. *We* will make *them* visible before they appear, since we have reason to assume they are the new DWB (driving while black/brown) with WMDs (weapons of mass destruction). In other words, we saw a historical ghost of race racing out of the Oval Office of evasion and amnesia and marching into a new domain of black and white grammar: "they" who terrorize versus "we" who are terrified. We saw a post–9/11 reemergence of the "one drop rule," the racist policy enforced and maintained during the Jim Crow era, which could be read as the white government's totalized attempt to symbolically phenomenalize "*invisible* Blackness,"[34] the invisible threat that is the black bloodline contaminating the white gene pool even with a drop, even "without a hint of Africa."[35] The undeconstructed white logic, of historical blindness and ideologized purity, unfolds on the reflexive urge to draw a line between the past and the present: black and white, pure and simple. Ground Zero has become sanitized ground.

The post–9/11 United States has transcoded Du Bois's "color line" into a color bar, or a colorful barcode; right there, the twenty-first century is merging with the twentieth century. In the name of a political decision (*krisis*) animating the traumatic cut of 9/11, the nation is restaging race panic, wanting a psychopolitical protection not of but from truths. We rarely have a principled protection of bare truths obscured by historicized assumptions, pernicious prejudices, and political smokescreens. But we do have a digitalized protection from dark truths, violently ambiguous and contagious like the prehistoric intention of Hitchcock's birds waging a war of the species for no apparent reason. We the people have become numb, have caught the bird flu already—and virtually. Unable to grasp where they come from and why they come to us, gripped by the fear of fear, the United States is losing its ability to judge without being judgmental; the affectivity of race panic is being converted to a moralized excuse for systematic, symbolic, and literal violence exercised in the name of state sovereignty. The United States, the global "promoter of democracy,"[36] has even become suspicious of and hostile to the faculty, the *art*, of judgment that is arguably the most important human resource and building "block" for participatory democracy—a block that, as I will illustrate shortly, when rhetorically liquidated could turn into the experimental object of gunpoint democracy.

That is, terror has become real through a codified surrealization of the conflicting psychical energies of and within the collective. The visible war on invisible terror is both the cause and the effect of the color codification of dangerous strangers within belongers. That seems to be how the *homeland* security advisory system operates, parallel to the racial profiling happening inside the *homeland*. Through the classificatory inscription of colors on the national body, the immanent futurity of terror seeks momentary stability: the emergency of the present is prescribed through the reflexive logic of self-fulfilling prophesies, that is, a round-trip of sanctioned paranoia from "We know it, you will see" to "We knew it, I had already shown you" and back to the presumption. A cancerous result of this tautologized fear of the taxonomized other is the escalation of race-based xenophobia. Schizophrenic dichotomy fueled by race panic is destroying the progressive ideals of and commitment to the construction of the egalitarian and pluralist society that the founding fathers of the United States promised, blindly.

The fact that rainbows, emblematic of a multicultural and multiethnic utopia of American modernity, are not "bows" but rays or circles is worth remembering at this point. Worth pondering also is this question posed by Carl Friedrich in 1963: "Are nations really built? Or, rather, do they grow?"[37] The questions, thus combined, are Do the rainbows stack? Or do they spill over into each other? Are the rainbows not *infinite* braids of light, of hope? Will the children of immigration, or transportation, notice that difference between the word and the world? Or could that irreducible difference be, perhaps, precisely the origin of their preschooled fascination with the materiality of the world?

> Children are fascinated by color, texture, shape and design. You can attract the children to the art center by including activities that promote each of these. For example, invite the children to make a collage (pasting objects together onto a surface) of varying yellow colors found in magazines. This activity encourages preschoolers to cut, glue, look for and discover that any color can have many shades;[38] for younger [c]hildren, it is helpful to start with one color at a time. Have them use the primary colors of red, blue, and yellow.[39]

Given the formative role that pedagogy plays in nation-building, primary education of this kind is a dual source of despair and hope. In the rest of this chapter, I shall explain some of my philosophical issues with the nation's "color" education; then I shall explore some reasons why it is too soon for us to give up, to "renounce" our philosophical "interference . . . in the ever-changing production of what is always the same."[40]

The digitalized abuse of color in colorful education is a reason for despair. The aesthetic conditioning of neurological responses to solar and significatory wavelengths facilitates the production of advanced citizen automata seamlessly integrated into the socially constructed system of classification and representation.[41] Such prejudicial social programming of the political body happens at the semiotic, that is, prelinguistic or presymbolic, level of ideological engineering. Physical experiences have become woven together with social meanings and values, producing gestalt reflexes within racial and gender consciousness. The measurability of colors, in the hands of behaviorist technicians, translates into the malleability and predictability of colored perceptions that, in turn, sedimentizes the genealogical materiality of dominant social rhetoric. The ontological complexity of color gets lost in the socioepistemological reduction of its gradational vibrancy to snippets of useful truths such as racial and racist stereotypes.

So the United States, as was once suggested by a fellow academic jester, is in fact a bowl of gumbo rather than a melting pot.[42] This alternative metaphor effectively discloses the lies, illusions, and pitfalls of "multicultural" education that end up typecasting rather than liberating the sociopolitical imagination of the United States today. Simply put, in "a world of rainbow students in which people often see race or color first and only afterward move on to the content of a person's character,"[43] the promise of social justice can be as easily fulfilled as that of virtualized reality. Thus, in the world of political drama scripted by the imperial "tyranny of expectations,"[44] both the assimilated stranger and the unassimilated invader play a role; the former as a counterbalancing extra, a model minority, and the latter as the antagonist. If the former fulfills the social expectations by "continually negotiating role expectations based on (skin) pigmentation,"[45] the latter does so by refusing to negotiate. The former internalizes the inclusive-exclusive logic of racial integration in order to survive, and the latter, in order to retaliate; *both* "the good guy" and "the bad guy" originate from white America's suspicion over dual or fuzzy identities. An extreme and extremely disturbing case in point is the image of the rainbow "pedagogically"[46] exploited by the Ku Klux Klan that uses black as a color of racial mixing, which is "bad," and rainbow as a color of racial integration (read: placing), which is "good";[47] good enough to represent the colors of their goods at "Kstore. . . . Coming Soon!"[48]

We have just glimpsed the logic of terrorized justice that keeps intact and fragile the facade of the colorized nation-state, which tends to be slighted, if not ignored, by the idealized philosophy of nonracial identity such as the "color-blind" version that Anthony Appiah proposes as a futural vision.[49] But the fact is, in this garden variety world of pick and mix, the use value of phenotypical and ethnocultural stereotypes can save us or kill us, not simply misidentifying or at best amusing us; more precisely, the problem of blind pretension or justice in colored thinking or social policy lies in a systematically "unfair"[50] or asymmetrical activation of color consciousness, which is where the ideal of blind justice remains insufficiently and inadequately blind to the concrete realities of its own randomly self-contradictory behaviors. Consider, for instance, "the inconsistencies between the color blindness that is invoked against affirmative action and the color consciousness that becomes apparent in the denunciation of immigration."[51]

Here is an illustration of the simple yet complex shifty color of racialized terrorism, again from *September 11, 2001: The Day That Changed America*. Two consecutive chapters, "Pitching In" and "The Roots of Hatred,"[52] show two faces of the potentially terrifying other. A bearded man in a blue turban, faintly smiling or perhaps squinting, is holding up an American flag bigger than him, about to hoist it in front of the door that bears the sign "Under 18 . . . Tobacco"; another American flag, smaller, is hitched behind the door, and so the reader has a parallel view of the miniflag and the megaflag, back and front. The caption reads: "Showing the Colors: A Sikh immigrant from India puts up an American flag outside his shop in downtown Manhattan."[53] What colors? It is hard to tell because we only see a subtly coerced, overdetermined display of "color-blind" patriotism among the colored. Next, a partially scarfed, youthful, Middle Eastern face, on which the camera zoomed in, is revealing its black, screaming mouth; the outstretched fist above the face, which forms the only and fuzzy background, completes the scene of some sort of fury. The caption helps: "Anger Boils Over: A Palestinian protester shows his hatred of Israel and the United States." What hatred? It is hard to tell because we only have an isolated representation of "unyielding hatred" that remains incomprehensible, that is, that which "few people could understand."[54] Puzzling as well as illuminating is the fact that the writer could not or did not make an effort to visually verify the geohistorical information—is that screamer locatable in Manhattan too, or is that person possible only in Palestine? The phenotypical similarities between the two characters are rhetorically apparent. Yet in the first picture, the focus is on the flag, the very act of verticalizing it and multiplying it, and the second, the face itself: the eyes, the nose, the gaping mouth, the terrifying youth. The corner shopkeeper of America can occasionally become an American *although* he is not really American; the Palestinian madman, wherever he ends up being, can never become an American *because* he is really not. Between those two images that speak two dis/similar languages, one a hyperbolic assurance and the other a heightened assault, we see the back of the neck of a white male New York City firefighter with a paper flag hitched on his helmet, "surveying the wreckage of the World Trade Center,"[55] as if surveying the United States for clues.

Here is another example. Take *New York's Bravest*. The legendary firefighter from the 1840s, named Mose Humphreys, employee No. 40, is multiplied by contemporary legends, "all eight feet tall and able to swim the Hudson River in two strokes."[56] This tall tale, dedicated "to the memory of 343 New York City firefighters who gave their lives to save others on September 11, 2001," is historically accurate to the extent that the accompanying illustrations blacken only three or four faces among about a hundred featured therein. What is curious is the last page of the book where the moral of the story is summarized, "Whenever we save folks, he saves them, too. You see, that firefighter—he'll never leave us. He's the very spirit of New York City"; there suddenly appears a small girl with East Asian features held in the arms of, and holding onto the neck of, none other than the one and only but also many Mose Humphreys who apparently just saved her. On a charitable reading, the ahistorical eruption of this alien character from the Far East could be deciphered as a pictorial gesture toward the racially inclusive, rainbow future of New York City. Still, however, structurally problematic is the incoherence, impossibility, and predictability of its paternalistic rhetoric, symptomatic of the economized desire for a sudden, selected continuity with the past; as the text is "originally" from the idealized past, the new Mose could not have been Mose Wang, and the new rescuee could not have been Mohammed Humphreys.

Lest you think the reading so far is too arbitrary and exaggerated, I suggest we visit *This Place I Know: Poems of Comfort. This Place* has been explored in various ways by eighteen renowned picture artists, who offered visual reflections on poems of their choice. Some consistent efforts at diversifying the facial colors of the families and friends within each pictorial space are visible, quite unremarkably. The notable part is the cover picture that represents the overall tone of the anthology. Here we have the face of an unshaven pale male with a hat on, *on* which the whole of gray Manhattan sits, and he is gazing vacantly at the poem on the opposite page: Walt Whitman's *Song of the Broad-Axe*.[57] That is the only page on which a male adult appears and does so broodingly. Is this place I know, then, created and inscribed initially and finally by the white man's burden, and in his headache? Is this reading of paternalistic guilt and authority in post–9/11 discourse biased?

Consider this too. Next to the poem by Susan Swanson, *Trouble, Fly*, is a quilt of houses where everyone is sleeping, including cats and dogs inside and outside.[58] The focal point of this picture is the united nations of a nursery room: a white mother is asleep, with her arms around brown, yellow, and white children altogether bundled up in one bed; the sleeper series begins with the blond mom and ends with a blond kid who too had to stretch his or her arm (one of his or her arms) in order to bring closure to that dreamy space. If New York City is protected by the father, homes are managed by the mother who will breed and feed the next Mose Humphreys. Now, what does this ready evocation of the motherland do and not do in the given context? Who else has access to that immediately and ultimately huggable über mom?

Here is a more curious and most troubling part: the visible exclusion of specifically "Muslim" or "Middle Eastern" or "Arabic" markers, pictorial or narrative, from almost all of the child characters in the books I surveyed, which were conscientiously or correctly "multicultural." One very colorful and poetic exception I could locate is *We Are All the Same Inside*, where an extraterrestrial sage, reminiscent of Dr. Seussian characters, "comes to us, a person like you and me, but with only the inside we can see," with "a goal, . . . a soul, . . . with no outside skin (because the sage came from the 'planet where we are all kin')."[59] And,

> Sage was all alone and needed a home.
> Without any fear, Sage looked far and Sage looked near.[60]
>
> Will they think I'm Dwight when my outside is all white?
> Will there be a scar due to Dasha's black and violet hair?
> What about Safia's veil. . . . I wonder if it will fail?[61]

> The insider heard some chatter. So you know Sage went to see what was the matter.[62]

The matter is, again, the systematic post–9/11 exclusion of the emerging other. Another example: the picture diary book put together by the first-grade students of H. Byron Masterson Elementary School, Kennett, Missouri, (Heartland, USA), *September 12th: We Knew Everything Would be All Right*, which received "Kids Are Authors Award, 2002," seems not quite right. Given the geohistorical and demographical background of that region, it is unsurprising that the pupils photographically represented here are "black" or "white" with one "Hispanic" boy added to one corner of the pictorial list. But what remains troubling is the symbolic clue this prized model provides: now, the Muslim other is the new black, for blacks have been politically united with, that is, recruited supplementarily into, whites in this time of crisis, as exemplified by Darwyn al-Sayeed in *Sleeper Cell* (Showtime drama series, 2005), an undercover FBI agent, an African American Muslim hero who infiltrates an Arab terrorist network that is plotting to bomb Los Angelese. No father or mother or even ex-slave of the United States can and will protect those with markers of terrifying otherness, not even Humphreys who will go as far as rescuing a Chinese girl. Suddenly, U.S. citizens, residents, and visitors of Middle Eastern and South Asian origin/face/name find themselves terrified orphans, totally inside *and* outside the laws of protection and exclusion.

Is it then shocking that the nation, thus mediated and united, is complicitly following the sanctioned hunt for those who deserve torture when necessary? Does not such ethnosocial zoning, distancing and outcasting, which is a function of race panic, as discussed earlier, reproduce the fugitive culture of a United States paradoxically yoked to provincial familialism, the root of which dates back as far as the days of slavery? Given the color-coded boundaries of inclusion/exclusion and lines of flight, which constitute the sociohistorical ontology of the United States, what kind of social justice and hope can be multilaterally envisioned? How can we think across, and act against, the line? Can we even show a book of "We are all the same inside" to our "Mom and Dad"[63] who don't think the alien Sage is or should be in and among us? Where can we go from here?

In Place of Conclusion: This Place I Imagine

One book I kept in view while writing this chapter is Walter Benjamin's *Berlin Childhood around 1900*.[64] Perhaps the origin of the present piece is dis/locatable in that "blue onion pattern,"[65] which seems to have left a lasting impression on the child reader in me. Young Walter, or the legendary guardian angel in him, is delivering this message to us via the diary entry "Society," which describes the hustle and bustle of a house hosting a dinner party:

> The doorbell began to ring. . . . And it was in keeping with this demand that, for the time being, the door was opened immediately and quietly. Then came the moment when the party, though it had barely gotten underway, seemed on the point of breaking up. . . .[66]

> The mirror-bright dress shirt my father was wearing that evening appeared to me now like a breastplate, and in the look which he had cast over the still-empty chairs an hour before, I now saw a man armed for battle. . . . Then I had been given permission to help set the table. In doing so, not only was I honored by having utensils like lobster forks and oyster knives pass through my hands; but even the familiar everyday utensils called into service. . . . All had a festive air about them. . . . I was suddenly touched to the quick by the small sign of peace that beckoned to me from all the plates. It was the pattern of little cornflowers that adorned the set of flawless white porcelain—a sign of peace whose sweetness could be appreciated only by a gaze accustomed to the sign of war I had before me on all other days. I am thinking of the blue onion pattern. How often I had appealed to it for aid in the course of battles that raged round this table which now looked so radiant to me![67]

> And when my mother—although she was staying at home this evening—came in haste to say goodnight to me, I felt more keenly than ever the gift she laid on my bedspread every evening at this time. . . . When my father then called to her from outside my room, I felt only very proud, as she departed, to be sending her thus arrayed into society. And without quite realizing it, I grasped there in my bed, shortly before falling asleep, the truth of a little enigma: "The later the hour, the lovelier the guests."[68]

Or rather, the later the hour, the scarier the guests, one might still think. By now, the reason why this little gem remains inspirational should be fairly obvious to the reader too. How about learning an ethics of hospitality from young Walter? Why do we, the post–9/11 children of hope, risk becoming smaller by doubling the fear and sanitizing the bloody battles? Could we not, as Maurice Merleau-Ponty would suggest, allow our perceptions to "bleed"[69] a little bit? Could that be a way of accessing the vibrating pattern of a blue onion?

In "a load of books," an allegorist of the enduring end of childhood writes:

> The Little Duke is dead and betrayed and forgotten; we cannot recognize the villain and we suspect the hero and the world is a small cramped place. The two great popular statements of faith are "What a small place the world is" and "I am a stranger here myself."[70]

After all indeed, it seems the liminal strangeness of awakening that turns fully functioning adults into dislocated children over and over again, as captured by Graham Greene's metaphysical miniaturization of the progressive-regressive rhythm of cultured life. An estranged child, I too find myself rereading, compulsively, a story of *Bravemole*, intended "for those who, in a dark and terrifying hour, saw what needed to be done—and did it":[71]

> Once upon a time, there was a wicked dragon. . . . So begins the bedtime story that Mole tells his little babymole. And dragons do seem far away for this ordinary mole and his family, living out their lives in the usual way.[72]

> They too need a story. Something safe, that they could pick up and read, or keep out of sight on the shelf, as they wished. A story for them alone. And, since this is my work, I wrote them one.[73]

Notes

1. Michael Cart, Marc Aronson, and Marianne Carus, *911: The Book of Help*, 1st ed. (Chicago: Cricket Books, 2002), 138–141.
2. *Teacher's Guide for 911: The Book of Help* (cited September 11, 2006); available from http://www.cobblestonepub.com/resources_bks_911.html
3. Ibid.
4. Ibid.
5. Ibid.; Mitchel Levitas et al., *A Nation Challenged: A Visual History of 9/11 and Its Aftermath*, 1st ed. (New York: New York Times/Callaway, 2002); Marc Gellman and Harry Bliss, *And God Cried, Too: A Kid's Book of Healing and Hope*, 1st ed. (New York: HarperTrophy, 2002); Lynne Jonell, *Bravemole* (New York: Putnam's Sons, 2002); Mary Pope Osborne, Steve Johnson, and Lou Fancher, *New York's Bravest*, 1st ed. (New York: Knopf, 2002); Jill C. Wheeler, *September 11, 2001: The Day That Changed America*, *War on Terrorism* (Edina, MN: Abdo, 2002); Carol Marsh, *September 11, 2001: When America Was Attacked by Terrorists: Factual, Tactful Information to Help Us All Help All Kids!*, *The Hear & Now Reproducible Book of the Day That Was Different* (Peachtree City, GA: Gallopade International, 2001); H. Byron Masterson Elementary School

(Kennett, Missouri), *September 12th: We Knew Everything Would Be All Right* (New York: Scholastic, 2002); Rosina Schnurr and John Strachan, *Terrorism: The Only Way Is Through: A Child's Story* (Ottawa, ON: Anisor, 2002); *Teacher's Guide for 911: The Book of Help*; Georgia Heard, *This Place I Know: Poems of Comfort*, 1st ed. (Cambridge, MA: Candlewick Press, 2002); Timothy D. Bellavia, *We Are All the Same Inside* (New York: T.I.M.M.-E. Co., 2000).

6. Ellen Willis, "Bring the Holy War Home," *The Nation*, December 17, 2001; emphasis added.

7. H. Byron Masterson Elementary School, *September 12th*.

8. Theodor W. Adorno, *Prisms: Studies in Contemporary German Social Thought* (Cambridge, MA: MIT Press, 1981), 23, 29.

9. Ibid., 30.

10. Ester Cohen, "Play and Adaptation in Traumatized Young Children and Their Caregivers in Israel," in *Psychological Interventions in Times of Crisis*, ed. Laura Barbanel and Robert J. Sternberg (New York: Springer, 2006), 151–179.

11. Ibid., 174.

12. Ibid., 156.

13. Ibid., 155.

14. Schnurr and Strachan, *Terrorism*, 33.

15. Wheeler, *September 11, 2001*, 52; this passage is from the chapter entitled "The Roots of Hatred," 50–53. Numbers added for sequential analysis; the original source is accompanied by an illustration, "Target: Bin Laden; A photo of Osama Bin Laden taken sometime in 1998."

16. Secretary of State's speech addressed to U.S. troops ready to move into Kosovo as peacekeepers: "You are being asked to make it possible for those people to return to their villages, reunite with their families, and rebuild their lives. I know the Balkans are a long way from your families and your homes. But that is a price Americans pay for being the best. . . . Your job is to help us transform this region from a breeding ground for war into a source of stability, to put the last piece in the puzzle of a Europe that is stable, united and free. And to send a message to bullies like Milosevic that *the good guys don't back down*. In so doing, you will make a huge contribution to the security of future generations of Americans. And you will make this a better and safer world. Thank you for what you are doing. You will be doing God's work" (emphasis added). See Madeleine K. Albright, *Remarks to U.S. Troops in Operation Sabre, Camp Able Sentry near Skopje, Macedonia, 11 June 1999* (cited September 11, 2006); available from http://secretary.state.gov/www/statements/1999/990611a.html.

17. Kroger Grocery Stores.

18. A reproduction of this image is found in Wheeler, *September 11, 2001*, 14., with which the chapter "Mourning in America" begins.

19. Heard, *This Place I Know*.

20. Marsh, *September 11, 2001*. This series teaches "things kids want to learn about today."

21. Schnurr and Strachan, *Terrorism*, 33.

22. Luis Alberto Urrea and John Lueders-Booth, *By the Lake of Sleeping Children: The Secret Life of the Mexican Border* (New York: Anchor Books, 1996).

23. "After he recovered, Zubaydah was defiant and evasive. He declared his hatred of America." George W. Bush, *Transcript of President's Speech on the Global War on Terror* (The White House Office of the Press Secretary, 2006, cited September, 11, 2006); available from http://usinfo.state.gov/.

24. David Grubin, "Theodore Roosevelt, 26th President," an episode in the PBS series *American Experience* (1996). The official Web site includes some "fun" facts about Roosevelt: PBS, *Theodore Roosevelt* (1997–2002; cited September 11, 2006); available from http://www.pbs.org/wgbh/amex/presidents/26_t_roosevelt/index.html.

25. John B. Judis, "Imperial Amnesia," *Foreign Policy*, no. 143 (2004): 53.

26. See for instance David Ray Griffin, *The New Pearl Harbor: Disturbing Questions About the Bush Administration and 9/11* (Northampton, MA.: Olive Branch Press, 2004).

27. Matthew Frye Jacobson, "Imperial Amnesia: Teddy Roosevelt, the Philippines, and the Modern Art of Forgetting," *Radical History Review* 73 (1999): 117–127.

28. Judis, "Imperial Amnesia."

29. Cart, Aronson, and Carus, *911*, 101–107.

30. "We have seen our vulnerability—and we have seen its deepest source. For as long as whole regions of the world simmer in resentment and tyranny—prone to ideologies that feed hatred and excuse murder—violence will gather, and multiply in destructive power, and cross the most defended borders, and raise a mortal threat." George W. Bush, *Inaugural Address: President Sworn-in to Second Term* (2005; cited September, 11 2006); available from http://www.whitehouse.gov/news/releases/2005/01/20050120-1.html.

31. "We will persistently clarify the choice before every ruler and every nation: the moral choice between oppression, which is always wrong, and freedom, which is eternally right. . . . We have confidence because freedom is the permanent hope of mankind, the hunger in dark places, the longing of the soul." Ibid.

32. Anna Deavere Smith, *Anna Deavere Smith on Art and Politics* (PBS, 2006; cited September 11, 2006); available from http://www.pbs.org/now/shows/232/index.html.

33. "So I'm interested in having all—having an arsenal at my disposal, or at the military's disposal, that will keep the peace. We're a peaceful nation and moving along just right and just kind of having a time, and all of a sudden, we get attacked and now we're at war, but we're at war to keep the peace." George W. Bush, *Press Conference by the President, the James S. Brady Briefing Room, March 13, 2002* (2002; cited September 11, 2006); available from http://www.whitehouse.gov/news/releases/2002/03/20020313-8.html.

34. Frank W. Sweet, Legal History of the Color Line: The Notion of Invisible Blackness (Palm Coast, FL: Backintyme, 2005), 3; emphasis added.

35. Ibid.

36. Joshua Muravchik, *Exporting Democracy: Fulfilling America's Destiny*. Aei Studies 513 (Washington, DC: AEI Press, 1991), 221.

37. Carl J Friedrich, "Nation-Building," in *Nation Building*, ed. Karl Wolfgang Deutsch, William J. Foltz, and The American Political Science Association (New York: Atherton Press, 1963), 27–28.

38. Hilda L. Jackman, *Early Education Curriculum: A Child's Connection to the World*, 3rd ed. (Clifton Park, NY: Delmar Thomson Learning, 2005), 171.

39. Ibid., 1.

40. Adorno, *Prisms*, 23.

41. See empirical research data on color/gender awareness among children ages two to five noted in Joel H. Spring, *The Intersection of Cultures: Multicultural Education in the United States and the Global Economy*, 3rd ed. (Boston, MA: McGraw-Hill, 2004), 177.

42. "[T]he United States is not a melting pot but a rather unstable gumbo in which pieces of okra sometimes rise up, onions shift to the bottom, sausage bits hover at the middle . . . well, most metaphors do wear out." Emily Toth, *Ms. Mentor's Impeccable Advice for Women in Academia* (Philadelphia: University of Pennsylvania Press, 1997), 121. From the chapter entitled "When Culture Collides," 105–128.

43. "Ms. Mentor agrees that you (a 'tall Norwegian American female professor moving from the Dakotas to a big city community college') won't ever pass as a woman of color. But she can help you feel less uncomfortable with your suddenly high visibility. She can assure that everyone will instantly know who you are. You'll encounter jovial inquiries you've rarely heard before ('How's the weather up there?') and field odd queries ('Are you a guard or a forward?'). If there's another tall blonde, you'll be instantly and forever confused with her. If she teaches German, people will forever be jabbering in German at you. All of which should sensitize you to a world of rainbow students in which people often see race or color first and only afterward move on to the content of a person's character. You're also living in a time of great, often unspoken, racial

tension, in which any classroom discussion of race is apt to generate a vast, brooding, hostile silence. Everyone's afraid to be called a racist; everyone's afraid to be attacked; and you, by yourself, can't handle, soothe, or solve problems that have festered for hundreds of years." Ibid., 112–113.

44. Anthony Appiah and Amy Gutmann, *Color Conscious: The Political Morality of Race* (Princeton, NJ: Princeton University Press, 1996), 7.

45. France Winddance Twine and Jonathan W. Warren, *Racing Research, Researching Race: Methodological Dilemmas in Critical Race Studies* (New York: New York University Press, 2000), 1.

46. "On the front of our web site we have an illustration of a multi-colored rainbow and a black and white rainbow. It piques a lot of interest from young people who visit the site. It very simply illustrates that God's design was for different colors and different races to exist, each with their own abilities, culture, and innate differences. God does not hate the races He created and as children learn the basics then you need to build upon it so that they do not become filled with hatred. Race mixing destroys the rainbow God created. It is Satan who works to amalgamate the races upon the earth—to reduce all to a common level that can be easily controlled." Rachel Pendergraft, *Raising Your Children to Have Racial Integrity* (2006; cited September 11 2006); available from http://www.kkk.bz/raising_your_children_to_have_ra.htm.

47. Ku Klux Khan, *Love the Diversity of God's Creation* (cited September 11 2006); available from http://www.kkk.bz/NA00682_1.gif.

48. Ku Klux Klan, *K Store* (2006; cited September 11 2006); available from http://www.kukluxklan.bz/.

49. Appiah and Gutmann, *Color Conscious*.

50. See Gutmann's point of contention in "Responding to Racial Injustice," ibid., 109–110.

51. Frank H. Wu, *Yellow: Race in America Beyond Black and White* (New York: Basic Books, 2002), 28.

52. Wheeler, *September 11, 2001*, 46–49 and 50–53, respectively.

53. Ibid., 46.

54. Ibid., 51.

55. Ibid., 49.

56. Ibid., front flap.

57. Heard, *This Place I Know*, 34–35.

58. Ibid., 18–19.

59. Bellavia, *We Are All the Same Inside*, 6–9.

60. Ibid., 13.

61. Ibid., 17–19.

62. Ibid., 21.

63. To whom *We Are All the Same Inside* is dedicated; ibid., 38.

64. Walter Benjamin, *Berlin Childhood around 1900* (Cambridge, MA: Belknap Press of Harvard University Press, 2006).

65. Ibid., 138.

66. Ibid., 136.

67. Ibid., 137–138.

68. Ibid., 139.

69. Maurice Merleau-Ponty, *The Prose of the World* (Evanston, IL: Northwestern University Press, 1973), 152.

70. Graham Greene, *The Ministry of Fear, Entertainment* (New York: Penguin, 1993), 89.

71. The opening sentence of Jonell, *Bravemole.*

72. Ibid., front flap.

73. Ibid., back flap.

3

Muslim Women and the Rhetoric of Freedom

Alia Al-Saji

THE APPEAL TO the liberation of "other" women, specifically Muslim women, forms part of the rhetoric that seeks to justify the United States' so-called war on terrorism. Whether explicitly evoked as part of the justification for the continuing war in Afghanistan, or implicitly used to establish a certain moral superiority with regard to Muslim cultures, this rhetoric defines Muslim women as passive victims (or pawns) of their religion or culture from which they require liberation. Their freedom can only come through the intervention of an external—in this case United States or "Western"—force that can bring about this liberation, because as "free" societies these have a genuine understanding of freedom, an understanding that Muslim societies supposedly lack. The argument for "exporting" freedom for women, whether to Afghanistan or, even less convincingly, Iraq,[1] seems easily questioned when invoked by the Bush administration.[2] In particular, this move is criticized for its opportunism and bad faith in light of the same administration's disregard of women's rights and concerns in general. Yet such criticism does not address the representation of Muslim women at work in U.S. rhetoric. The reaction to U.S. policies, even on the part of mainstream feminists, is often accompanied by a belief that Muslim women are indeed in need of liberation; it is merely the means of liberation that is at issue.[3]

What goes unquestioned is the underlying assumption that Muslim women should be helped to freedom. On closer consideration, the assumption is twofold: First, Muslim women are oppressed—the oppression of women being seen as essential to Islam. The symbol of this social, cultural, or religious gender oppression is identified with the "veil." In this sense, it is the "veiled" Muslim woman who is the target of attempts at liberation (unveiled Muslim women are seen as "escapees" of their religion and implicit "allies" of liberating forces). Second, the "freedom" promised to Muslim women is universally desirable, both for Muslim women and for "Western" women who are understood to already possess, or at least be working toward, such freedom.

These two premises, though posited as separate, in fact rely on and mirror each other. Although "Western," liberal freedom is put forward as the natural remedy to the oppression of Muslim women, I would argue that this freedom is already conceived and valorized through the representation of that oppression, and hence cannot pretend to be a neutral recourse. In this regard, the image of the "veiled" Muslim woman is posited as antithetical to "freedom" (whether assumed to be actually available to Western women or progressively attainable by them by means of advances within Western society). The oppression of Muslim women is naturalized, specifically with respect to the "veil," just as the "freedom" of Western society and the ideal of Western womanhood are naturalized. This concept of "freedom" confronts Muslim women with an impasse, a choice between their religion or culture, on the one hand, and their supposed liberation or full subjectivity, on the other hand.

This chapter attempts to unravel the logic of representation that defines "Western" and "Muslim" in oppositional terms—a logic that at once elides the constitutive interdependence of these representations and positions "woman" as the contested terrain between them.[4] For women like me with complicated personal connections to both identities, this poses a false and sometimes intolerable dilemma. This dilemma is reinforced by the way feminist discourse, in its colonial and imperialist forms, assumes rather than deconstructs the dichotomy of Islam and the West, taking the latter to be the only appropriate and perfectible ground for feminist subjectivity.[5] At stake is not only the normalization of a particular Western construction of gender and selfhood, but the exclusion of other modes of subjectivity, differently structured desires, and hybridized forms of lived experience that do not fit neatly into the oppositional grid of religious-modern, oppressive-free, or Islamic-Western.

The obsession with "the veil"—which often works metonymically to designate Islam and "Islamic fundamentalism"—sustains just such an oppositional and exclusionary logic. I observed this obsession not only in media coverage but also in personal communications around the events of 9/11 and the wars in Afghanistan and Iraq.[6] As a Muslim-Canadian woman of Iraqi origin who has lived most of her life in the West and was a resident of the United States until 2002, I found myself called on to respond to questions, confirm hypotheses, and give an "insider's" perspective on Muslim women and their veiling practices. Why, for instance, is the veil (*abaya*) worn by Iraqi women always black?[7] What makes this seemingly straightforward question about customs of dress problematic is revealed if I attempt to pose an equivalent question to a U.S. individual: why do women often wear high-heeled shoes in the United States? Or even, why do U.S. men wear trousers? Several troubling elements emerge.

The question about the blackness of the veil demands a level of generalization that makes it difficult to introduce any historical, contextual, or experiential nuance. A static and homogenizing representation of the veil is assumed, whose value is not itself open to question; not only *is* the veil black, but this material feature *must be* salient to understanding women's veiling experiences and Iraqi society as such. Though Middle Eastern dress is not my field of expertise, the question puts me in the position of an expert, or what Uma Narayan has called an "authentic insider," simply because I hail from that region.[8] That the hermeneutical frameworks of social conventions are not so transparently accessible, and that situated knowledge may resist reformulation into essentialist explanations of the sort demanded, do not seem matters of concern. This brings me to a third worry: the lack of self-reflexivity that permits such questioning to appear as simple curiosity on the part of the questioner.[9] When I asked after the motivation for the aforementioned question, this was articulated as a concern for the well-being of Iraqi women: black seems so stifling in the heat of the Middle East. A paternalistic attitude is thus revealed behind the simplicity of the question. Although I believe that those who asked me such questions did not self-consciously adhere to a discourse of U.S. nationalism, of us versus them, they inadvertently and implicitly inscribed the rhetoric of freedom that sustained such nationalist identification. The call for a cohesive nation, for a "united America," requires the representation of an other (here Islam) as fundamentalist and oppressive, in order to maintain its appeal. These questions, and representations of the veil more generally, are part of a rhetoric of freedom that positions "the Muslim woman" as victim and foil; such rhetoric, I will argue, works to hide the gendered and racialized dimensions through which national and colonial discourses are formed.

It should be noted that the use of representations of Muslim women in the rhetoric of freedom has roots in colonial and orientalist discourses and is certainly not limited to the United States post–9/11, though it has become acutely visible in justifications of the continuing war in Afghanistan. Frantz Fanon's study of the French colonial project in Algeria, the British framing of the "woman question" to justify its colonial presence in Egypt, the forced de-veiling of women in movements of "modernization" in the 1930s in Iran and Turkey,[10] but also the more recent law banning the "Islamic head scarf" in French schools and debates surrounding the wearing of the "veil" in Quebec,[11] point to the fact that more is at stake here than the attempted justification of one nation's war. In this chapter, I will more broadly follow a line of questioning that asks after the representation of Muslim women in the "Western" imaginary (an imaginary shared by, though not limited to, the United States). The term "West" is an admittedly inadequate notion that I do not intend to defend here. What I wish to indicate is, however, the way in which the representation of Muslim women (as veiled, oppressed, unfree) plays a role in this geographical and cultural formation, and hence supports the binary of "us" and "them," of West and non-West (or, more narrowly, Muslim). To the degree that I use the term, this qualification should be kept in mind. "The West" is invoked in this chapter as an imaginary construct in formation, rather than an ontological entity with predefined boundaries and identity.[12]

In what follows, my focus will be on one dominant representation of Muslim women in the Western imaginary, a representation that is both contemporary and colonial: the Muslim woman as "veiled."[13] The use of the term "veil"—instead of "*hijab*" for instance—is itself open to debate, since this term covers over and reduces to a single representation what are culturally heterogeneous and historically dynamic phenomena.[14] In using the term "veil," it is precisely this representation that I aim to study critically. This chapter does not have within its scope the presentation of empirical cases, histories or descriptions of "veiling." It is neither an apology for nor a condemnation of the "veil," but an analysis that attempts to reveal the structures that sustain the Western representation of the "veiled" Muslim woman. In other words, what is the mechanism that produces the representation of Muslim women as veiled, and simultaneously overdetermines the image of the woman "hidden behind her veil" as oppressed, unfree, invisible, and anonymous? Indeed, the motivation for this chapter lies in understanding the hold and force of this representation on the Western imaginary. Surprisingly immune to counterexamples, able to stretch to incorporate individual, cultural, and historical exceptions, as well as attempts to redefine it, this largely homogeneous and reductive representation has a hold that, I believe, reflects its investment in Western constructions of femininity, freedom, and self.[15]

I take as my starting point the colonial discourse on the veil described by Frantz Fanon in his essay "Algeria Unveiled"—partly because of the clarity of his account, but also because of what he leaves unsaid.[16] By reading "Algeria Unveiled" together with *Black Skin, White Masks*, I critically extend Fanon's analysis by asking how dimensions of gender and race mutually support one another in the representation of the "veil."[17] Drawing on French and British colonial discourses on the veil as well as contemporary U.S. discourses around the "war on terrorism," I aim to go beyond Fanon's French example to unearth the mechanisms of othering at work in "Western" representations of the veil—what I will call the "racialization" of the veil. My purpose is to reveal the ways in which this racialization is already at work in Western discourses of subjectivity, gender, and even nationhood (as we shall see in the case of the United States). My claim is that images of Muslim women are much more than idle fictions woven around the bodies of other women, who may be located inside or outside that amorphous and imaginary construct called "the West." These representations are constituted as the support for that imaginary construct itself, in particular for Western society's self-representation as a "free" society, soliciting women's complicity. That is, representations of veiled Muslim women are the negative mirror in which Western constructions of national identity and gender can be positively reflected.

In "Algeria Unveiled," Fanon describes the French colonial project to unveil Algerian women, a project that took on explicit dimensions from the 1930s onward. Fanon's analysis of this colonial project allows us to understand the degree to which the veil was identified, for the colonizer, not only with Muslim women but with Algerian culture and Islam as a whole. The "unveiling" of Algeria was, then, a project to destroy its culture, as Fanon explains.[18] What comes through clearly in Fanon's account is the *homogeneity* of Western perceptions and reactions to the veil, whether at the level of colonial governance or individuals.[19] Fanon's explanation of the unity of reactions to the veil attributes it to the material unity of the veil itself: "The woman seen in her white veil unifies the perception that one has of Algerian feminine society. Obviously, what we have here is a uniform that tolerates no modification, no variant."[20] Yet in the footnote on the same page, Fanon admits the wide variation in veiling practices in Algeria: women in rural areas are often unveiled, as are Kabyle women, except, he notes, in large cities.[21] The Algerian *haïk* (the white body covering described by Fanon above), applies then only to women in urban centers. What Fanon has said of masculine garb could also be said of Algerian feminine dress: it undergoes regional modifications, allowing "a certain margin of choice, a modicum of heterogeneity."[22] Why, then, the homogeneity in colonial perceptions of and reactions to the veil? What remains in question throughout Fanon's essay, despite the explanations that he gives, is why it is the veiled Muslim woman in particular who becomes the focus of the colonizer's cultural attack. Fanon does, however, provide hints, which I will use to construct an answer.[23]

For this, we must scrutinize the *visibility* of the veil. Fanon's description of the colonial perception (or representation) of Muslim women is rendered in terms of the visibility and invisibility that the veil—as a material and symbolic sign of cultural difference and barrier to possessive vision—operates for the colonizer. Fanon begins: "The way people clothe themselves, together with the traditions of dress and finery that custom implies, constitutes the most distinctive form of a society's uniqueness, *that is to say the one that is most immediately perceptible.*"[24] What is most visible is thus essentialized as the marker of a society's difference. But most visible to whom? As Fanon writes, "In the Arab world, for example, the veil worn by women is at once noticed by the tourist. . . . For the tourist and foreigner, the veil demarcates both Algerian society and its feminine component."[25] Fanon explicitly inscribes the seer—an outsider, tourist, Western subject—in this perception. Visibility/invisibility are not in themselves properties of objects but are meaningful only relative to the position of the seer, to a desire to see and a way of looking.[26] The perception of the veil is no innocent seeing, but a gaze made possible by a world order where Western subjects can travel to, reside in, and "observe" Algeria.[27]

In answer to the question of why it is the veil that becomes the "essential" marker of Algerian cultural or Islamic difference, we then have the response that it is the most visible feature of that society. Why it is so visible, however, brings us to the already constituted field of vision of the Western observer. This field of vision has been structured by colonization, overdetermined by the colonial apparatus of knowledge and representation. As Fanon says: "It is on the basis of the analyses of sociologists and ethnologists that the specialists in so-called native affairs and heads of the Arab Bureaus coordinated their [policy with respect to the veil]."[28] Orientalist knowledge and media, "written accounts and photographic records or motion pictures," allow the Western subject to already know the colonized society before she or he has any direct contact with it.[29] This apparatus of representation, combined with economic and political hegemony, is the lens through which the Western observer sees Muslim society. We must turn to this lens, for, as I will try to show, the lens is in fact a mirror—a negative and distorting one.

To understand the mechanism of colonial or neocolonial representation whereby the veil becomes the essential marker of Muslim woman and of her culture's otherness, we must turn to Fanon's account of racialization in *Black Skin, White Masks*. Reading this together with "Algeria Unveiled" will allow us to see how the veiled woman is "othered" in the Western imaginary. Behind the visibility of the veil to the colonial and neocolonial regard, a process is revealed that makes the veil differentially visible and overdetermines it with a particular negative sense. This is the mechanism of othering by which Muslim women are racialized in the Western gaze. The attack on the veil is then not only the means by which the colonizer aims to destroy the colonized society; it is also the means by which colonial or neocolonial society constructs its self-representation, the counterimage or negative mirror image in which it perceives itself.

In chapter 6 of *Black Skin, White Masks*, Fanon describes the way in which the antiblack racism of white culture constitutes the "black" as other to the "white" self through a mechanism of projection or abjection. Here, the undesirable alterity of the self is projected or transferred onto the other.[30] In this process of othering, both "white" and "black" identities are constructed, and though they are constituted relative to one another, these identities are taken to be mutually exclusive. Excluded from the "white" self are any perceived impurities, undesirable incongruities, and differences that may trouble its univocity, stability, and sameness. These qualities are projected onto the "other," now seen in these terms. Only through this exclusion, which operates to essentialize both black and white identities, can whiteness be seen as pure and unified, as a stable identity. The essentialist logic of racist society thus sees the relative constructs of "black" and "white" in absolute terms; it does this by naturalizing race as a property of the black, material body, and specifically of skin color. In this way, race becomes seen as a natural category and not as a historical construct; the mechanism by which "black" and "white" identities are produced is effaced. The seeming naturalness of these categories works to justify the very racist logic that produced them. The myth or representation of the "black" as naturally inferior structures the visual field and overdetermines "normal" perception in racist society; "black" is seen as inferior and superiority, including moral superiority, is by default a characteristic of white identity.[31] It is then, on Fanon's account, racist society that creates the "black" and, we can say, colonial or neocolonial society that creates the "native." As "other" in the Western imaginary, the black or native plays the role of "scapegoat" for the collective guilt of white society.[32]

In "Algeria Unveiled," Fanon reveals a comparable racist logic in the French colonial representation of both Muslim men and women—though one that may be more accurately called cultural racism as we shall see later. The Muslim woman's condition is taken to be essentially conveyed by her veil, the material symbol of her oppression. As Fanon notes, the woman behind the veil is "pictured as humiliated, sequestered, cloistered . . . transformed by the Algerian man into an inert, demonetized, indeed dehumanized object."[33] Thus, in a move that anticipates U.S. representations of Islamic fundamentalism, the Muslim man is "denounced and described as medieval and barbaric."[34] His resistance to "liberating" colonial policies is "attributed to religious, magical, fanatical behavior," to an "Islam" that is posited in opposition to Western culture and values.[35] The othering of Muslim society extends to the characterization of its family life, seen as secluding the woman in the home. Curiously, all these colonial representations can be seen to relate back to the Muslim woman and her veil. Muslim families, men, and women are defined relative to the veil—and to its associated connotations of seclusion, oppression, invisibility, and lack of subjectivity. The man is he who imposes the veil to "keep [women] out of sight";[36] the family and home are the prisons where she hides or abides; and the Muslim woman is "she who hides behind a veil."[37] In these representations we see the identification of Muslim society with woman and of woman with her veil, itself overdetermined as oppressive.

To turn to the more recent U.S. "war on terrorism" and the rhetoric employed to justify the war in Afghanistan in particular, a similar focus on the veil (here *burqa*) can be discerned. Here, the image of the veil allows the demarcation of Islamic otherness in a visible and immediately identifiable form. By functioning as a metonym at once for Islam and for the oppression of women, the representation of the veil produces a slippage between these two concepts, making the identification of Islam with "fundamentalism" possible. It should be noted that "fundamentalism" is an amorphous and ill-defined term.[38] As Charles Hirschkind and Saba Mahmood have shown, the trope of "Islamic fundamentalism" collapses disparate currents of Islam into a "singular socio-religious formation."[39] This reductive schema crystallizes around certain stereotypical images, notably the image of the veiled Muslim woman.[40] This image, I claim, works in large part to provide "Islamic fundamentalism" with a particular (negative) affective and moral sense, despite the difficulty of defining the term. At the same time, since the representation of the veil is largely homogeneous—lacking in historical, contextual, or lived specificity—the amalgamation of fundamentalism to Islam more generally is supported by the image itself. Although arguably the term "fundamentalist" is supposed to designate only regressive or traditional versions of Islam, it is *only* in the context of Islam that forms of extremism so clearly oppressive to women are *represented* as developing.[41] The implication is that such fundamentalism and oppression are natural developments of this religion (unless safeguards are put in place and "progressive" forces encouraged by the West).

It should be noted that this construction of "Islamic fundamentalism"—and the image of the veil that in part constitutes it—plays a more complex role in U.S. self-representation than is at first visible. Once this Islamic otherness is rigidly defined, a cohesive sense of U.S. nationalism can be posited as desirable. Repeating the racist logic that Fanon discovered in French representations of Algeria, U.S. nationalism is here oppositionally defined in relation to an abjected other. The rigid disidentification with this other allows the borders of "Americanness" to be drawn. A striking example of this imaginative exclusion can be found in Laura Bush's radio address of November 17, 2001: the "blessings of American life," its desirability, are evoked largely by means of the contrast with the "brutal oppression of women" and inhumanity of "the terrorists and the Taliban," seen as incapable of loving their "women and children." It is significant here that the evocation of "Americanness" is gendered. The way that gender functions within the self-presentations of U.S. nationalism and colonialism requires us to look more closely at the role of the veiled Muslim woman as foil.

What I want to suggest, going beyond Fanon's analysis of othering, is that the Western representation of the Muslim woman is not posited in the same way as that of the Muslim man, nor is it a symmetrical representation. Though both are racialized, the othering undergone by the "veiled woman" is what Mohja Kahf calls a "double othering."[42] This means that our analysis must extend to include other subject positions, so far invisible, specifically that of the "Western" or U.S. woman. For the "veiled woman" is not only the other to Western man, but also to Western woman.

In this regard, the colonial and neocolonial use of feminist discourse to justify its project needs to be scrutinized. The British colonial construction of the "Woman Question" has been described by Leila Ahmed in the context of the discourse on the veil in Egypt in the late nineteenth and early twentieth centuries.[43] Ahmed points out that it is in the colonial context that "the issue of women emerged . . . as the centerpiece of the Western narrative of Islam."[44] The way in which colonial rhetoric combines the discourses of orientalism and, ironically, of feminism leads to a conflation of other women and their cultures; more specifically, a conflation of the colonial representation of other women as oppressed and their culture. As Ahmed notes, "The idea that Other men, men in colonized societies or societies beyond the borders of the civilized West, oppressed women was to be used, in the rhetoric of colonialism, to render morally justifiable its project of undermining or eradicating the cultures of colonized peoples."[45] This is what Fanon observed in the case of French colonial policies in Algeria and what we can see repeated in U.S. representations of Islamic fundamentalism/terrorism/the Taliban.[46]

Key to this "colonial-feminist" discourse is the representation of the colonized society as essentially inferior *because* it oppresses women—hence the purported aim of liberating or saving these women, an aim that can only be achieved by destroying their culture.[47] The implied thesis is that only in a Western or Westernized (read: civilized, liberal, enlightened, open) culture can women be truly free. That this is the implied thesis tells us that the "colonial-feminist" discourse—and its contemporary neocolonial U.S. counterpart—have another purpose. The moral justification that this discourse seeks to impart is not limited to the colonial or neocolonial project abroad but extends to a justification of patriarchal constructions of gender in the home society. This discourse serves simultaneously to normalize the position of women in the home society, to construct other societies as inferior, and to justify the colonial or neocolonial domination of those societies in the name of civilization, progress, and the liberation of women—hence the triple function of this discourse: patriarchal, orientalist, and colonialist. It is in this way that the identification of Muslim society with the veil, overdetermined as the symbol of women's oppression, can be understood. Given this framework, it should not be surprising that the United

States' rhetoric of freedom maintains the same apparent contradiction with respect to gender relations that one finds in the discourses of many former colonial powers. U.S. nationalist discourse can at once uphold patriarchal structures at home while invoking the freedom of other women as a reason for intervention abroad. In this sense, U.S. nationalism is a gendered project that is constructed through the racialization of other cultures, as we shall see.

We are now a step closer to understanding why it is the veiled Muslim woman who is the focus of the Western rhetoric of freedom, whether in the case of French and British colonialism or U.S. neocolonialism. But what, specifically, is the role of the image of the "veiled woman" in the Western imaginary? In her book, *Western Representations of the Muslim Woman*, Mohja Kahf argues that the Western representation of the "Muslim woman" is posited as a counterimage to the ideal of Western woman (itself also a representation). She is hence able to trace historical changes in this image that mirror shifting Western norms of femininity and gender.[48] Most importantly, Kahf shows that this image is formed at the intersection of two discourses of Western cultural history, "the discourse on Islam and the discourse on gender."[49] The image of the Muslim woman is hence constituted both in terms of the West's relation to Islam, its self-definition in connection to Islam, and in terms of the Western construction of "woman," the West's self-definition in terms of particular gender norms. Crucial to my reading of Kahf is that these discourses do not merely intersect—as if each were articulated separately and came into contact with the other only provisionally—but mutually support and define one another. As such, the Muslim woman is doubly othered in the Western imaginary; she is constructed at once as "woman" and "Muslim." This complex difference means that the veiled woman is the symbol of an "Islamic [feminine] otherness," whose role is to allow a certain representation of "woman" to be posited in the Western imaginary as desirable, normal, and ideal.[50]

Reading Kahf in conjunction with Fanon, we can extend our understanding of this "double othering" further. The veiled woman, as I mentioned, is "othered" relative to the Western woman. The double othering of the veiled woman hence presupposes another othering, that of the "Western woman" constructed as the gendered other within Western patriarchal society. This "other within" is, however, posited in opposition to an "other without"—to the representation of the veiled Muslim woman (who, though she may in fact be living within Western society, is imaginatively projected as external to it, as belonging to a different and alien Muslim society).[51] This other woman is then not only a gendered but also a racialized other. The process of double othering, in fact, puts both Western and Muslim woman in their peculiar places, as other within and other without. The relative subject-positions constituted in this way involve complex differentiations that need to be unraveled.

To adopt Fanon's framework from *Black Skin, White Masks*, we could say that it is the undesirable alterity in woman that is projected onto the "veiled woman." This projection or abjection thereby constitutes the identity of "Western woman" as a unified and pure ideal. But since Western woman has already herself been othered, I believe a further process is at play. Projected onto the "veiled woman" is not simply what is undesirable in femininity from the patriarchal perspective, that is, what is excluded from the norm of womanhood, but also, I argue, the mechanism of gender oppression of patriarchy itself. This is significant and helps explain the positive valence of the norm of "Western woman" so constructed. Here, we have a constitution that takes place on two levels. There is the constitution of the patriarchal norm of woman with particular qualities (e.g., a particular construction of a "liberated" female sexuality and body), seen in negative form in the image of the Muslim woman (e.g., seen as suffering from an overly modest, hidden, and imprisoned sexuality).[52] At the same time, all the weight of the process of gender othering or domination, the very mechanism that sets up the norm of woman, is projected onto the shoulders of the Muslim woman, and specifically onto her veil. This racialization of the veil renders it hypervisible. It is in this way that it becomes the most visible marker of Muslim society in Western eyes, for the veil is seen as the symbol of the gender oppression of *that* society. Focus on the veil deflects attention away from the patriarchal structures of Western society itself. But, more than this, it hides the othering mechanism that characterizes the subject-position of Western woman and it fosters the impression that this subject-position is not itself problematic or socially controlled, that is, that Western woman is "free."

A representation of Western womanhood is thus constructed as desirable for women in general, as an ideal that solicits women's complicity. Indeed, this representation is presented as desirable for other women as well (hence the colonizer's or occupier's belief that native women will welcome him).[53] This is because the ideal of Western woman implicitly excludes her gender oppression at the same time as it repeats features of the Western norm of femininity that are oppressive. This paradoxical and complex mixture of features—at once normalizing the patriarchal definition of woman and idealizing it as what women, including other women, would want and reclaim—reflects the subversion of feminism by orientalist and neocolonial discourse. As in the U.S. rhetoric of freedom, combining a feminist discourse of liberation in regard to "other women" with an implicit (or even declared) patriarchal attitude to women at home is possible, since these attitudes mutually support one another.[54] This is because the representations of the United States or "Western" woman and the "veiled woman" are implicitly constructed relative to one another; the veiled woman is criticized and saved in the name of (Western) woman, while the norm of Western femininity is posited in opposition to the veiled woman. This ultimately means that the subject-position assigned to Western woman is one where she can see herself as free, or as becoming free, only to the degree that she sees other women as oppressed—that is, to the degree that she accepts the "othering" of veiled Muslim women. She must accept her Western society as the only potential place where freedom can be actualized.

The subject-positions of Muslim women are marked by an even more paradoxical construction. As the abjected other to Western woman, her double othering can be understood in an additional way: it is not only the colonizer who seeks to save her, but also Western women. From the colonial-feminist perspective, the veiled woman can only become "free" by casting off her veil (and her society), that is, by accepting the ideal of Western womanhood, by becoming "Westernized." But her attempt to pass as Western will encounter limitations, for the subject-position of the Muslim woman remains marked by otherness, allowing for continued paternalism in her regard. Significantly, the discursive position from which the unveiled Muslim woman can speak about her culture is scripted in advance: as "escapee" of her religion or culture, she is expected to speak for its victims; if she argues for a more complex position, she is seen as a "pawn" still in its grips.[55] As for the subject-position of the veiled woman, she is denied individuality and voice in the colonial and neocolonial imaginary, even in relative terms. While the veil becomes hypervisible, Muslim women are posited as invisible, passive, and anonymous, as oppressed almost to the point of lacking subjectivity behind their veils. A marked example of this is the description in the U.S. press of burqa-clad Afghan women as "downtrodden ghosts."[56]

Significantly, this places Western and Muslim women in opposed, asymmetrical, and nonreciprocal subject-positions—even though their identities are constructed relative to one another. This exclusion means that commonalties between women and between societies are hidden from view. In particular, it obscures the recognition that what we may have to deal with are differently structured patriarchies with different complex specificities.[57] The nonreciprocity of Western and veiled women's subject-positions within the Western imaginary means that the "Islamic" difference of the veiled woman takes on an absolute sense and precludes the possibility of her being seen otherwise. Once the attribute of being "veiled" is attached to woman, her commonality with Western woman is severed. This exclusion also means that the identity of Western woman can be posited in an unproblematized and seemingly stable way—that the tension and othering, which we have seen are part of this identity, can be effaced.

The racialization of veiled Muslim women hence sustains and stabilizes gender dichotomies in the West—rendering them seemingly innocuous and "natural" to the subjects constituted therein.

The U.S. context provides a striking example of how gender, race, and culture are put in play in service of a neocolonial and nationalist project. Here, a gendered construction of the nation is made possible through the racialization of Islam as other. U.S. (read: Western and white) constructions of gender and family are normalized by eliding the mechanisms of gender oppression at work within U.S. society. This society is represented either as having already attained gender equality, or as the perfectible ground for such equality, *the* terrain for freedom; in contrast, Muslim cultures are conceived as stagnant and closed, repeating the same fixed patterns of gender oppression (continually reinvented in the ahistorical image of the veil).[58] Curiously, U.S. gender roles are understood as unoppressive and hence go unremarked (even though there is no question of eliminating gender altogether), yet signs of gender difference (e.g., veiling) are seen as oppressive when they belong to Muslim cultures. This representational contrast allows moral superiority and emotional content to be ascribed to a U.S. nationalism that is otherwise only vaguely defined, while at once justifying the neocolonial project with respect to certain Muslim countries. In this sense, the presentation of "Islamic fundamentalism" as oppressive to women and hence rigidly other—as a practice with which "free" subjects and women in particular would disidentify—works implicitly to sustain the call for a cohesive identification with "Americanness" as liberatory.

What is noteworthy in both the United States and the colonial rhetoric of freedom is that racialization proceeds by way of gender and is not immediately visible as "biological" or color racism. Rather, it takes the form of what I argue is "cultural racism." What is differentially visible is not race or skin color as such, but culture—defined largely through the perceived presence of gender oppression (ostensibly embodied in veiling practices). Since the hypervisibility of the veil is configured as gender oppression, the racism that structures this perception is covered over by the manifest antisexist and feminist concern for the freedom of Muslim women. It is this imbrication of racism with gender that confronts U.S. feminists with an apparent dilemma in the case of the veil.[59] It has been my aim to show that the rhetoric of freedom, which poses such a dilemma, not only perpetuates a paternalistic attitude toward Muslim women but also reinforces blindness to gender oppression in the context of the United States. The politics it inscribes is hence not only racist, but, I would add, antifeminist.

As with the mechanism of racialization described by Fanon in *Black Skin, White Masks*, Islamic otherness is here essentialized. Islam, as we have seen, is represented as essentially oppressive to women and thus essentially inferior. This essentialist logic has as its focus the veil. Islamic difference, its perceived oppression of women, is projected as a property of the material piece of clothing, the "veil." This defines a *cultural racism* that, it has been argued, is continuous with color racism.[60] Though differences clearly exist in how "race" is understood or seen in each case—whether as biological inheritance or as cultural genealogy and belonging—it is important to note that bodily difference plays a role in both cases. Cultural racism is not merely intolerance of the "spirit" of another culture; it is directed at bodies, which this racist vision materially inscribes and perceives as culturally different. This racism naturalizes cultural difference to visible features of the body, including clothing, hence the backward belief that it is the ostensible visibility of bodily difference, in this case veiling, that "causes" racist reactions in Western societies.[61] To imply that the solution to this racism is to forcibly or voluntarily change one's clothing, so as to dissipate racist attitudes, is both to elide the way in which clothing functions as an integrated part of one's lived sense of bodily space and also to misconceive the kind of racism involved.

Clothing is often seen as an artificial envelope that can be removed to reveal a "natural," biological body. What is missed in such a picture is the way in which clothing constitutes a bodily extension that cannot be removed without transforming one's lived sense of embodiment. As phenomenologists such as Maurice Merleau-Ponty have shown, clothing, through habituation, is no longer seen as an object apart from the body, but comes to form an integrated part of one's body schema. Bodily extensions (which include articles of clothing but also tools) become themselves dimensions through which the subject perceives and interacts with the world and others.[62] Crucial for my argument, such extensions affectively and kinaesthetically transform and recast one's sense of bodily space (as well as one's body image). The limits of my body are felt not at the skin, but at the surface and edges of the clothing I wear, redefining my sense of "here."[63] In navigating my surroundings, it is in terms of this "here" that a sense of "there," an external space, is configured. Though I do not mean to reduce veiling to a simple article of clothing—since it takes part in subject-formation in arguably more complex ways, at once spiritual, religious, conventional and cultural—both veiling and clothing more generally must be understood as more than mere superficial "cover." None of this is to imply an essentialist or static view of veiling, or to assign a univocal meaning to veiling experiences. What I mean to point out are the ways in which veiling can be formative of a bodily sense of self, so that instead of being liberatory, unveiling comes to be experienced as bodily disintegration and immobilization.[64]

In addition, the recommendation that Muslim women unveil in order to eliminate the reactions of intolerance directed against them misconstrues the kind of racism involved. In cultural racism, culture becomes nature. The veil is seen as both a marker of Muslim culture and an explanation of its inferiority, just as, in color racism, skin color is seen as the site of racial difference and biological determinism. Bodies are not only perceived as belonging to a different culture; they are also seen as culturally determined and inferior as a result.[65] In the sense in which culture is seen as nature, it is not merely the veil but the veiled body as a whole that is racialized[66]—along with any phenotypical differences that would otherwise have been seen as indifferent but that are in this way overdetermined. Phenotypical difference plays a supporting role in the racialization of veiled women. It is no coincidence that the image of the veiled Muslim woman is also of a "nonwhite" woman, and that "white" women who choose to veil pose a problem for the Western imaginary.[67] Moreover, culture becomes nature, since the determinism that characterizes cultural racism implies a definition of the other culture or religion (here Islam) as static, closed, and incapable of progress—in contrast to Western societies that are understood to be "open" and hence perfectible, to be spaces that enable, rather than determine and limit, individual expression and clothing choices. It is in terms of such cultural racism that the United States' rhetoric with respect to the "liberation" of Muslim women can be understood as continuous with colonial discourses on the veil.[68]

I have argued that the conception of "freedom," held open to Western women, is dependent on the counterimage of the veiled Muslim woman as oppressed. Given this distorting play of mirrors, what can we as feminists do? It seems simple enough to point out that oppression is not intrinsic to veiling, that gender cannot be understood univocally, and that relations of gender and veiling have had multiple historically and culturally differentiated forms. The perception of veiling as synonymous with gender oppression (and unveiling with freedom) has roots in Western constructions of freedom and gender that result in a persistent disregard for such correctives. I want to suggest that there are no easy routes for feminist analysis or solidarity here, but that we should start with a form of bracketing (to borrow a method from phenomenology). What needs to be bracketed is the framework of freedom and oppression that prefigures the representation and knowledge of Muslim women. Such bracketing neither adopts nor rejects freedom as a category of analysis, but attempts to reveal the structures that motivate and sustain its normative force and the "natural" belief in it. Hence, the bracketing I propose questions the ways in which concepts of freedom, woman, Muslim, and Western are constructed. This translates into an initial hesitation, an impulse to listen rather than act.[69] This hesitation forms an antidote to the uncritical application of ready-made binaries (freedom-oppression, but also modernity-religion and West-Islam) to the lives of other women in feminist analysis.

A critique of representation of this sort admittedly risks becoming a narrative that is only about "the West," perpetuating the exclusion already at work in that construct.[70] In contrast, by showing how what is so often presented as progressive and liberating for Muslim women in fact partakes of a colonial and paternalistic logic of representation, it is the aim of this chapter to open up feminist imagination. In its racialization of other cultures, U.S. rhetoric on freedom is not an isolated phenomenon. Indeed, colonial and imperialist feminist discourses perpetuate representations of Muslim women that posit Islam and feminism as mutually exclusive, silencing voices that blur these binaries (whether self-identified as Muslim and/or Western). Significantly, my hope is that the method of bracketing I propose can be useful in dispelling certain seemingly paralyzing dilemmas (in my view false) that confront feminists when it comes to Muslim women: in condemning the Taliban, should feminists support the United States' war on Afghanistan? Does a commitment to gender equality imply advocating a law banning the Muslim veil in schools (as in France)?[71] These questions only have a hold when the logic of representation that naturalizes oppression to the veil is left unquestioned. It allows such dilemmas to be posed without the difficult work of concrete communication, self-critical reflection, and attention to historical and contextual specificity being carried out. In contrast, the hesitation I propose is productive; it aims to destabilize representational frameworks that close down the imagination and limit the possibilities for feminist solidarity. The work of this chapter has been to make possible other ways of seeing ourselves and each other, Muslim and Western—different modes of understanding subjectivity and ways of thinking freedom.[72] Such radical rethinking can only take place, I believe, once we understand the exclusions and blind spots upon which the United States, and more broadly Western, self-representation of freedom has been constructed and the misperceptions that it sustains.

Notes

I wish to acknowledge the support of the Social Sciences and Humanities Research Council of Canada and to thank Florentien Verhage for her research assistance for this chapter.

1. See Lila Abu-Lughod, "Saving Muslim Women or Standing with Them? On Images, Ethics, and War in Our Times," *Insaniyaat*, 1, no. 1 (Spring 2003); available at http://www.aucegypt.edu/academic/insanyat/issue%201/I-article.htm. I should note that the rhetoric of "freedom" was used extensively with respect to Iraq, but applied mainly to "ethnic" populations (specifically Shi'a and Kurds). Although this meant that the war was not portrayed as a "feminist" cause (as Abu-Lughod observes), it

inscribed a paternalism with respect to Iraqi women (and Iraqis in general) that structured U.S. attitudes toward the war in implicitly gendered ways (as the personal example I will give illustrates).

2. The most memorable example of this appeal to the liberation of Afghan women on the part of the Bush administration can be found in Laura Bush's delivery of her husband's weekly radio address on November 17, 2001, more than a month after the beginning of the bombing of Afghanistan and the first time that a president's entire radio address had been delivered by a first lady. But this justification of the war in Afghanistan can also be found interspersed in George W. Bush's State of the Union Address in 2002. Cf. Dana L. Cloud's analysis in "'To Veil the Threat of Terror': Afghan Women and the <Clash of Civilizations> in the Imagery of the U.S. War on Terrorism," *Quarterly Journal of Speech* 90, no. 3 (August 2004): 297–298.

3. See Sharon Lerner, "Feminists Agonize over War in Afghanistan," *The Village Voice*, November 1, 2001. Lerner describes the war on Afghanistan as posing an "excruciating dilemma" for feminists. One aim of my chapter is to show how this dilemma is a false one. Once its gender politics are scrutinized, the U.S. war on Afghanistan is revealed as *antifeminist* (in line with other colonial and neocolonial interventions). For a summary of the campaign against the Taliban by the "Feminist Majority" and their stance with respect to the war in Afghanistan, see Charles Hirschkind and Saba Mahmood, "Feminism, the Taliban, and Politics of Counter-Insurgency," *Anthropological Quarterly* 75, no. 2 (Spring 2002): 339–340.

4. I scrutinize this oppositional logic from the perspective of Western self-presentations that work by representing "Islam" as other. It can be argued that some Muslim and Arab nationalist self-definitions also make use of this logic in reaction to colonial and neocolonial policies, defining their societies as inherently "anti-Western."

5. To draw on Marnia Lazreg's argument in "The Triumphant Discourse of Global Feminism: Should Other Women be Known?" in *Going Global: The Transnational Reception of Third World Women Writers*, ed. Amal Amireh and Lisa Suhair Majaj (New York: Garland, 2000), 30–31.

6. I do not mean to imply that these are the only events around which Western, or United States, stereotypes of Islam and veiling have crystallized. The Iranian revolution and hostage crisis in 1979–1981 were also such events. See Edward Said, *Covering Islam: How the Media and the Experts Determine How We See the Rest of the World* (New York: Random House, 1981). Nor is it my contention that the relation between stereotypes and events is simply causal.

7. This is by far one of the least problematic questions I received. Others had to do with kinship relations, marriage customs, and their relation to veiling.

8. With all the pitfalls that such a speaking position implies. See Uma Narayan, *Dislocating Cultures: Identities, Traditions, and Third-World Feminism* (New York: Routledge, 1997), 142–149.

9. My reverse question about U.S. men and trousers usually provokes surprise, if not hostility, since it makes visible the conventional and culturally contextual character of what is a naturalized, gendered practice.

10. For the case of de-veiling in Iran, see Homa Hoodfar, "The Veil in Their Minds and On Our Heads: The Persistence of Colonial Images of Muslim Women," *RFR/DFR* 22, no. 3/4 (1993): 5–18. Both the French and the British colonial manipulation of the question of the "veil" will be discussed later.

11. The law banning the wearing of "conspicuous" religious signs in public schools was passed in France on March 15, 2004. Both the debate leading up to the passage of the law and the majority of cases to which it has been applied have concerned girls wearing the "Islamic veil or head scarf" in schools. In Quebec, Canada, girls were banned from wearing the *hijab* (head scarf) during sports tournaments for purported safety reasons (soccer in February 2007 and Tae Kwon Do in April 2007), and a political controversy arose around women being allowed to wear the *niqab* (face veil) while voting (March–October 2007). Though the hijab has been permitted in public schools in Quebec since 1995 after a recommendation by the Quebec Human Rights Commission, the case of women employed in civil service or public administration, who wear the "veil," has been a subject of debate during the hearings of the commission on "reasonable accommodations" in the province in 2007.

12. See Talal Asad on the "West" and "modernity" as political projects in *Formations of the Secular: Christianity, Islam, Modernity* (Stanford, CA: Stanford University Press, 2003), 13–15.

13. As Mohja Kahf shows, the Western image of the Muslim woman as veiled and victimized is not timeless. Medieval images were quite different, representing her as termagant, aggressive, and transgressive. Kahf shows how the Western representation of the Muslim woman has changed, locating the appearance of the oppressed Muslim woman in the eighteenth and nineteenth centuries' discourses of orientalism and colonialism. See her *Western Representations of the Muslim Woman: From Termagant to Odalisque* (Austin: University of Texas Press, 1999), 1–9.

14. Veiling practices are multiple and complex, with different names, forms, uses, and contextual, as well as individually varying, meanings. A nonexhaustive list would include *haïk* (Algeria), *chador* (Iran), *abaya* (Iraq), *burqa* (Afghanistan), *niqab* (face veil), and *hijab* (head scarf); these are materially and culturally different forms of veiling, some of which cover the whole body, others the face, and some only the head. For an analysis of the complexity and history of the term "hijab," see Barbara

Freyer Stowasser, "The *Hijab:* How a Curtain Became an Institution and a Cultural Symbol," in *Humanism, Culture, and Language in the Near East: Studies in Honor of Georg Krotkoff*, ed. Georg Krotkoff, Asma Afsaruddin, and A. H. Mathias Zahinsen (Winona Lake, IN: Eisenbrauns, 1997), 87–104. Today, the Arabic term "hijab" designates a piece of cloth that covers the hair and neck, though not the face.

15. Muslim women who do not veil, non-Muslim women who veil, masculine instances of veiling, and historically different representations of Muslim women—all constitute exceptions to the dominant image of the Muslim woman as veiled. When such exceptions are raised, however, the image can be stretched to accommodate them (even if sometimes stretched almost to its breaking point). For she who is Muslim but does not veil is represented as having *escaped* it. Non-Muslim women who wear an article of clothing materially similar to a veil are wearing "ethnic" dress and are thus not represented as wearing the same veil, the supposedly rigid and religiously mandated "Islamic veil." And the veiling of men (e.g., the Tuareg) is construed as originating for climatic and pragmatic reasons.

16. In Frantz Fanon, *A Dying Colonialism*, trans. Haakon Chevalier (New York: Grove Press, 1965). The French edition: *L'an V de la révolution algérienne* (Paris: La Découverte, 2001). Henceforth cited as *A Dying Colonialism*, followed by the English and the French page numbers, respectively.

17. Frantz Fanon, *Black Skin, White Masks*, trans. Charles Lam Markmann (New York: Grove Press, 1967).

18. Fanon, *A Dying Colonialism*, 37–38/19.

19. Ibid., 37/18.

20. Ibid., 36/17.

21. Ibid., 36n/17n.

22. Ibid., 36/17.

23. In taking up Fanon's analysis in this way, I also mean to point to some of its shortcomings: most importantly to a certain elision of the complex difference that characterizes the position of the Muslim woman. Her role is too frequently reduced to her participation in national struggle in "Algeria Unveiled." For example, though Fanon famously points to the historical dynamism of the veil, he presents this dynamism as limited to the context of colonialism and revolutionary struggle (*A Dying Colonialism*, 63/47). There is an ambiguity in Fanon's account whereby precolonial Algeria is sometimes posited as the silent and static foil (or prehistory) in contrast to which revolutionary Algeria is defined as a historically dynamic and progressively liberatory society. An instance of this logic can be found in Fanon's discussion of the Algerian woman prior to the revolution as a "minor," in comparison to her revolutionary "entry into history" ("The Algerian Family," *A Dying Colonialism*, 106–107/91–93).

24. Fanon, *A Dying Colonialism*, 35/16; emphasis added.

25. Ibid., 35–36/16–17.

26. The veil is not visible for everyone, as Fanon points out. The Algerian, he says, does not see it. This is part of a differential way of seeing women that distinguishes the European from the Algerian in Fanon's essay (*A Dying Colonialism*, 44/26).

27. As Edward Said points out, "to reside in the Orient is to live the privileged life, not of an ordinary citizen, but of a representative European whose empire (French or British) *contains* the Orient in its military, economic, and above all, cultural arms." See Said's *Orientalism* (London: Penguin Books, 1978), 156.

28. Fanon, *A Dying Colonialism*, 37/18.

29. Ibid., 35/16.

30. Fanon, *Black Skin, White Masks*, 190–191.

31. Ibid., 194.

32. Ibid.

33. Fanon, *A Dying Colonialism*, 38/19.

34. Ibid., 38/19.

35. Ibid., 41/23.

36. Ibid., 38/19.

37. Ibid., 36/18.

38. Said, *Covering Islam*, xvi–xvii.

39. Hirschkind and Mahmood, "Feminism, the Taliban, and Politics of Counter-Insurgency," 348.

40. See Cloud's analysis of these images in "To Veil the Threat of Terror," 289–296.

41. Though she says "the terrorists and the Taliban," rather than "fundamentalism," Laura Bush's radio address of November 17, 2001, performs both moves. At once pointing to how other Muslims condemn the treatment of women under the Taliban, yet noting that "[o]nly the terrorists and the Taliban forbid education to women. Only the terrorists and the Taliban threaten to pull out women's fingernails for wearing nail polish." No comparison is possible to other forms of religious fundamentalism or "terrorism," and U.S. involvement in Afghanistan is elided. Rather, it is Islam who bears the guilt for this form of extremism.

42. Kahf, *Western Representations of the Muslim Woman*, 63.

43. Leila Ahmed, *Women and Gender in Islam: Historical Roots of a Modern Debate* (New Haven, CT: Yale University Press, 1992), 149–168.

44. Ibid., 150.

45. Ibid., 151.

46. Fanon, *A Dying Colonialism*, 37–38/19.

47. This discourse is of course in bad faith. As Ahmed shows with respect to the British in Egypt, the discourse on the liberation of women from

the veil was accompanied by a curtailment of women's opportunities for education (*Women and Gender in Islam*, 152–53). I owe the term "colonial feminism" to Ahmed (ibid., 151).

48. As well as the shifting relation of the West to Islam. See Kahf, *Western Representations of the Muslim Woman*, 7.

49. Ibid., 9.

50. Ibid., 163. This is a variant on what Chandra Talpade Mohanty has called the constitution of "third-world difference" that serves to produce the representation of "the third-world woman" as foil to that of Western woman. See her "Under Western Eyes: Feminist Scholarship and Colonial Discourses," in *Feminism Without Borders: Decolonizing Theory, Practicing Solidarity* (Durham, NC: Duke University Press, 2003), 22, 40–42.

51. Kahf, *Western Representations of the Muslim Woman*, 9.

52. As Fanon noted, the veil represents for the Western imaginary the "demonetized [*démonétisé*]" status of Muslim women, their removal from circulation (*A Dying Colonialism*, 38/19). That the freedom constructed as desirable is that of the free circulation, or sexual currency, of women's bodies helps explain some of the fascination with the veil in the Western imaginary. It is, however, not the whole story—as I try to show.

53. This can be seen in the colonial and neocolonial ideal of "*femmes dévoilées et complice de l'occupant*" (Fanon, *A Dying Colonialism*, 39/20).

54. It is thus not surprising that "a reversion to traditional gender roles" accompanies the rhetoric for the War in Afghanistan; cf. Lerner, "Feminists Agonize over War in Afghanistan."

55. For an elaboration of the roles into which Muslim women are constantly scripted in the Western imaginary—oppressed victim, pawn of her society, or escapee—see Mohja Kahf, "Packaging 'Huda': Sha'rawi's Memoirs in the United States Reception Environment," in *Going Global: The Transnational Reception of Third World Women Writers*, ed. Amal Amireh and Lisa Suhair Majaj (New York: Garland, 2000), 148–172.

56. Barry Bearak, "Kabul Retraces Steps to Life before Taliban," *New York Times*, December 2, 2001. For an analysis of this dehumanizing image of veiled women, see Kevin J. Ayotte and Mary E. Husain, "Securing Afghan Women: Neocolonialism, Epistemic Violence, and the Rhetoric of the Veil," *NWSA Journal* 17, no. 3 (Fall 2005): 119.

57. See Ahmed, *Women and Gender in Islam*, 215. It is unclear whether using the term "patriarchy" is useful here; to be precise, I am not assuming a universal patriarchal schema.

58. See Lazreg, "The Triumphant Discourse of Global Feminism," 30–31.

59. For more on this dilemma in other Western contexts, see Hoodfar, "The Veil in Their Minds and on Our Heads," 13; and Christine Delphy,

"Antisexisme ou antiracisme? Un faux dilemme," *Nouvelles Questions Feministes* 25, no. 1 (2006): 59–83.

60. Though these authors have different accounts of this continuity, see Etienne Balibar, "Is There a 'Neo-Racism'?," in *Race, Nation, Class: Ambiguous Identities* (London: Verso, 1991), 17–28; David Theo Goldberg, *Racist Culture: Philosophy and the Politics of Meaning* (Oxford, UK: Blackwell, 1993), 70–74; and Tariq Modood, "'Difference', Cultural Racism and Anti-Racism," in *Race and Racism*, ed. Bernard Boxill (Oxford, UK: Oxford University Press, 2001), 238–256.

61. By naturalizing racist conduct toward, and intolerance of, other cultures, cultural racism according to Balibar displaces biologism one degree but does not eliminate it ("Is There a 'Neo-Racism'?," 26). The belief that it is the veil that provokes racism is widespread, and can be found in some feminist reactions, see, for example, Julia Kristeva, *Nations without Nationalism*, trans. Leon S. Roudiez (New York: Columbia University Press, 1993), 36–37.

62. Maurice Merleau-Ponty, *Phenomenology of Perception*, trans. Colin Smith (London: Routledge and Kegan Paul, 1962), 143. Merleau-Ponty's examples of bodily extensions include a woman's hat and a blind man's stick, as well as cars, typewriters, and musical instruments.

63. Lila Abu-Lughod's description of veiling (specifically burqas) as "mobile homes" (drawing on Hanna Papanek's term "portable seclusion") seems particularly apt in this regard. See Abu-Lughod's "Do Muslim Women Really Need Saving? Anthropological Reflections on Cultural Relativism and Its Others," *American Anthropologist* 104, no. 3 (2002): 785.

64. Frantz Fanon and Homa Hoodfar have pointed to the immobilizing effects of de-veiling on previously veiled women. See Hoodfar's description of her grandmother's experience in the context of compulsory de-veiling in the 1930s in Iran in her "The Veil in Their Minds and on Our Heads," 10–11. For Fanon's description of Algerian women's unveiling in the context of revolutionary struggle, see *A Dying Colonialism*, 59/42.

65. Balibar, "Is There a 'Neo-Racism'?," 22.

66. The racialized construction of the veil, as univocally oppressive, means that veiled bodies are objectified and perceived to be passively determined by their culture. This racializing perception covers over the heterogeneity and dynamism that lived senses of veiling—such as those described in the previous paragraph—can take.

67. This needs to be examined further. For Tariq Modood, for instance, cultural racism is a distinctive phenomenon that relies on and adds to color racism. It is the racialization of "non-Whites" based on cultural difference. But Modood takes the term "non-White" to be evident. Though he shows how cultural difference renders one less "White," he does not address how "Whiteness" is already defined in opposition to

other cultures, as well as "races," and hence cannot be understood to be a neutral, phenotypical given. See his "'Difference', Cultural Racism and Anti-Racism," 247–249, 252. Though beyond the scope of this chapter, I want to imply that cultural racism is already at work in the definition of "Whiteness" as it is in the understanding of "Western."

68. In other words, this racism is not new; Balibar, "Is There a 'Neo-Racism'?," 23–24; Goldberg, *Racist Culture*, 70–71.

69. For more on hesitation as an initial strategy, see Linda Alcoff, "The Problem of Speaking for Others," *Cultural Critique* 20 (Winter 1991–1992): 24.

70. This chapter only begins this bracketing. To the degree that it remains at the level of Western representation, it shows how other ways of being are systematically and structurally misperceived; it does not describe how representations may be internalized and lived differently, or what experiences escape them. As such, it necessarily calls for further work. See Narayan, *Dislocating Cultures*, 137–138.

71. See Christine Delphy on the paralyzing effects of this dilemma on French feminists ("Antisexisme ou antiracisme?," 60–61).

72. Notably, Saba Mahmood's nuanced anthropological study of the women's mosque movement in contemporary Egypt, in her book *Politics of Piety: The Islamic Revival and the Feminist Subject* (Princeton, NJ: Princeton University Press, 2005), attempts just this: to challenge the normative framework of freedom that univocally constructs "Muslim women" as oppressed and to open up alternative ways for conceiving subject-formation (by examining the "architectures of the self" that are concretely embodied in the lives of particular women, without assuming "Muslim women" to be a homogeneous group).

Part 2
Unity

4

Faith in Unity

The Nationalist Erasure of Multiplicity

María Lugones and Joshua M. Price

THE TIME OF *day when I drive from or to my place every day is a solitary time when I think in unstructured, spontaneous, reflection. My own relation to U.S. politics, values, relations, living—which is complex, tense, solidarious in some directions, resistantly hostile in others—always finds some place in this thinking things through. For months after 9/11, continuously with the war with Afghanistan and the first year of the war in Iraq, the road that took me back and forth—I live in the mountains—was lined with those small paper American flags, about three feet apart from each other. Many people also hung huge, waving, American flags somewhere on their property—by the mailbox, or close to the house. I drove through a space flagged, constrained, rigidified, patriotically judgmental with a sense of having my mind silenced, thoughts not easily expressible to my neighbors, to folk I encounter casually in the business of living in this town. Thoughts silenced in their credibility, validity, and sense among the people and their flags. The U.S. flag is not my flag. I am not a citizen of the United States, but I have lived here most of my life. I think of myself as a U.S. Latina.* (María)

Hurricane Katrina has unavoidably, undeniably, unveiled some of the depth of racial inequality and oppression that many Americans and many of them white-Anglo have erased from their social landscape. They repeat to themselves like an incantation that the United States is no longer a racist country. Sometimes they do so in my presence and sometimes to my face and sometimes not just defiantly and assertively but also with hostility. I cried for days seeing people from the Ninth Ward in New Orleans getting their bodies burned by the hot roofs on which they were waiting for hours and days to be rescued, or crowded on bridges, or floating in the waters no longer alive having died in desolation and despair. This is certainly one of the largest neighborhoods of African American–owned housing. Everywhere I go other folks of color are overwhelmed by the sadness. Media commentators narrate the desolation and keep on saying that this does not look like the United States, but the Third World. This is foreign to them, this racialized poverty. (María)

May 1, 2006. Thousands upon thousands took to the streets all over the United States. In the small towns, where there were no densely peopled convergences against nationalist racism, one had a strong sense of possibility: ill defined, but clearly not just a spectacular, radical politics of events. Un día sin inmigrantes/A Day without Immigrants. Over one and a half million immigrant workers and their allies came out in the biggest demonstration in U.S. history. They continued to do so for days, weeks. Student activists, labor, human rights, and immigrant activists, pushing against the once-again rise of nativist and racist xenophobic legislation under consideration in the U.S. Congress. The inward, toward each other, sense of the strike spoke of a crossing, a heterogeneous, multivocal, solidarity. South Asians, Chicanas/os, Mejicanas/os crossing the border, Salvadoreños, Koreans, a manyness that does not stand up for each other in the streets with frequency. It is that sense that kept my attention, the one that promised that which is both difficult and necessary: Asian Americans, Native Americans, African Americans, and Anglos, as well as Latinas/os mattering to each other against nationalist unity. One recognizes a cognitive openness that cannot be contained within the epistemology of empire; a cognitive openness that signals a defiant exteriority within. (María)

I (María) began Linda Alcoff's and Mariana Ortega's invitation to reflect on the conjunction of "American nationalism" and "the pressure for patriotic unity" with a narration, a juxtaposition of my experience of three events that stand out in my mind as connected by the conjunction. I offer that narration as the context within which I want to reflect on both the cognitive practices that need to be adopted or reinforced to make the "pressure for patriotic unity" efficient and on the epistemological shift necessary to a solidarity that is multivoiced.

In line with the dialogical, plural voicing of the resistance to the nationalist, patriotic unity, I felt a need for a conversation with Josh Price, another activist radical intellectual with whom I have history, including a history of thinking through and writing together what "multiculturalism" needs to mean to make our lives sufficiently complex, sufficiently free, sufficiently interdependent, engaged, solidarious, respectful, ready to listen and respond from intertwined histories that are woven from distinctly different ways of living under racialized oppression.

Ten years ago we wrote "Dominant Culture: El deseo por un alma pobre" at the time of the culture wars.[1] In that piece we thought that the manyness of cultures/values/economies/senses of person and relation necessitates a structural, not an ornamental, multiculturalism. We thought that this manyness also necessitates the exercise of cognitive practices that select a complex reality, an expanded, enriched sense of the present, that see the refractions in the lived and organized social as power and resistance constantly recreate, alter, or transform it.

In drawing the distinction between structural monoculturalism and structural multiculturalism and arguing for the need for structural multiculturalism, we argued for the importance of altering practices of cognition. That is, the structural institutional change needs to be accompanied by a structural cognitive change. By "cognitive practices" we mean the attitudes and expectations that constitute our attention as selective, that underlie our perceptions, evaluations, and choice of action. Cognitive practices lead people to privilege some ways of thinking and reject others in their everyday lives, at home, at work, in the formation of foreign policy, and so on.

We understand these practices as both learned and as changeable. A crucial ingredient of being inculcated and formed into monoculturalism is learning practices of cognition that incline one to seek certainty, simplicity, and the kind of agreement that is mediated by compromise. If one has been inculcated into such ways of cognition, such cognitive practices, one would be inclined to see structural multiculturalism as nonsensical, impossible, chaotic, politically suspicious, necessitating fragmentation and division instead of unity. That is, monoculturalism is constituted by the institutional erasure and devaluation of subalternized people's languages, traditions, knowledges, and practices. They are erased in favor of a national, official language and those practices and Eurocentered knowledges prized as expressive of the United States as a nation.[2]

But monoculturalism is not only constituted by that institutional erasure and relegation of all nonhegemonic practices to the private. It is also constituted by learned attitudes of cognition that in our peopled everydayness affirm and maintain the monocultural nature of the selection and are repelled by multiplicity and complexity. The monoculturalist, from within a mode of cognition that seeks simplicity, certainty, agreement, is repelled by linguistic manyness. For example, having several official languages—languages that are fully embraced and practiced in public and government institutions—or a complexity of legal practices and approaches within the legal system is cognized as leading to muddle, anarchy, incomprehension, balkanization, Babel.

Exercising the cognitive practices that incline one to complexity, uncertainty, and open-ended understanding, one would see structural monoculturalism as reductive, constraining, impoverishing, undemocratic. Those who have come to or have been forced into double consciousness/double vision have a particular relation to what is erased and devalued. They live within the erasure and devaluation of practices and knowledges crucial to their own peopled line of survival and flourishing. They cultivate practices of cognition that are consistent with structural multiculturalism. They live the cognitive practices that constitute monoculturalism as reductive, impoverishing, and tyrannical. They are constantly being pressed against, brutally cognitively assaulted by the reduction not just of the knowledges and practices crucial to their protagonism, their agency, but also of the very possibility of sense.

In revisiting the distinction we drew, we now wonder whether the nationalism that calls for patriotic unity would feel at home with the cognitive practices of structural monoculturalism as we had theorized it more than a decade ago. The militarization of the border, the "war on terror," the USA PATRIOT Act, new forms of racial profiling, all speak to new social and racial formations.[3] Other social changes during the last fifteen years are equally important: a consolidation of residential and educational segregation, the explosion of the incarceration of women of color, and the abolition of bilingual education in large parts of the country. These political, social, and economic struggles shape, and are shaped by, emerging patterns of racialization, not just of Arabs and Latinos, but also of South Asians, African Americans, whites, and others, as all reshuffle and shift, or are forced to shift, their political, economic, and racial positions.

These developments are mirrored by important changes in cognition and perception. The change that we want to explore in the cognitive practices of structural monoculturalism have to do with a significant shift from the "rational" negotiation process of compromise to the use of faith to ground dogmatic claims, positions, and decisions.

Looking for a common ground through compromise has been a valued test of an American pragmatic approach to politics since the founding fathers entered the Mephistophelean Three-Fifths Compromise. Angling for a successful compromise has been treated as an art; striving for common ground a civic value; and reaching commonality a goal for successful living in a liberal democracy. We find the practice of compromise to be morally and politically suspect and at times repugnant. If nothing else, the history of compromise in this country should be warning enough: the Missouri Compromise of 1820 and the Compromise of 1850 were also exercises in compromise that guaranteed unfreedom and subverted democracy in the name of democracy. Compromise as a structurally monocultural cognitive attitude leaves too much room for the give and take of "rational" negotiation of interests when seen from the dogmatism and narrowness of faith. We write "rational" instead of rational, because the compromise process is a simplifying process in line with the subalternization of people and knowledge characteristic of the Eurocentered modern racial nation-state.

The cognitive practices that we described in "Dominant Culture" are in line with what Boaventura de Sousa Santos has called "lazy reason."[4] Sousa Santos tells us that social experience in the world is much wider and more varied than what the Western understanding of the world knows and considers important, and that this social experience is being wasted.[5] Compromise as a decision-making process is in line with what Sousa Santos calls a "contracting of the present" produced through lazy reason. The common ground reached through the process of compromise is one that impoverishes, contracts the present. It is not the common ground that may be found through the tense, long-range project of transforming social institutions toward an egalitarianism wrought through a desubalternization and decolonization of the social.

The present turn calls for the imposition of American unity through an identification of American unity with the adoption of a secularized fundamentalist Christianity at the level of the state, not just at the level of individual religiosity that replaces compromise with the resoluteness of faith. Certainty is "arrived at" through faith. This is a process of conversion, not a negotiation. The certainty of faith is unshakable. When we are told from the lay pulpit of the presidency that America represents democracy and freedom, joined with an "I was not chosen to listen to people," we can understand the smoothing out of the inconsistency by seeing "democracy and freedom" as an indisputable article of faith.

The characteristics of "faith" that we are highlighting here constitute it as an epistemic state where judgment precedes the particularities and richness of the cognitive situation. Thus faith is not open to dialogue and does not require justification. Faith can be unshakable, and to that extent it is like unbroken pottery: internally consistent, it holds together and comes as a complete package. Through the set of cognitive practices that ground the new monoculturalism, other ways of viewing the world are not just unseen or disregarded as unimportant. They are imagined as dangerous and antagonistic. Things are polarized. The Manichean understandings of morality, and the identification of morality with fundamentalist Christianity, Occidentalist thought, Anglo culture, and whiteness, impinge deeply on the struggles of people of color in America. These understandings contract the present further, expanding the range of irrational ways of imagining the Other. This is a deepening of the irrationality of monoculturalism.

Those who speak with certainty have the underlying faith that their perceptions, speech, and actions are undoubtedly correct or true. Certainty expels doubt. The world is monistic. Reality is not multiple and it is not complicated. Certain judgments simplify the richness of the world and displace subtlety, contradiction, and especially irony. From the standpoint of simplicity, elaborate views of the world are suspect since they suggest moral relativism, elitism, dissimulation, indecision, even cowardice. Simplicity, in this view, is coextensive with honesty, with frankness, and with popular democracy. Simplicity thus becomes a sine qua non of social interaction and public debate. In the old monoculturalism, we identified certainty, simplicity, and the search for a common ground as monocultural practices. In the new monoculturalism, certainty and simplicity have come to fit even tighter together than they had, through fundamentalist faith. A cognitive practice of not compromising through the prejudgment of faith entails rather than arrives at certainty. That is why it is unshakable, though faith itself may be shakable. The Manichean quality of fundamentalist faith ensures simplicity. Boundaries are sharpened and thrown into further contrast—boundaries between good and evil, heterosexual and homosexual, man and woman, white and black (other racializations are practiced—including through tokenism—but cognitively erased), English and alien tongues, Western civilization and the dark, inferior cultures. Anglo culture, "our" culture as a nation, has a referent, it has a content, it has contours, limits, characteristics. George W. Bush reminds us of the extreme narrowness of patriotic cognition in his famous words shortly after 9/11: "You're either with us or against us in the fight against terror."[6] It is important to point out the practical compatibility of these cognitive practices with a color blindness that is accompanied by a racial tokenism that is strictly assimilationist.

Freedom has become infused with religion: freedom from evil rather than freedom from want or even, as in classical liberal theory, from interference. In this worldview, other cultures are striving toward our culture, other cultures that are defined as less free, more chauvinistic, or internally ethnically homogeneous, with strange, antiquated values vis-à-vis the best nation in the world, the great democratic experiment, the nation of immigrants, the melting pot: American Exceptionalism, America as beacon. Other cultures and societies are retrograde. They pull us back, they need us as an example. "We" are clear, democracy is clear, its workings are clear. "We" have it. "We" do not see counterevidence: the fundamental problems with our society and how it functions, hypocrisy, structural oppression, social amnesia of past social trauma, residential and educational segregation, and so on. "We" have a world mission.

We see, then, that the starker set of cognitive practices that we describe here deepen the ones we described almsot fifteen years ago. But like them, these three practices "work together to form not just indifference and misunderstanding, but positive violence in political 'union.' We can see how these cognitive practices are invested in cultural domination."[7]

So, why is May 1, 2006, evoked here? What is the connection with American nationalism and the pressure for patriotic unity? The connection is "an unhinging from," "a resistance to," nationalist unity imposed through a racist criminalization of "alien" labor. The marches form a resistance through a heterogeneous, cosmopolitan, multiple, egalitarian solidarity. If structural multiculturalism is ever to be, it is through a radical transformation of the social toward an egalitarianism that goes well beyond the recognition of difference and inclusion in terms that cannot be one's own, terms that highlight the unreason of the Other. The egalitarianism that would be coconstructed with structural multiculturalism infuses the economic, interpersonal, and political social. What we are stressing is not the May 1 marches as addressed to power, but as addressed inward, toward the formation of a solidarity against power. The solidarity stands together against enormous pressure. This is what is promising: the heterogeneity of the oppressed standing together.

As Catherine Walsh says, *interculturalidad* is a counterhegemonic process of long-range transformation of social relations, and public structures and institutions.[8] It is better thought of as *interculturizar*, an ongoing process. She sees this process as including cognitive struggles between hegemonic and subaltern positions relegated to invisibility and the nonmodern. "These are not knowledges frozen as ancestral. Rather they are built in the present from the interpretation and reinvention of a historical memory located in subjectivities, spaces and places that find their sense in the present."[9] She tells us that this is a proposal from the bottom up that "reflects the need to promote processes of reciprocal translation of knowledges in the plural. But their goal is not a mixture, or a hybridization, nor an inventing two possible worlds. It rather represents the construction of new epistemological frameworks that incorporate, negotiate and *interculturalizan* both knowledges."[10]

The march of May 1 is also from the bottom up. It may well point in many directions. It could result merely in inclusion in an inegalitarian, monocultural, capitalist nationalism. From the standpoint of structural monoculturalism, the protests are seen as a threat to the consolidation of a unitary, white, patriotic hegemony. Through the cognitive lens of structural multiculturalism, we see multiple movements whose potential is contingent, emergent, whose contours are not defined. The potential of the marches rest in part on practices of interculturalidad built on reciprocal exchanges. But its form and process begins to exhibit the process of interculturalidad that we see as connected intimately with what we call structural multiculturalism. The sense of possibility lies in the presence of Asians and Asian Americans, Native Americans, African Americans, Anglos, Chicanas/os, Afro-Caribbeans, Latino Americans born in the United States, and migrant Mexicans, Asians, and Central Americans in a process, not just of confrontation with the state, but an inward multivoiced process of egalitarian challenge to the marriage of global capital and the racial nation-state.

The promise here lies in those in the May 1 marches unhinging from the neoliberal, ornamental, multiculturalist strategy that, again in Catherine Walsh's voice, "does not point to the creation of more egalitarian societies, but rather to the control of social conflict and the preservation of social stability toward the goal of impelling the economic imperatives of capitalist accumulation."[11] Control of social conflict is achieved through a mirage that treats cultures as totalities maintained in a utopian, mythical time under the appearance of tolerance and equality. Fernando Coronil's account of what he calls "Occidentalism" stresses this understanding of cultures and groups as monadic, separate totalities.[12] Ella Shohat and Robert Stam detail what they call a "polycentric multiculturalism" that also stresses the need to undo the understanding of cultures and groups as monadic totalities.[13] They also stress the need to understand the subordination of knowledges and the process of subalternization as one that places the subaltern in a privileged epistemic position, the one that sees the historical process of domination. These processes, structural multiculturalism, polycentric multiculturalism, and interculturalidad are all necessary and adumbrated in these times of American nationalism and of pressure for fundamentalist patriotic unity. If the streets lined with American flags have come to represent nationalist patriotism for many of us pressured into self-erasure toward a procrustean unity; if Katrina has already blended into the weak, mythmaking, color-blind memory of the hegemon but remains the stark present of racial inequity for many with a historical memory; then the May 1 marches of the strike of *un dia sin immigrantes* stand as that "Not Yet" that Sousa Santos tells us will only come from an expanded present and it will not be taken for granted, but crafted with care. Therein lay our possibilities and the freedom of our imaginations.

Notes

1. María Lugones and Joshua Price, "Dominant Culture: El deseo por un alma pobre," in *Multiculturalism from the Margins*, ed. Dean A. Harris (Westport, CT: Bergin and Garvey, 1995).

2. For a theorized understanding of the meaning of "Eurocentered," see Anibal Quijano,"Coloniality of Power, Eurocentrism, and Latin America," *Nepantla: Views from the South* 1, no. 3 (2000): 533–580. For Quijano, Eurocentric knowledge is a theoretical perspective that privileges the idea of race to naturalize colonial relations between Europeans and non-Europeans. Race is deployed as a way to legitimize asymmetrical

social and economic relations by casting them as following from intrinsic or natural hierarchies of inferior and superior. In a Eurocentric concept of knowledge, rationality and modernity are uniquely European (354ff).

3. By "racial formation" we refer to the process by which social, economic, and political forces determine the content and importance of racial categories, and by which they are in turn shaped by racial meanings." See Michael Omi and Howard Winant, *Racial Formation in the United States* (New York: Routledge, 1986), 61. We have in mind the racial formation that combines xenophobia, state security, and religious panic in the demonization of Arabs and Arab Americans and that perceives Arab women as passive, super-oppressed, and in need of help from Westerners. For an account by Arab American feminists, see Nadine Naber, Eman Desouky, and Lina Baroudi, "The Forgotten '-ism': An Arab American Women's Perspective on Zionism, Racism, and Sexism," in *The Color of Violence: The INCITE! Anthology* (Cambridge, MA: South End Press, 2006). For an account that is part of the xenophobia, see for example, Samuel Huntington, *The Clash of Civilizations* (New York: Free Press, 2002). Another example of a racial formation is emerging from the social movements of migrant Latinos. They are faced with withering congressional debates that frame migrants as a "problem." In these debates, untethered neoliberalism jousts with explicit white supremacy: agrobusiness argues for temporary permits for guest workers because they need an inexpensive, exploitable migrant labor pool that does not receive many of the rights of citizenship. These business interests are opposed by a resurgent nativist radical right that fears losing a white English-speaking Protestant hegemony. See Samuel Huntington, *Who Are We? The Challenge to America's National Identity* (New York: Simon and Schuster, 2004).

4. Boaventura de Sousa Santos, "A Critique of Lazy Reason: Against the Waste of Experience," in *The Modern World-System in the Longue Duree*, ed. Immanuel Wallerstein (Fernand Braudel Center Series (Boulder, CO: Paradigm, 2004).

5. Based on his research, Sousa Santos concludes: "First, social experience in the world is much wider and varied than what the [W]estern scientific or philosophical tradition knows and considers important. Second, this social wealth is being wasted. On this waste feed the ideas that proclaim that there is no alternative, that history has come to an end, and such like. Third, to fight against the waste of experience, to render visible the initiatives and the alternative movements and to give them credibility, resorting to social science as we know it is of very little use. After all, social science has been responsible for concealing or discrediting alternatives. To fight against the waste of social experience, there is no point in proposing another kind of social science. Rather, a different model of rationality must be proposed" (ibid., 3), Sousa Santos links the waste of social experience

to larger struggles against hegemonic globalization: "Discrediting, concealing and trivializing counter-hegemonic globalization go largely hand in hand with discrediting, concealing and trivializing the knowledges that inform counter-hegemonic practices and agents. Faced with rival knowledges, hegemonic scientific knowledge either turns them into raw material (as is the case of indigenous or peasant knowledge about biodiversity) or rejects them on the basis of their falsity or inefficiency in the light of the hegemonic criteria of truth and efficiency." See Boaventura de Sousa Santos, "The Future of the World Social Forum," *La Rivista del Manifesto* 47, February 2004; available at http://www.larivistadelmanifesto.it/originale/47A20040203.html.

6. Available at http://archives.cnn.com/2001/US/11/06/gen.attack.on.terror/.

7. Lugones and Price, "Dominant Culture," 121.

8. Catherine Walsh. "(De)Construir la interculturalidad. Consideraciones críticas desde la política, la colonialidad y los movimientos indígenas y negros en el Ecuador," in *Interculturalidad y política: desafíos y posibilidades*, ed. Norma Fuller (Lima: Red para el Desarrollo de las Ciencias Sociales en el Perú, 2002), 115–142. *Interculturalidad* is a social, political, and epistemological project that arises from contemporary indigenous movements in Ecuador and Bolivia, and has become centrally linked to *plurinacionalidad*. The principle of interculturalidad in Ecuador respects the diversity of indigenous peoples and nations and other sectors of society in struggle against colonial and imperial hegemony, demanding unity in economic, social, cultural, and political terms toward the transformation of present structures and the construction of the new plurinational state within a framework of equality of rights, peace, harmony, and mutual respect among the nations. Interculturalidad implies a permanent rupture with monocultural, exclusive practices and emphasizes processes of reciprocal translation of plural knowledges without mixture or hybridization as the goal, but rather building a democracy of diverse cosmologies. It represents the construction of new epistemological frameworks that do not ossify ancestral knowledges but are knowledges being built from the interpretation and reinvention of a historical memory located in subjectivites and places that find their meaning in the present. It rejects the neoliberal multiculturalist strategy that hides the coloniality of power and that presents cultures as totalities kept in a mythical time. These processes are built from below, looking for social transformation through processes of interculturalization in multiple directions, emphasizing the social, political, and cultural subalternization of peoples and knowledges, thus emphasizing the process of desubalternization and decolonization (summary of Walsh, "(De)Construir la interculturalidad," by María Lugones).

9. Ibid., 136.

10. Ibid., 137.

11. Ibid., 122.

12. Fernando Coronil, "Beyond Occidentalism: Towards Non-Imperial Geohistorical Categories," *Cultural Anthropology* 11, no. 1 (February 1996): 51–87. With Occidentalism, Coronil refers "to the ensemble of representational practices that participate in the production of concepts of the world, which (1) separate the world's components into bounded units; (2) disaggregate their material histories; (3) turn difference into hierarchy; (4) naturalize these representations; and thus (5) intervene, however unwittingly, in the reproduction of existing asymmetrical power relations" (54) Thus Europe and America are understood as separate and their material histories are disaggregated. The same is true of groups and individuals (56–57).

13. Ella Shohat and Robert Stam, *Unthinking Eurocentrism* (London: Routledge, 2004). Shohat and Stam contrast "polycentric multiculturalism" with the historical unilinearity of "Eurocentrism" that renders history as a sequence of empires. Polycentric multiculturalism sees all cultural history in relation to social power; does not preach a pseudoequality of viewpoints; its affilitations are clearly with the underrepresented, the marginalized, and the oppressed; thinks and imagines "from the margins," seeing minoritarian communities not as "interest groups" to be "added on" to a preexisting nucleus but rather as active, generative participants at the very core of a shared, conflictual history; grants an "epistemological advantage" to those familiar with "margins" and "center" (or even with many margins and many centers), and thus ideally placed to "deconstruct" dominant or narrowly national discourses; rejects a unified, fixed, and essentialist concept of identities (or communities) as consolidated sets of practices, meanings, and experiences; it sees identities as multiple, unstable, historically situated, the products of ongoing differentiation and polymorphous identifications and pluralizations; goes beyond narrow definitions of identity politics, opening the way for informed affiliation on the basis of shared social desires and identifications, affiliations that have to be forged; is reciprocal, dialogical. It sees all acts of verbal or cultural exchange as taking place not between essential discrete bounded individuals or cultures but rather between mutually permeable, changing individuals and communities (see Shohat and Stam 300–301).

5

Muslim Immigrants in Post–9/11 American Politics

The "Exception" Population as an Intrinsic Element of American Liberalism

Falguni A. Sheth

> The "alien" is a frightening symbol of the fact of difference as such, of individuality as such. . . . The danger in the existence of such people is twofold: first and more obviously, their ever-increasing numbers threaten our political life, our human artifice.
>
> —Hannah Arendt, *The Origins of Totalitarianism*

Emergencies and Exceptions

The phenomenon of outcasting select populations has often been understood as the consequence of the hypocrisy of liberal democracies. The accusation of hypocrisy emerges when a liberal democratic nation's claim to extend rights equally to its entire population is shown to be untrue or when equal treatment for certain populations is rescinded in the name of some urgent political concern. In this chapter, through the example of populations who are loosely recognized as Arab or Muslim in the post–9/11 United States, I argue that such a practice is not hypocritical but rather an intrinsic element of Western liberalism.[1] The United States can understand itself *consistently* as aspiring to the liberal democratic project of equal treatment and protection of its members, even when simultaneously marginalizing or ostracizing certain populations within its midst. The consistency of these two practices might be usefully understood as a long-standing mode by which certain ethnically, culturally, or racially conspicuous groups—seen as a threat to a national population that understands itself as internally united, stable, and secure, *but for this group*—are outcasted politically and legally. In the context of the political and ideological framework of the United States, which takes its lead from classic liberal political philosophy, this practice of ostracizing certain groups is not necessarily collectively or societally self-conscious. Rather, it is one that depends on a dual (judicial) interpretation of the term "person." Such a dual interpretation in turn corresponds to a vacillating interpretation of constitutional protections.[2] Ultimately, the promise of equal protection is extended to all residents of a polity, so long as they are seen to qualify for membership—not in the polity—but in the set of human beings we call "persons."

In December 2002, Attorney General John Ashcroft began a focused agenda to round up, question, and detain hundreds of mostly male Muslim immigrants in the United States—under the aegis of the newly created category of "potential" terrorist—for the purposes of "intercepting and obstructing terrorism." This agenda was carried out without extending the benefit of constitutional protections routinely offered to non-Muslim American citizens (and often indulgently granted to noncitizens during times of relative peace and security) such as writs of habeas corpus and various Fourteenth Amendment rights such as the right to an attorney, due process, and equal protection.[3] The aegis for this action came from the USA PATRIOT Act, otherwise known as "Uniting and Strengthening America by Providing Appropriate Tools Required to Intercept and Obstruct Terrorism."[4] As is well-known today, it is a several-hundred-page document that takes as its premise the idea that terrorism can be duly understood and eradicated through preventive and preemptive measures.[5] The USA PATRIOT Act authorizes a striking increase in the scope of police powers afforded to the attorney general's office and to the recently created Department of Homeland Security (and the new overseer of the Bureau of Citizenship and Immigration Services (BCIS).

In many ways, the increasing restriction of movement of Muslim immigrants and increasing erosion of the civil liberties and protections of Muslim Americans bears an uncanny resemblance to Hannah Arendt's description of the treatment of Jews by various European states prior to the onset of World War II. She points to statelessness as that condition in which the country of one's origin will no longer claim members of a certain (ethnic) population as its own, disenfranchising them entirely, casting them away, and leaving them to appeal to the mercy of another nation for protection. Her analysis describes the reluctance of other nations to claim the unwanted as their own, and the unwillingness to extend them active economic or legal protections, leaving them in effect "undeportable."[6] The stateless, as Arendt points out, were constituted by minorities who could not claim membership in a nation on the basis of origin or blood, thereby requiring a "law of exception" to guarantee them both recognition and protection in spite of their "insistence" upon claiming a different nationality.[7] On such grounds, the law was transformed from an instrument of the state to an instrument of the nation, thereby transforming human beings into members of ethnic groups rather than members of polities, that is, citizens.[8] Statelessness becomes evident through "denationalization," and through the constitutional inability to guarantee human rights to those who have lost "nationally guaranteed rights." The final evidence of statelessness—and this seems to be the consequence of the first two moves—is that the claim to "inalienable human rights" becomes a demonstrably empty one.[9]

It is difficult to apply fully all the elements of Arendt's understanding of statelessness to Muslims. It is certainly the case that the "denationalization" of Muslims is a post-facto phenomenon, one that appears to have gained momentum as diasporic Muslim immigrants have found themselves under increasing scrutiny by immigration officials. This scrutiny, along with the absence of judicial review, has led to the deportation of scores of immigrants to their "countries of origin" without warning, welcome, or community.[10] The phenomenon of denationalization appears to be closely linked to American attempts to reinforce an "outsider" status for Muslims in the United States by constructing a certain descriptive conflation of Muslims with terrorists, namely, by institutionalizing a belief that Islam is a religion that should be suspected of sowing the seeds of a "terrorist psychology" in the minds of its adherents.

The plight of Muslims in the United States has not yet escalated to that of Jews prior to and during World War II. However, Arendt's discussion of statelessness clearly has a certain resonance with various events in contemporary American political discourse.[11] The most important implication of Arendt's analysis of statelessness is its fundamental implication of rightlessness.[12] The Bush administration has, according to certain political observers, planned its next round in the war on terrorism to resemble yet another stage in the creation of statelessness and rightlessness—not only for immigrants but even for those born in the United States.[13] The powers of the USA PATRIOT Act are only possible in a social and political context, as Arendt points out, where rightlessness has become the order of the day, and the distinction between human being and citizen has been eradicated—in a milieu that foreshadows totalitarianism as a condition where the distinction between the public and the private no longer exists, because the possibilities of action and difference, once protected by constitutional rights, have been effectively eliminated by the state's restriction of those rights.

Even Arendt's caveat that human rights can be reintroduced for minorities by special law becomes a fruitless avenue of appeal when the condition of human rights—namely, that they be universally extended to all members of the same class—is rendered null and void through the creation of exception populations, as I will discuss. The notion of exceptions, which Arendt uses to describe the social perception of the pariah, seems to be particularly insightful here. Arendt discusses the creation of exceptions as the method by which members of an outside group can assimilate themselves into a dominant group—namely, by showing oneself to be superior in some trait valued by the dominant group. However, I would suggest that "exception," understood as the avenue by which one is seen as inferior in some respect in comparison to another group, dominant or minority, is a particularly powerful weapon in selectively realigning the boundaries of universal human rights.[14] Such possibilities occur in a world where "exceptions" are routinely made in the extension of "human rights" to all members of the human class, through the irrationalization, the inferiorization, and delegitimation based on ad hoc differences—by creating "an illusory line between alien and citizen,"[15] and between enemy and friend. The practice of creating exceptions, as the state has been able to do most recently with Muslims, be they immigrants, potential terrorists, or enemy combatants, seems to be an intrinsic impulse of societies that wish to reconcile the mythological tolerance of liberalism with the fear of extreme cultural heterogeneity in the name of defending rational values, establishing security, and eradicating the threats to freedom within our midst.

Exceptions as the Condition of and Counterpart to American Liberalism

How does the ideological self-understanding of American liberalism remain consistent with its promise of universalism while constituting exceptions to the society whose members will be awarded full legality and protections? Dialectically speaking, it is only possible to recognize the set of members who are granted rights when we have a clear idea of who is excluded. Liberal political philosophies tend to offer a catalog of interests and characteristics of those human beings who are intended to be the recipients of natural or inalienable rights. John Locke, for example, refers to "reason" as the intellectual faculty and condition by which men know which rights are inalienably theirs. Reason, combined with the need to protect property interests, forms the basis of the argument for the Lockean social contract.[16] The extension of rights in classical liberal thought is neither universal nor inalienable, as feminists have long argued. The circle of membership—the set of individuals who are recognized as citizens and for whom the promise of rights *is indeed universal and inalienable*—

often depends on the attentive and obedient subordination of women (in the household, as free labor, mothers, sex partners) and of slaves (who, for Locke, have been granted their lives in an altruistic gesture by their victorious vanquishers, after a war of aggression has been fought).

And those who are excluded are excluded "justifiably"—either because their proper roles preclude them from claiming citizenship or rights, or because they have forfeited their rights by misbehaving (i.e., criminals), or because they are not entitled to claim rights because they do not qualify by virtue of some set of political, social, or ontological reasons. In other words, liberalism's promise of universal and inalienable rights is often intimately connected to the justified exclusion of some population, that is, an "exception" population.[17]

And so, the state understands or constitutes certain ethnically, culturally, or racially conspicuous groups as not quite capable of engaging in political interaction or not eligible for "citizenship," the standard trope denoting "full rights and membership in a polity." In a contemporary liberal society such as the United States, this mode of self-understanding involves the selective awarding or privation of certain rights and protections that are normally afforded to citizens and noncitizens alike; it functions by vacillating between an understanding of rights as political (and thus afforded primarily to those who are full members or citizens) and universal (and thus to be extended to individuals in a polity, regardless of their legal status in the polity).[18]

But liberal polities do not engage in a self-conscious creation of exception populations; rather, the creation of "exceptionalism" is justified through recourse to certain already given understandings of what constitutes reasonable values. This is often a self-referential and circular move, since the question of reasonable values is precisely always what is under scrutiny in debates between heterogeneous populations. As William Galston states,

> Liberal public institutions may restrict the activities of individuals and groups for four kinds of reasons: first to reduce coordination problems and conflict among diverse legitimate activities and to adjudicate such conflict when it cannot be avoided; second, to prevent and when necessary punish transgressions individuals may commit against one another; *third, to guard the boundary separating legitimate from illegitimate variations among ways of life*; and finally, to secure the conditions—including cultural and civic conditions—needed to sustain public institutions over time.[19]

By preempting the possibility of challenging a prevailing set of norms, the question of reasonableness is already instantiated by those who understand themselves as "full members of the polity." And so, a dominant population can create the conditions by which to reproduce itself and its norms while defending itself as extending full and equal rights to all "members" of the polity—that is, others like themselves. The practice of distinguishing "legitimate from illegitimate variations among ways of life" enables the state to justify why certain populations—especially if the members of that population are seen to be culturally homogenous—are not entitled to its promise of "universal protections." As Galston says, "Value pluralism is not relativism. The distinction between good and bad, and between good and evil, is objective and rationally defensible."[20]

The American state's justification for the exclusion of certain populations is necessary for several reasons. First, by continually redrawing the boundaries that circumscribe the set of members who are entitled to the liberal promise of "full, equal, and universal treatment," the state can emphasize and promulgate to members and nonmembers alike the import of its protections. If we were to extend the economistic argument that the value of a good increases in proportion to its scarcity, then it would make sense to say that equal and universal treatment can hardly be recognized and valued unless it is understood to be acquired through difficulty. Otherwise, the truly "universal" and equal treatment of all individuals would be transformed into a ubiquitous, transparent material that enveloped everyone, like air. Second, it is only by identifying an enemy or stranger that a liberal polity can understand itself and its function—the collective and collaborative function of maintaining an internally united, stable, and secure society. Thus, the selective criteria by which "members" are constituted enables the state to mark certain populations as insiders and others as enemies. By engaging in a selective extension of rights, the state is able to legitimate its inconsistent treatment of different populations while appearing to conform to its supposed promise of universal and identical treatment of all human beings.

Carl Schmitt's discussion of the political, whose existence is predicated on the distinction between friend and enemy, illuminates this point. According to Schmitt, the political is essentially defined through the identification of those who are considered to be an enemy.[21] An enemy does not need to be evil or ugly, and can even be an economic partner. "But," as Schmitt writes, "he is, nevertheless, the other, the stranger; and it is sufficient for his nature that he is, in a specially intense way, existentially something different and alien, so that in the extreme case conflicts with him are possible."[22] Thus, an enemy, because he is precisely what the polity is not, is necessary to engender a collective self-recognition.[23] The enemy, for Schmitt, is what the polity understands itself against. The case of Muslim immigrants enables the self-recognition of the United States as an internally united population, whose identity can only be understood through the ostracization of the "enemy" within its midst—that population which is not only culturally heterogeneous, but also appears to constitute a threat to the self-preservation of the polity.

Why must the enemy be internal? Why is it not sufficient for internal self-cohesion for a polity to regroup against an external enemy? Of course, it is certainly possible for the latter to occur. But the creation of internal enemies can be a tactic by which sovereign authorities can regulate potentially "unruly" or threatening populations by reorienting other subpopulations to understand them as a threat to "themselves."[24]

Schmitt's reading of the dynamic between the polity and its enemy is especially astute. However, I wish to go one step further and suggest that the polity must set the enemy outside the law that pertains to members of that polity in order to continually reinforce this recognition. And this is why the concept of "exception" plays a crucial role in the creation of an enemy group, particularly in a liberal context, where rights are considered the inalienable property of all human beings. The ethos of such universalism is important precisely for its promise of eliminating the capacity to find new groups to marginalize. This is why the notion of exception is crucial to the creation of new outsiders and insiders, that is, because it can justify why rights thought to belong to all human beings should be withheld from some group. The strength of "exceptionalism" lies in showing why the group in question does not meet the requisite criteria for protection by the state. In the case of Muslims, as once was true for Black Americans,[25] they are seen to be not sufficiently human, or, if human, then not sufficiently manageable by a dominant political authority or dominant social group to be extended the necessity of human rights. Here, the term "enemy" refers to that group which must be cast out by being marginalized and deprived of the protection of the state. And thus, the enemy represents that group which constitutes an "exception" to the population that the state ostensibly exists to protect.

An "exception" is typically understood as a deviation from the standard. On this reading, we understand the enforcer of the law to be either hypocritical or inconsistent. But what if we were to understand the "exception" as an intrinsic element of the standard *qua law*, as Giorgio Agamben does? For Agamben, the basic expression of sovereignty simultaneously circumscribes the polity, those who will be acknowledged by and subject to the law, as well as those who will be forced outside those parameters.[26] The latter group does not "incidentally" become the exception, but rather is intrinsic to the instantiation of the former group, that is, the group who will be included or protected.[27] Exceptions are intrinsic because they enable sovereign authorities to manage and secure their own claims to power. That is, through the creation of potential vulnerability for all populations, sovereign authority gives an incentive to them to avoid being targeted, by being able to focus on another group as a scapegoat. The concept of exception, understood as a "routine exclusion," enables us to understand how certain subject populations can be marginalized or eradicated as a matter of fact or procedure. If the American state convincingly renders Muslims a new race of "evildoers" with an inherent psychology of terrorism,[28] then it can constitute Muslims as some kind of "exception" population, a population who is simultaneously subject to the law, but not entitled to its protection. As Agamben points out, "It is literally not possible to say whether the one who has been banned is outside or inside the juridical order."[29] As a result, the vulnerability of such a subject in relation to the sovereign renders it possible to be eradicated or marginalized without such destruction being seen as a "sacrifice."[30] By extension, then, exception populations can be abandoned as a matter of "unexceptional" practice.

Constitutional Rights: Political? Human?

Drawing on some of the aforementioned political frameworks by which enemy populations are understood, I wish to apply the concept of "exception" to the American political and legal context. Exception populations are instantiated and demarcated from a core polity through a dual interpretation of constitutional protections as political and human rights. In this reading, it seems that the normative significance of the universalism of "natural" or "human" rights can be retained while extending them to select groups and depriving others of them. Thus, by reading the Constitution as a document that enumerates those rights extended to individuals as human beings, but by offering this reading only to its citizens, the state de facto insists on a second meaning of constitutional protections that illuminates them as political and, hence, selective rights that can be extended only to "friends," and not enemies, which corresponds to a distinction, simply put, between "us" and "them."

The ambiguous status of constitutional protections as both political rights and human rights is concealed during times of peace by the generally indulgent extension of a bulk of these protections to citizens and (legal) noncitizens alike.[31] This ambiguity refers directly, if implicitly, to the question of how to understand the figure of the immigrant. There are several parts to this story. The first part is about immigration as read through the history of American immigration law. The status of immigrants in American legal history is crucial to understanding how pariah groups are created and exceptions are legitimated, because immigration law confirms that arriving outsiders ("aliens") will be generally viewed and treated with suspicion because of their ethnic and cultural dissimilarities from the general U.S. population and because of their distinct geographical origins. The current moment deals with Arab immigrants of

Muslim origin, but it resembles in important ways the treatment of other ethnic groups who arrived from the mid-nineteenth to the end of the twentieth century—the Chinese, Sikhs, Mexicans, Irish, Italians, Slavs, Pakistanis, Indians, among countless others—for whom inclusion in the national political imaginary was often an arbitrary, elusive process and coincided with a concurrent outsider status.

One of the concerns about the way that (mostly male and primarily Muslim) Arab immigrants are currently being treated by the Office of Homeland Security is that they are not being extended the general constitutional protections that are considered "inalienable" for American citizens and often cautiously extended to immigrants during times of relative domestic peace. This division between the constitutional rights extended to American citizens and those most often arbitrarily extended or withheld from immigrants has its origins in the development of American immigration law.[32] Through a set of strategic administrative and legislative moves beginning in the late 1800s,[33] immigrants became subject to a body of law and to a mode of treatment that is separate and mostly distinct from the rest of American and constitutional law.[34] These moves enabled the cementing of certain norms in immigration procedures. Various rights implied under the Constitution were not required to be extended to immigrants: the writ of habeas corpus, the right to due process, routine judicial review, the right to an advocate or an attorney.[35] There is an enormous burgeoning literature begun well before 9/11, authored by liberal and communitarian scholars from various fields, that debates whether rights such as those listed above should be rights of membership rather than fundamental moral claims due any human being.[36] While I cannot possibly treat this literature adequately here, it is *the fact of the debate* that is itself of central importance to the argument here.

The tension over whether rights are political or human emerges from the central question of liberalism, namely, that of how "membership" should be understood. The narrowest interpretation of this question is that membership is based on claims to legal recognition by the state. The broadest interpretation is that membership is based on a community of human beings. Membership then connotes at least two different sets of individuals and possibly many more. But more fundamentally, the tension over the meaning of membership stems from whether it is being read from the "inside" or from without. Kunal Parker terms the former reading of "membership" as a liberal "insider" narrative about citizenship, that is, one that rests on the uncritical (and mistaken) premise that "members" of a group have the right to exclude or deprive "outsiders" of citizenship rights.[37] Read from the "outside," of course, that is, as pertaining to all human beings, membership would lose its central import, since it would thus render all rights as human rights to be awarded independently of legal status.

Yet, Hannah Arendt recognizes the central problem of securing rights as human rights when she points out that the recognition of one's human rights is predicated not on one's status as human, but on one's recognition as a member of a polity. One must be afforded some vehicle by which to mediate between oneself and the state. It is that recognition upon which the rhetorical discourse of human rights is predicated, namely, that human rights are to be accorded to all human beings under any and all conditions. And it is this premise that is betrayed in the absence of national rights:

> If a human being loses his political status, he should, according to the implications of the inborn and inalienable rights of man, come under exactly the situation for which the declarations of such general rights provided. Actually the opposite is the case. *It seems that a man who is nothing but a man has lost the very qualities which make it possible for other people to treat him as a fellow man.* This is one of the reasons why it is far more difficult to destroy the legal personality of a criminal, that is of a man who has taken upon himself the responsibility for an act whose consequences now determine his fate, than of a man who has been disallowed all common human responsibilities.[38]

In this excerpt, Arendt challenges the very assumption of international human rights that we in the contemporary world accept uncritically. Arendt draws on Edmund Burke's point that even "savages" are accorded human rights, but unless there is a state that recognizes and guarantees them, they remain ineffectual, indeed nonexistent. And here, I would go one step further than Arendt: it is not only the absence of political rights, but the absence of the dual recognition that political rights are human rights, that renders the distinction between human being and animal collapsed, such that one becomes a political and legal nonentity.[39]

The conception of human rights, based on the assumed existence of a human being as such, broke down at the very moment when those who professed to believe in it were for the first time confronted with people who had indeed lost all other qualities and specific relationships, except that they were still human. The world found nothing sacred in the abstract nakedness of being human.[40] To be human is meaningless within the context of a polity if it is not accompanied by certain political protections. Thus, human rights can only be secured through the recognition of one's political status as a member of a community. The absence of this dual recognition, then, is especially devastating for the figure of the immigrant.

The case of the American treatment of Muslims follows consistently from the history of its standard treatment of immigrants. In the American context, constitutional rights are often read either as human or political (membership) rights. Yet, the distinction between human rights and political rights emerges not only from the Arendtian point that one must be recognized in the latter sense, that is, as a member, in order to receive recognition of one's human rights. It also emerges from the ambiguous reading of the central category of individuals to whom rights are thought to be extended: persons. In the standard legal literature, the debate over whether immigrants should receive certain rights of due process and equal protection is thought to rest on the category of "persons," a category found throughout the U.S. Constitution.[41] The powers and equal protections of the Constitution are most famously defined as applying to "any person" within the territorial jurisdiction of the United States, as seen in the Fourteenth Amendment.[42]

But this debate emerges from another source as well, the central ambiguity over the meaning of the term "person." As Charles Mills points out, this category, of central importance in the philosophical literature, emerges in challenge to the world of rank and ascribed status as a way of denoting the central equality of human beings.[43] As a conceptual category, the term "person" has an ambiguous dual meaning, one that refers to both a legal and an ontological status. How this term is read again connects back to the distinct ways in which membership can be read—from the inside or outside. From the former perspective, "person" is a legal category whose recognition is cemented by the set of laws that liberal institutions uphold and promote. Thus to be a citizen is to be a "legal person," and thus to be an "official" member of a polity, distinguished from "unofficial" or "illegal" denizens of a polity. From the latter, that is, from the "outsider's," perspective, a "person" is an ontological category that entails automatic legal recognition. On this reading, then, constitutional rights are human rights, which must be extended to all who live within the polity—"members" or not.

However, there is a third dimension that attaches itself to this dual reading of "person." It is a dimension that neatly connects to the ambiguous and shifting reading of constitutional rights as political or human. The question of whether to grant rights as human rights or political rights depends not only on how the term "person" is read constitutionally, but on whether to read the person in question—in this case, the figure of the immigrant—as merely a human being or as a legal person also. The condition of reading the immigrant in the latter sense requires that they satisfy one crucial criterion: not only must they be "human," but they must be "human-like-us."

Heterogeneity in this case is expressed through the existential status of the immigrant, who lives neither inside nor outside the polity, but hovers on the edge. To clarify, the figure of the immigrant expresses existential heterogeneity through simultaneous or vacillating allegiances to multiple cultures, conventions, nations, or territories. Such plural affinities preclude the immigrant from fitting neatly and easily into the conventions of the society into which he has immigrated, and thus render him undependable, an uncertain ally in the quest for the unity, conformity, and stability of any given society, especially during times of crisis. For the dominant "rational" society, then, cultural heterogeneity—in the figure of the immigrant—is again interpreted as the existential inability to live neatly within the community, that is, the inability to be human-like-us. Thus, both existential and cultural heterogeneity are perceived as a potential threat to the internal stability of a society. And this combination, in turn, renders new immigrants particularly susceptible to being identified as the new enemy.[44]

The most obvious evidence of this reading emerges from the history of the plenary power doctrine with regard to immigration law, which grants "a unique immunity from judicial review."[45] For over a century, the Supreme Court has ruled that federal power needs no oversight with regard to making immigration law. Gabriel Chin argues that immigration law is the last stronghold of racial segregation in the United States, owing largely to the Court's attitude that "aliens of a particular race" may be excluded or removed from the United States and have no constitutional rights when seeking admission to the United States.[46] Further, the Justice Department, one of the venues through which immigration law is made, has argued that "citizenship" can be refused to immigrants by reason of inadequate habits, culture, or "deficiency of race." Referring to Chinese immigrants, the Justice Department insisted that color-blindness did not extend to aliens: "[T]he Chinese are a people not suited to our institutions, remaining a separate and distinct race, incapable of assimilation, having habits often of the most pernicious character . . . a people of such a character and so inimical to our interests as to require that their coming shall be prohibited."[47]

In effect, then, by holding that Congress had an absolute power to regulate immigration, a power not articulated in the Constitution, and one not subject to judicial review, the Court effectively deemed immigrants as unworthy of the status of "legal person," and hence unworthy of "inalienable" protections such as judicial review. This reading of both the immigrant and the Constitution is echoed by Charles Mills, when he astutely points to the implicit presence of nonwhites as crucial to the reification of (white) persons in the Racial Contract of the liberal polity. Labeling them "subpersons," Mills says,

> Subpersons are humanoid entities who, because of racial phenotype/genealogy/culture, are not fully human and therefore have a different and inferior schedule of rights and liberties applying to them. In other words, it is possible to get away with doing things to subpersons that one could not do to persons, because they do not have the same rights as persons.[48]

Whereas Mills argues this point with regard to raced persons generally, others, such as Natsu Taylor Saito, illustrate the double standards of liberal protections with specific regard to immigrants. Speaking with respect to Asian immigrants and their continual depiction as non-American, un-American, and "foreign," Saito suggests that the

> identification of those that race as foreign must be understood as part of the larger process of maintaining our particular social, racial, and economic hierarchies. Matters of citizenship and foreignness—who is a member of this polity, who should be allowed to live here, who should pay which social costs, and who should receive which benefits—are . . . closely tied to deeply held beliefs about what it is to be an American and what America should be.[49]

And yet the absence of an explicit confession on this front seems best explained by Alexander Bickel, who writes, "It has always been easier, it will always be easier to think of someone as a non-citizen than to decide he is a non-person."[50]

In the American context, that is, as understood through the ethos of immigration law, one can only be recognized as a legal "person" or a member of a community when one is not merely human, but "human-like-us." The message of the American polity is that Americans will be afforded political rights as if these are human rights, but non-Americans, because they are not-yet-human-like-us, will, at least until such time as they become American, be granted human rights only as political rights.[51] That is, until such point as membership is afforded, one can only be construed as an enemy, or that "Other" qua not-yet-human-like-us to whom, therefore, we have no obligation to extend human rights. Hence, constitutional rights are understood as natural rights only for members of the American polity.

Here we see an instance of how a category is instantiated through sovereign power that simultaneously becomes "exceptionalized"—the sovereign protection of the state is extended to "all persons," but the question of who is fit for "personhood" is continually and implicitly modified and reconstrued to reproduce certain fundamental divisions between populations. These divisions are predicated on a division between nonpersons (the enemy or the stranger or the foreigner, per Schmitt) and persons (the set of individuals who constitute the polity). And here is where the tension of liberalism is necessary to continually reproduce its self-understanding as maintaining the promise of universal rights: under this view, every human being is potentially eligible for recognition as a member of a polity, as long as he or she meets the (fairly rigid—and constantly changing—set of) criteria by which member qua person is defined. And, by implication, one can reside in a polity, one can even participate in many practices that citizens do, but one cannot be a full member of the polity—entitled to full protections and rights—unless and until one fully meets the criteria of what it means to be human. Before that moment, one can be understood in various modes that fall short of the definition of human being: stranger, alien, enemy—but most importantly as "an exception" to the set of individuals in this polity that we call citizens. That is, whatever "it" is, "it" is not "one of us," and therefore we are not obligated to award it constitutional protections or rights.

Thus, the effect of the stark division between the set of rights afforded to members versus nonmembers is to reinforce the collective self-recognition of a national political imaginary for a set of core constituents who were continually informed that they "are lucky enough to live in a country that believed in democracy and freedom."[52] The right of freedom, in this trope, often implied that it was a human right that human beings in other countries are not lucky enough to be afforded, but what is omitted is that other human beings who were not lucky enough to be natural-born American citizens, or, given the correct political times and circumstances, to be "naturalized," are also not lucky enough to be extended this protection by the American government except by fiat and selective judgments during times of international instability. Non-American immigrants are susceptible to the urgent drawing of lines between friend and enemy, which occurs (in a legal context) primarily through the suspension of procedures that are normally utilized to ascertain the grounds for indicting someone of a crime, or of judging him guilty of one.

The process of "nationalizing" the rights enumerated in the Constitution, and thus correlating the extension of human rights with the condition of citizenship, effectively elides the issue of whether human rights can ever be logically and consistently considered merely political rights, and whether political rights can ever be justified as less than universal human rights. But what we do know is that this elision also creates the opportunity to turn any given group—natural-born or immigrant—into an enemy population. By insisting on the enemy alien *exception*, the attorney general during the Bush administration resorted to a long-standing political framework whereby (human) rights would only be given to those deemed human-like-us, and those deemed not-quite-human-like-us, whether for just or unjust cause (we will never know since their causes will no longer be stated, much less tried, publicly), would be deprived altogether of the moral claims that are thought to be granted to all human beings in a liberal context, the claims to respect, dignity, and recognition.

Muslims as the New Exception Population

How have Muslims,[53] in the American public mind, become the new exception population? Muslims, following the argument of Agamben, constitute the newest population whose status is that of "bare life" in the American discourse, because they are not-American and (simultaneously) not-yet-human-like-us. And so, they are not worthy of being American, the sign of which is being extended constitutional protections on the ground of moral claims, that is, as human rights. This ambiguity refers directly, if implicitly, to ambivalence over how to understand the figure of the immigrant. The immigrant's nebulous status, as one of "us" in that he is human, but not (or not yet) human-like-us, seems to facilitate the distinction between friend and enemy during times of crisis. Again, it is not just cultural difference, but cultural difference perceived as a potential threat that seems to legitimate the generally popular trend of stripping a new group of political and legal protections, as in the case of immigrants of Arab descent or Muslim faith.[54] The moment constituted by the two years after 9/11 facilitated the Bush administration's promulgation of a crisis situation extreme enough to legitimate the ad hoc legal distinctions such as "terrorists," "enemy combatants," and "evildoers" versus "Americans," "citizens," and "friends" in direct reference to Muslims.

Briefly, I wish to identify some of the discursive mechanisms by which Muslims in the United States are understood as the most recent outcast(e) group.[55] There are several traits that have been ascribed to Muslims since 9/11—traits that, when combined, form a powerful public indictment of Muslims as an exception to the universal race of (rational) human beings. These three traits are enumerated as follows: (1) affiliation with a religion (Islam) that is equated with the ubiquitous goal of the destruction of non-Muslims generally (and Americans in particular); (2) in light of (1), ontological status as terrorists, which follows from a perceived moral, political, and cultural obligation to commit violent acts); and (3) political, cultural, and "existential" status as immigrants. These three traits take on a singular potency when understood as part of an effort to create a new pariah. Through these traits, Muslims have begun to be depicted as a new race, an evil and less rational race. In turn, this transformation has been parlayed into their depiction as a new pariah group, and has legitimated the withholding from them, as a group, of the "universal" protection of human rights and constitutional law.

The first trait was evident in the immediate aftermath of 9/11 in both moderate and fundamentalist positions. Moderate concerns could be found in myriad newspapers and magazines, including *Newsweek* and the *Atlantic Monthly*. Journalists asked the question of what about Islam led to 9/11, suggesting that the seeds of destruction were embedded in Islam as a political ideology, rather than a certain interpretation of Islam promoted by certain ideological factions for the purposes of a certain political agenda. Scholars also offered similar suggestions. Paul Berman traces the reaction of the events of 9/11 to the cultural appeal of Sayyid al-Qutb, an Egyptian religious scholar, member of the Muslim Brotherhood, and "the Arab world's first important theoretician of the Islamist cause," who called for a return to the principles of Islam.[56] Fawaz Gerges offers an excellent review of writers including Gilles Kepel, Bernard Lewis, Amos Perlmutter, Daniel Pipes, and others, who assert that Islam is a culture that "produces" terrorists, and is fundamentally incompatible with liberalism and democracy.[57] A third example is that of John Rawls in his book *The Law of Peoples*. Rawls continually uses the imaginary example of Kazanistan to illustrate the case of decent but illiberal peoples. He idealizes the rulers of Kazanistan because they, "[u]nlike most Muslim rulers, have not sought empire and territory. This is because their theologians understand *jihad* in a moral and spiritual sense, and not in military terms."[58]

These visions of Islam do not distinguish the interpretation of religious principles from a political agenda. They have been compounded by statements in the fundamentalist camp as well. At least two well-known Christian leaders, Jerry Falwell and Bob Graham, openly equate Islam with evil and destruction. It is the identification of Islam as a destructive political ideology and the corresponding identification of Muslims as being imbued with a "terrorist psychology" that is perhaps the easiest to locate, since it emerges from various comments by well-known religious leaders as well as generally in the policies enacted and enforced by the Bush administration.[59]

The second trait, namely, the identification of all Muslims as terrorists, and their perceived obligation to commit violent acts, is best illustrated through the dictates of former Attorney General Ashcroft: thousands of Muslim men—unless they were naturalized—were required to register with the Immigration and Naturalization Service since fall 2002, on the suspicion of having knowledge of or being associated with terrorists, by reason of their religion. The categories of "enemy aliens," "enemy combatants," and "suspected terrorist" have become commonplace in the days since 9/11. The last term has been used to detain two thousand people as of October 28, 2002. The term "enemy aliens" has been used to hold 598 Taliban and Al-Qaeda detainees at Guantanamo Bay U.S. Naval Station. None of these detainees were prisoners of war.[60] The term "enemy combatant" has been used to indict and convict at least one American citizen, John Walker Lindh, a convert to Islam, on scant and dubious evidence, according to one prominent terrorism scholar, who is convinced that Lindh knew nothing about Al-Qaeda's plot on 9/11.[61] The same term, "enemy combatant," has been used to detain Jose Padilla "until the end of the hostilities," according to a district court judge, although the judge overturned Attorney General Ashcroft's decision to deprive Padilla of the right to meet with his attorney or review the evidence against him.[62] Yasser Hamdi, an American citizen, has also been subject to the same treatment on the same grounds. The claim that the Bush administration treated all Muslims as if they were, de facto, terrorists is substantiated not only through the reawakening of the category of "enemy aliens" and "enemy combatants," but myriad other events, including the night raids on Muslims in graduate student housing at the University of Idaho; the mass rounding up of Muslims in Lackawanna, New York; the mandatory registration of all Muslim immigrants in the United States; the incarceration of John Yee, a Muslim chaplain in the U.S. Army; and the abandonment of the prisoners at Guantanamo Bay by a federal district court. Another obvious instance of such identification of Muslims as terrorists might best be seen in a CBS/*New York Times* poll, in which 42 percent of those polled thought that Saddam Hussein was responsible for the events of 9/11 (April 2003), suggesting an interchangeable set of "evil" Muslim leaders.

The third trait is a crucial substantiation of the exception narrative as discussed above. Their identification as immigrants facilitates the indictment of Muslims as outcast(e)s or an evil race. There are two dimensions to their status as immigrants: one is the *association* of immigrants with *outsiders* or the "not–quite-one-of-us," through phenotypical and cultural differences.[63] The second dimension is that of their nebulous status as immigrants, namely, a population who is not-quite-one-of-us.

In our modern culture of liberal toleration,[64] cultural difference alone is not a sufficient reason to deprive a group of rights. It is significant cultural difference—seen as a *threat* to other reasonable and hence law-abiding members of the polity—that is understood as holding the potential for criminality. In the case of Muslims, the actions of a group of nineteen men on 9/11, have become a synecdoche for the "nature" and unique cultural practices of all members of that ethnic and cultural group. And thus, this synecdoche reinforces the perception of the entire group as engaging in a set of culturally heterogeneous practices that emerge through the affinity for another tradition or "another" God, and thus another law than the culture that binds us as a community. Hence, these practices are seen as profane or criminal practices, that is, as transgressing or departing from the common culture that members of a group should share. If we can ascribe this interpretation to a given group, then we might better understand the logic behind the preemptive hunt for "potential terrorists," qua enemies: the idea of "innocent until proven guilty" does not apply to those who are "not-like-us" or "not-human-like-us." What is important to take away from these newly "characteristic" marks of Muslims, however, is a crucial perception that enables the recognition of this group in its cultural heterogeneity as being unworthy of the protection afforded by a reading of constitutional rights as human rights.

Conclusion

It is, on one level, a historical commonplace of liberalism that the promise of equal protection has not been extended universally. But the rationale of these "commonsensical" exclusions as "mere" exceptions to the American constitutional promise of equal treatment and universal protections of all persons within its borders raises deep suspicions. The transhistorical constancy, the consistent presence of exceptions within the political and legal history of the United States, compels one to ask whether these exceptions really are unwitting or accidental. I suggest, instead, that exclusion is an intrinsic element of American liberalism, emerging from the impulse to circumscribe and valorize the liberal subject as a privileged member of that polity, granted a treatment that, incredibly enough, is considered elite, and is one for which few are eligible unless they can meet a rigorous and stringent set of criteria. The criteria in question revolve around the reproduction of a set of implicit values and, at minimum, the cultural appearance of those who constitute the full-fledged members and who author the laws of the liberal polity. Through this lens, exclusion is intrinsic to the maintenance and reproduction of liberal values and practices. The figure of the Muslim immigrant is a precise threat to the cultural homogeneity (or limited heterogeneity) and political unity of the liberal polity. But since the self-understanding of American liberalism is at variance with the above description, the method by which such divergence is reconciled is through a vacillating interpretation of the person at the center of that quintessential document of American polity, the U.S. Constitution. There, through the judgment of the Supreme Court, the liberal person is sometimes understood as an ontological category and at other times, a normative one. This selective, always-convenient interpretation corresponds to an equally selective interpretation, namely, of the nature of the rights thought to ground a liberal polity; sometimes these rights are thought to be inalienable for everyone, and other times, they are thought to be so for members only. This reading of the intrinsic exclusionary impulse of liberalism has often been recognized by various liberal theorists as a necessary and justifiable impulse. It is one that is embedded in a worldview, as Kunal Parker points out, which leaves the burden of proving that one is worthy of membership on the claimant, always already the "outsider," rather than insisting that exclusion is not a rational impulse. In this logic, the burden of proving the legitimacy of exclusion from a polity should rest on those who wish to exclude, that is, on the "insiders."

Is there a remedy to the exclusion that is the counterpart to the rhetoric of American liberal universalism? The nature of exceptions might imply that such a solution is impossible; however, I do not think we need to be so pessimistic. Part of the reason behind the continual repetition of "exceptions" is that they are seen as accidental; that is, their intrinsic nature is concealed behind the superficial, if conspicuous, rhetoric of "equal rights." If we can crack open the façade and consider the creation of "exceptions" as a tendency of American liberalism, rather than a series of accidents, then we can anticipate this tendency by looking for warning signs. In so doing, we may be able to avert or head off the creation of potential scapegoats. In other words, solutions require a change of perspective. It is easy to deceive ourselves that atrocities—genocides, mass incarceration, inhuman treatment of various kinds—are "incidental" and "accidental" only when we refuse to understand them in a historically longer-standing context. Any time an atrocity occurs, it is tragic. But when tragedies occur repeatedly, then it behooves us to recognize them as part of a systemic pattern and to address them as such. Solutions to the problem of "intrinsic" exceptions can only occur by changing the way we understand such events, and by deeming them unacceptable and searching harder and longer for an extensive reconfiguration of the United States' political framework—one that addresses and rectifies the procedure by which political recognition is awarded by the state, that is, the vehicle of membership. Short of a change in perspective and a new framework, this remedy—and the fulfillment of the promise of liberalism—remains chimerical.

Notes

I thank Robert E. Prasch, Marcellus Andrews, Joan Cocks, Gordon Hull, Fouad Kalouche, Charles Mills, Matt Silliman, Gregory Velazco y Trianosky, and Barbara Yngvesson for their efficient and extensive feedback on various versions of this chapter. Thanks to Kimberly McGuire for her excellent research assistance. I also acknowledge audiences at the following forums for their helpful comments during the presentation of this chapter: Smith College, Massachusetts College of Liberal Arts, the North American Society for Social Philosophy, the American Philosophical Association, and Hampshire College School of Social Science Citizenship Conference. A different version of this chapter can be found in Sheth, *Toward a Political Philosophy of Race* (New York: State University of New York Press, 2009), chap. 5: "Producing Race: Naturalizing the Exception through the Rule of Law."

1. My claims here pertain to American liberalism. They might extend to other forms of liberalism, but with significant caveats. For an extended discussion of what I mean by liberalism more specifically, see Sheth, "Introduction," *Toward a Political Philosophy of Race*.

2. Michael Scaperlanda points out that at times the United States Supreme Court has interpreted the "person" of the Fourteenth Amendment

as a category that applies to all denizens of the United States, citizens or otherwise; at other times, it has also interpreted it much more narrowly, and thus applying only to citizens (and occasionally only to certain kinds of citizens. See the Court's decision in *Yick Wo v. Hopkins* 118 U.S. 356 (1886) for an expansive interpretation, and *Chae Chan Ping v. U.S.* 130 U.S. 581 (1889), for a much narrower interpretation of "person." See Scaperlanda, "Partial Membership, Alienage, and the Constitutional Community," Iowa Law Review 81, 707ff (1996). But it is important to note that in each of these cases, the decision is implicitly ascribed to the proper interpretation of the "rule of law," that is, an objective and rigorous interpretation of the Constitution.

3. BBC Web site (www.bbc.co.uk), December 19, 2002; ACLU Web site (www.aclu.org), December 19, 2003.

4. Passed October 26, 2001. The USA PATRIOT Act defines domestic terrorism as "activities that (A) involve acts dangerous to human life that are a violation of the criminal laws of the United States or of any State; (B) appear to be intended—(i) to intimidate or coerce a civilian population; (ii) to influence the policy of a government by intimidation or coercion; or (iii) to affect the conduct of a government by mass destruction, assassination, or kidnapping; and (C) occur primarily within the territorial jurisdiction of the United States" (H.R. 3162, Sec. 802). The power to "hunt" terrorists has since been augmented by the Intelligence Authorization Act of 2004 and the 2006 Military Commissions Act.

5. Among the list of actions authorized by the USA PATRIOT Act was the express requirement that immigrants from twenty-five countries (twenty-four of which are predominantly Muslim) register their presences with the Immigration and Naturalization Service, and "voluntarily" speak with federal agents about intelligence concerning Al-Qaeda, Osama bin Laden, terrorist organizations in general, and, more recently, about Iraq. The sole non-Muslim country included is North Korea.

6. Hannah Arendt, *The Origins of Totalitarianism* (1951; New York: Harcourt, 1968), 276.

7. Ibid., 275.

8. Ibid.

9. Ibid., 269.

10. Indeed, a number of cases have been reported whereby Muslim immigrants are sent to countries where they believe they are in danger of harm, undue incarceration, or losing their lives.

11. Another dimension of statelessness, namely, the reluctance of other states to consider asylum claims, has also found resonances in recent relevant actions. In particular, the Safe Third Country Agreement, which was signed in December 2002, renders the U.S.–Canadian border effectively closed for U.S.-residing refugees asking for asylum from the Canadian

authorities. This agreement requires immigrants seeking refuge in Canada to appeal for asylum to the U.S. immigration authorities first, and risking long-term incarceration—and most likely—eventual refusal of their appeals and deportation back to the country from which they were initially fleeing, to try to find their way to a consulate in their "home" countries from which to appeal for asylum. The third element of statelessness, namely, the inability to claim entitlement to the native country by origin or blood, is less relevant here. Claims to American citizenship—whether by country of origin or by special laws (such as the laws of naturalization)—have become much more unstable since 2002, leaving citizens of Muslim background fairly defenseless in claiming the constitutional rights normally afforded to other non-Muslim citizens, for whom as well these privileges are being starkly restricted.

12. Rightlessness stems from the inability to claim a set of rights that have been instantiated as human rights, that is, the rights of all persons and not merely the rights of American citizens—once a popular reading of the U.S. Constitution. See Gerald Neuman, *Strangers to the Constitution: Immigrants, Borders, and Fundamental Law* (Princeton, NJ: Princeton University Press, 1996), chap. 1 and David Cole, "Enemy Aliens and American Freedoms," *The Nation*, September 23, 2002, 20–23.

13. See note 12.

14. The description of the enemy or the exception that is being ascribed to Muslims, as I discuss further on, is a status that many groups have held during previous moments in American history. Prior cases where such enemy status has been ascribed include the Irish, Japanese Americans, Chinese, East Indians, Jews, and Italians. See Noel Ignatiev, *How the Irish Became White* (London: Routledge, 1995).

15. Cole, "Enemy Aliens and American Freedoms."

16. John Locke, *Two Treatises of Government* (1690; New York: Hafner Press, 1947), bk. 2, par. 6.

17. This argument has been found in different versions in recent scholarship on liberalism. Carole Pateman and Charles Mills have both argued that the "universal" right of the social contract in liberal theory intrinsically depends on a gendered or "raced" reading. Pateman argues that marriage rights are intrinsically sex rights that men hold to women's bodies. Mills argues that the Social Contract is a trope by which it is understood that only individuals of certain races (depicted by color, class, culture, or some other set of characteristics) are understood to qualify for the ability to consent to its enactment. See Carole Pateman, *The Sexual Contract* (Stanford, CA: Stanford University Press, 1988) and Charles Mills, *The Racial Contract* (Ithaca, NY: Cornell University Press, 1997). I discuss how exception populations are constituted in more detail in Sheth, *Toward a Political Philosophy of Race*.

18. I will discuss this method of selective awarding of rights more fully in the next section.

19. William Galson, *Liberal Pluralism: The Implications of Value Pluralism for Political Theory and Practice* (New York: Cambridge University Press 2002), 3; emphasis added. As a political philosopher, a deputy assistant to the president for domestic policy during the first Clinton administration, and an executive director of the National Commission on Civic Renewal, which was chaired by Sam Nunn and William Bennett, Galston might be a quintessential representative of the tenets of Western—or more specifically—American liberalism.

20. Ibid., 5.

21. Carl Schmitt, *The Concept of the Political* (1932; Chicago: University of Chicago Press, 1996), 26.

22. Ibid., 27.

23. Ibid., 28.

24. For more extensive arguments about these tactics, see Sheth, "*Toward a Political Philosophy of Race*, chap. 2: "The Violence of Law: Sovereign Power, Vulnerable Populations and Race."

25. Here I am thinking of the status of Black Americans in their initial introduction to this country as slaves, as well as their treatment at the hands of various state authorities in the postemancipation United States. For a fuller treatment of Black Americans as one of the original "exception" populations, see Falguni A. Sheth, "Stateless, Rightlessness and Black Americans," unpublished manuscript, 2003. The same understanding also can be applied to other groups in the history of United States immigration, such as Chinese migrant laborers, Mexican immigrants, and Irish immigrants. See Lucy Salyer, *Laws as Harsh as Tigers: Chinese Immigrants and the Shaping of Modern Immigration Law* (Chapel Hill: University of North Carolina Press, 1995), Tomas Almaguer, *Racial Fault Lines: The Historical Origins of White Supremacy in California* (Berkeley and Los Angeles: University of California Press, 1994), and Noel Ignatiev, *How the Irish Became White.*

26. "If the exception is the structure of sovereignty, then sovereignty is not an exclusively political concept, an exclusively juridical category, a power external to law . . . , or the supreme rule of the juridical order . . . : *it is the originary structure in which law refers to life and includes it in itself by suspending it.*" See Giorgio Agamben, *Homo Sacer: Sovereign Power and Bare Life* (Stanford, CA: Stanford University Press, 1995), 28; emphasis added.

27. Ibid., 15.

28. A pursuit that has been successful, as I will show further on in this chapter.

29. Ibid., 28–29.

30. Agamben, *Homo Sacer*, 83.

31. For exemplary if disparate readings of the selective reading of constitutional rights to "foreigners," "aliens," and other kinds of "strangers," see Peter Schuck, *Citizens, Strangers, and In-Betweens* (Boulder, CO: Westview Press, 1998) and Neuman, *Strangers to the Constitution.*

32. See Schuck, *Citizens, Strangers, and In-Betweens*, especially chapter 2, where he argues that immigration law is the vehicle by which the United States can maintain itself as a national community, which has the right to refuse admissions to enemies or outsiders.

33. During this time Congress returned from federal courts to the federal government the power to create immigration law, and also awarded "federal administrators the sole power to enforce immigration policy." See Salyer, *Laws as Harsh as Tigers*, 1.

34. Peter Schuck, "The Transformation of American Law," Columbia L. Rev. 84:1 (1984): 1–90; Owen Fiss, "The Immigrant as Pariah," *Boston Review* (October/November 1998); Salyer, *Laws as Harsh as Tigers.*

35. See Schuck, "The Transformation of American Law"; Salyer, *Laws as Harsh as Tigers.*

36. For example, Seyla Benhabib, drawing on Jürgen Habermas's distinctions, distinguishes these as legal rights, or claims of membership, rather than human rights, which are grounded on fundamental moral claims; see her "Citizens, Residents, and Aliens in a Changing World: Political Membership in a Global Era," *Social Research* 66, no. 3 (1999): 731. Benhabib credits Habermas with this distinction, although she offers no specific citation. And, yet, legal scholars such as Peter Schuck insist that the goals of community must be reconciled with the universal aspirations of liberalism, the U.S. Constitution's protections are extended to "all persons," living under its jurisdiction, that is, on U.S. soil, and not merely to those who can legally claim "citizenship," suggesting that these rights are moral claims rather than the privileges of legal membership. See Schuck, "The Transformation of American Law," 10. See also Michael Walzer, *Spheres of Justice: A Defense of Pluralism and Equality* (New York: Basic Books, 1983), whose work seems to inaugurate the most recent round of this debate over the past two decades, in philosophy, legal theory, and political science.

37. Parker identifies the liberal "insider" narrative as shared by scholars such as Peter Schuck, Rogers Smith, and Michael Walzer. Parker suggests that a more accurate, although less congenial, narrative would locate the United States' attitude toward immigrants as a "gesture of pure refusal," that is instantiated and institutionalized through a set of laws and policies set up to anticipate and preclude a "foreigner's" claim to citizenship rights. Parker says that "rather than conceiving of the relative moral urgency of individual's claims upon the community in terms of their location vis-à-vis a

territorial community already organized on the basis of citizenship, as various liberal historians of American citizenship have done, one should always conceive of the state's construction of citizenship as a barrier to the individual's territorial rights as itself being a strategy for defeating the individual's claim upon the community." See his "State, Citizenship, and Territory: The Legal Construction of Immigrants in Antebellum Massachusetts," *Law and History Review* 19, no. 3 (2001): 583–643.

38. Arendt, *The Origins of Totalitarianism*, 300.

39. Ibid., 298–302.

40. Ibid., 299.

41. See Jeremy Waldron, "Security and Liberty: The Image of Balance," *Journal of Political Philosophy* 11, no. 2 (June 2003): 191–210. Waldron points to an instance of this when he discusses section 214 of the USA PATRIOT Act, whereby "United States persons" will remain protected from searches "conducted solely on the basis of those activities protected by the first [*sic*] Amendment to the Constitution." As Waldron points out, "United States persons" refers to American citizens and legally admitted permanent residents, but not nonresident aliens living legally within the U.S. borders.

42. Most directly: " [N]or shall any state deprive any person of life, liberty, or property, without due process of law; *nor deny to any person within its jurisdiction the equal protection of the laws*." U.S. Constitution, amend. 14, sec. 1; emphasis added.

43. Mills, *The Racial Contract*, 57. He also points out that this category emerges within the context of Kantian literature on moral and natural rights that are thought to enshrine the sanctity of individuals "whose rights must not be infringed."

44. For excellent and detailed arguments that survey the literature on immigration law and scholarship and how "aliens" and "foreigners" are conceived of and treated within the American context, see Neuman, *Strangers to the Constitution* and Linda Bosniak, "Membership, Equality, and the Difference That Alienage Makes," 69 N.Y.U. L. Rev. 1047 (Dec. 1994).

45. Gabriel J. Chin, "Segregation's Last Stronghold: Race Discrimination and the constitutional Law of Immigration," 46 UCLA L. Rev. 1, 1 (1997).

46. Ibid., 4.

47. Quote taken from the Supreme Court's decision in *Fong Yue Ting v. United States*, 149 U.S. 698, as cited in Chin, "Segregation's Last Stronghold," 18–19.

48. Mills, *The Racial Contract*, 56. Mills is referring to mainstream political philosophy's rendering of the Social Contract. Mills also points to the inevitable interpretation that such treatment of subpersons is contingent

or accidental in order to render race marginal to the contract *rather than a central, intrinsic element.* Again, I would extend this reading to liberal polities more generally.

49. Natsu Taylor Saito, "Alien and Non-Alien Alike: Citizenship, 'Foreignness,' and Racial Hierarchy in American Law," 76 Or. L. Rev. 262, 344 (1997). Part of a symposium entitled "Citizenship and Its Discontents: Centering the Immigrant in the Inter/national Imagination (Part I): Section One: Race, Citizenship, and Political Community within the Nation-State."

50. Alexander Bickel, *The Morality of Consent* (New Haven, CT: Yale University Press. 1975), 53. I must acknowledge Linda Bosniak's article (cited in note 44) for first alerting me to this statement.

51. The figure of the immigrant is not the sole version of the "exception," or the not-yet-human-like-us, or the pariah. We saw a similar phenomenon during 1920s America. During the "Red Scare," serious consideration was given to denaturalizing scores of communists, anarchists, and other presumed "subversives," on the grounds that they were not fulfilling their responsibilities of citizenship by turning in potential insurgents—the then "enemy aliens." There are also the cases of the internment of Japanese Americans and, of course, U.S. slavery.

52. The Bush administration was consistent in promoting this link: Droves of immigrants were rounded up for being publicly critical of the Justice Department's procedures, as in the case of Yemeni Americans in Lackawanna, New York. See Joanne Wypijewski, "Living in an Age of Fire," *Mother Jones* (March–April 2003), while the administration emphasized its commitment to freedom and democracy.

53. The use of this fairly nebulous term is deliberate and, I hope, reflects accurately the population under consideration as treated by mass media and the various offices of the Bush administration (including the FBI, Homeland Security, the Attorney General's Office, BCIS). I use this term to connote the larger international trend toward the vilification of Islam; however, the term "Arab" might also be used to identify the same population. I wish to circumscribe this group in the following ways: they are generally neither natural-born nor naturalized U.S. citizens; they are often but not necessarily culturally conspicuous (e.g., through a religious commitment to Islam, dress, or physical marks such as beards), and often identified as being of Middle Eastern or Arab backgrounds, but not always Muslim (such as Palestinian Christians). These are only provisional guidelines. Obviously, there are significant exceptions to these guidelines; many men who have been required to register with the BCIS are of Arab background, but not Muslim. A number of detainees at Guantanamo Bay are U.S., Australian, or British citizens, and/or not of Middle Eastern background. There is also a significant population

of Black American Muslims in the United States. My argument does not address these populations.

54. Viewing terrorism as truly a fact of cultural difference seems to border on racism, but at the very least, this understanding is a fallacy that need not concern us here. I am interested rather in the perception of cultural difference.

55. I use the term "outcast(e)" to indicate the dual meaning of being "Untouchable" and marginalized. I am aware that the treatment of Muslims in the United States can be linked to the larger internationalist discourse on Islam, and I have attempted to illustrate this link elsewhere. See Sheth, *Towards a Political Philosophy of Race*. My focus in this chapter is the treatment of Muslims in U.S. domestic contexts.

56. See Paul Berman, *Terror and Liberalism*, 1st ed. (New York: Norton, 2003), 62.

57. See Fawaz A. Gerges, *America and Political Islam* (Cambridge: Cambridge University Press, 1999). See especially chapter 2, "The Intellectual Context for American Foreign Policy."

58. John Rawls, *Law of Peoples* (Cambridge, MA: Harvard University Press, 1999), 76. For a more extensive argument that illustrates the association of Muslims and destructiveness in Rawls and others, see Sheth, *Towards a Political Philosophy of Race*, chap. 3, "The Unruly: Strangeness, Madness, and Race." See also Jeffrey Paris, "After Rawls," *Social Theory and Practice* 28, no. 4 (2002): 679–699, who argues convincingly that Rawls's writings are a historical blueprint that reflect actual domestic and international politics of the latter half of the twentieth century.

59. What follows are a few quotes from some of these leaders, which exhibit the first two traits:

- Reverend Jerry Falwell: "The Prophet Muhammad is a terrorist" (CBS, *60 Minutes*)
- Southern Baptist Pastor Jerry Vines stated that Muhammad was a "demon-possessed pedophile" and that Islam teaches the destruction of all non-Muslims.
- Reverend Franklin Graham, son of Reverend Billy Graham, called Islam "a very evil and wicked religion."
- Pat Robertson, on Muhammad, "This man was an absolute wild-eyed fanatic. He was a robber and a brigand. And to say that these terrorists distort Islam, they're carrying out Islam. I mean, this man was a killer. And to think that this is a peaceful religion is fraudulent." (Quotes are taken from Fedwa Wazwaz, "Falwell, Graham and Friedman: Inexcusable Tolerance for Religious Extremism in America," *CounterPunch*, October 10, 2002.)
- Lt. General Boykin: "We are a Christian Nation leading a war against Satan" (*New York Times*, October 18, 2003).

60. Joseph Lelyveld, "In Guantànamo," *New York Review of Books*, November 7, 2003.

61. See Jane Mayer, "Lost in the Jihad," *The New Yorker*, March 10, 2003, 52).

62. Miles Harvey, "The Bad Guy," *Mother Jones*, March–April 2003, 32, 34.

63. First, they are neither legally nor "culturally" Americans already—since they are holding onto a distinct ethnic description: Arabs, Syrians, Iranian, and so on. Second, they appear visibly different—for reasons of skin color, language, food, cultural practices (holidays, prayer, mosques), dress, and so on, and thus threaten the general nebulous quality of "American culture," with such distinct and different practices. Third, their economic status, combined often with educated or skilled backgrounds, and perhaps an intragroup willingness to combine economic resources, renders them a threat to that group in the domestic labor force which also is educated (and thus not only to unskilled labor per se).

64. For exemplary arguments to this effect, see Will Kymlicka *Liberalism, Community and Culture* (Oxford, UK: Oxford University Press, 1989); Charles Taylor, *Multculturalism: Examining the Politics of Recognition*, ed. Amy Gutmann (Princeton, NJ: Princeton University Press, 1994).

6

Situating Race and Nation in the U.S. Context

Methodology, Interdisciplinarity, and the Unresolved Role of Comparative Inquiry

Mindy Peden

> Fellow citizens, above your national, tumultuous joy, I hear the mournful wail of millions! . . . What, to the American slave, is your 4th of July? I answer; a day that reveals to him, more than all other days in the year, the gross injustice and cruelty to which he is the constant victim. To him, your celebration is a sham; your boasted liberty, an unholy license; your national greatness, swelling vanity; your sound of rejoicing are empty and heartless; your denunciation of tyrants brass fronted impudence; your shout of liberty and equality, hollow mockery; your prayers and hymns, your sermons and thanks-givings, with all your religious parade and solemnity, are to him, mere bombast, fraud, deception, impiety, and hypocrisy—a thin veil to cover up crimes which would disgrace a nation of savages. There is not a nation on the earth guilty of practices more shocking and bloody than are the people of the United States, at this very hour.
>
> —Frederick Douglass, Independence Day Speech at Rochester, 1852

IN THIS CHAPTER I attempt two counterintuitive moves. The first is to suggest that political science should study the interplay of race and nation with the help of other disciplines. The second is to show how a good comparative analysis can function, with problems, to shed light on the experience of race and nationalism in the United States. As should be clear by the end, I think that there are two trends in thinking about race and nation in the context of the United States that have very ambivalent repercussions. The first is the tendency to think of the United States as an "exception." In that sense it is easy for Americans to see problems of nationalism as problems that other peoples face, but also to see the experience of U.S. identity as so profoundly unique that it borders on being inherently racist. The second is the desire to be scientific in the sense of universalizing observations. This scientific striving can overshadow nuanced philosophical and literary approaches that undermine the transhistorical pretensions of racial ideology.

The term "nationalism" has been given much historical and empirical scrutiny; however, one challenge for the student of national identity in the United States is that much of the literature is focused on European nation-states historically and so-called third world nationalisms in the contemporary world. These studies underscore the extent to which the doctrine of "American exceptionalism" affects the study of nationalism. One notable exception in the vast literature on nationalism is the way Benedict Anderson calls attention to North and South American national projects being led by "creole nationalism" (Ben Franklin being the central figure) that in turn asserts a presumed community of unitary national identity out of a hyphenated émigré one.[1] Other historically focused studies have drawn attention more sharply to U.S. national identity as contested on the basis of race.

The demands for cultural and national unity in the United States in the face of racial diversity have clear historical precedent that has been highlighted both by some historians of the United States and also by comparative studies.[2] Rogers Smith has pioneered historical institutionalist approaches to the question of U.S. nationhood by naming and tracing a tradition of "ascriptive hierarchy" in United States' legal discourse on citizenship.[3] For many thinkers, U.S. citizenship is at worst a form of civic nationalism, though Smith's work disputes this formulation and recasts the deep ways in which U.S. culture has been exclusionary on the basis of race and other ascriptive assignations, making the very project of citizenship itself inconsistent. Many scholars of slavery and emancipation in the United States can help us understand the distinctive history of African Americans and debates about national identity.[4] In what has been a mostly welcome move, contemporary scholars have scrutinized whiteness as racialized as opposed to the often assumed "naturalness" of whiteness.[5]

Academic writing about U.S. "civic" identity and the "dangerous" role of immigration certainly did not emerge only after September 11, 2001, but has been particularly successful in playing into nationalist fears of race that have become, somewhat oddly when one considers the hegemony of notions of "progress" in thinking about United States' history, more frequent in the public domain.[6] As a particularly good example, political scientist Samuel P. Huntington's "The Hispanic Challenge" argues explicitly for a noncivic U.S. national identity that is being obstructed by immigration from Mexico.[7] What is fascinating about Huntington's piece is precisely his recognition of what many scholars of U.S. nationalism have been pointing out for some time—namely, the profoundly racial and noncivic nature of U.S. identity. But rather than critique this conception of identity, Huntington wants to embrace it, and it is easy to assume that he is far from alone in that.

At stake in these discussions is the extent to which it is presumed that identity needs to be, or is by definition, unitary. For scholars of liberalism, this presents a problem for the articulation of difference, as Iris Marion Young makes clear in her critique of what she calls "the distributive paradigm" of justice.[8] In part because of her intervention, liberal thinkers have begun to try to rethink the status of group identity within the liberal individualist paradigm. The classic in this regard is Will Kymlicka's *Multicultural Citizenship*,[9] which, though written by a Canadian with many Canadian examples, also provides substantial insight into U.S. political identity and the often problematic ways in which group identity (of which race is a subset in this formulation) has been handled. More recent articulations of difference and identity (sometimes in the context of the United States) link race to political ideologies. For example, Paul Gilroy's earlier work has been influential in thinking through race and identity in modernity; Gilroy utilizes Du Bois's notion of double consciousness to help articulate a notion of transnational diasporas.[10] Though originally a theorist of race in the British context, he is increasingly using his sociological training and post-Marxist methodology to interrogate the use of "race" more generally. Additionally, since moving to the United States, his work more and more has been contextualized by his new home. For Gilroy, though "race" is clearly valuable for scholars as a tool, the concern seems to echo that of Hannah Arendt's in *The Origins of Totalitarianism*. That is, both Gilroy and Arendt suggest that race-thinking is responsible for the great disasters of the nation-state.

Reconciling the need for recognition based on identity and the fact that such recognition almost always entails a privileging of identities is deeply important to interrogate, especially at the level of nationality. However, philosophically rich analyses of race are not easy to come by. Particularly difficult to find would be examples of philosophy that focus on race in the U.S. context. This probably has more to do with disciplinary rather than racial prejudice, but the effect is virtually identical. Charles W. Mills's *The Racial Contract* is a rare exception that links race, U.S. national identity, and the contract tradition as political, moral, and epistemological.[11]

Emmanuel Chukwudi Eze's essay on Kant's anthropology is an excellent example of how important it is to show the race-thinking that was explicit in many works of philosophy, though often ignored or dismissed as a "symptom of the age."[12] While Eze's work on race represents a step forward in philosophical investigations, it is not clear how to use such work in investigating U.S. national identity. Part of the issue, it seems to me, is the disciplinary standard of universality for philosophy, where investigations of race and identity examine particularities that, almost by definition for many philosophers, are not philosophy at all. Among political theorists and philosophers, one way to talk about race without talking about particularities (in other words, how to get around the privileging of the universal) is to examine the status of outsiders, foreigners, and others in framings of nations and territories.[13]

However, in the end, most of the efforts work in relative isolation from each other, and the explicit, philosophically rich analyses for the most part do not call into question U.S. national identity explicitly. Such analyses may become more common as the issue of the United States as empire/imperial/national comes into sharper focus with decreasing civil liberties and increasingly common calls for closed borders and immigration reform. While most historians would probably dispute that 9/11 marks a unique turning point in terms of race and nationalism, it has brought the issue of race and national identity into more crucial public focus. One thing, however, is clear: nationalism based on race is neither a thing of the past nor a thing of other places. Comparative analysis can help bring this into focus, but the scientific pretensions of its question formation need very careful consideration.

In order to explicate the meaning and merit of interdisciplinarity in the study of race and nationalism, I submit an illustration from my own field of political science. I will be emphasizing the capability of philosophical and literary scrutiny to contribute to empirical studies of race and nationalism that have been influenced by the rise in behavioralism and that expect to be social "scientific" in a particular way. I chose Karl Deutsch's classic work on nationalism to make a point about the role of disciplinary methodologies. The reason why Deutsch's work makes sense in this context is precisely because he has influenced later generations of political scientists through his use of universalizing methodology. He is one pioneer in the use of scientific methodology in the study of political science in order to draw conclusions about things that one has not studied in depth. His work on nationalism certainly impacted how scholars have looked at national identity, but it has not had a legacy nearly as important in that way. I hope to show why this has to do with interdisciplinarity. In some ways it is neither odd nor unknown that disciplines can impact each other in positive ways. What I am suggesting is that in the study of race and nationalism in particular such interdisciplinarity is of singular importance in also potentially dismantling racist systems.

More significantly, though, U.S. national identity needs to be refocused in a way that can be done uniquely by comparative inquiry. In order to demonstrate this point, I will explicate in detail a particularly good example of comparative analysis by the president of Amherst College, Anthony Marx. I have chosen Marx's comparative work because it focuses explicitly on race and nationalism, and, in particular, calls into question the idea that the United States is so unique that any comparison to any other place makes no sense. As strange as it may sound to some people, the very idea of comparing the United States to other places makes some uncomfortable. The argument seems to be that the United States is so utterly unique in all ways that comparing it to other places suggests a sameness that cuts against the "American spirit." By contextualizing the United States in the world at large, however, and working against the American exceptionalism thesis, we are more clearly able to see the duplicitous pretensions to the assertions of uniqueness. However, there is nothing inherently constructive about comparative inquiry either, as my critiques of Marx's methodology will show.

Defining Questions

Methodological considerations are deeply important in the study of race and nationalism—not just for their own sake, but because of the implications of methodology for how we conceptualize the very meaning of the terms. In a significant piece of writing in comparative political science, Barbara Geddes shows that when one is selecting cases for analysis one can easily bias the outcome of research.[14] She demonstrates the need to investigate phenomena that differ from what one wants to study in terms of outcome in order to be able to draw conclusions. Before investigating her point in greater depth, and how it relates specifically to the study of race and nationalism, I would like to highlight that Geddes's point can also be included in a larger tradition of reminding scholars that our choice of question and object of study necessarily inform the type and scope of knowledge we can reach. So, for example, political scientists can often embark on research with the goal of saying something that applies not just to what one has studied, but to other, similar cases as well. In some sense this is the logic of any comparative investigation, but there is also a peculiarly universalistic assumption in political scientific study; phenomena can be explained and this explanation can be transported to other phenomena that we know nothing about. Given this logic, it is not odd that that would be the focus of the comparative political science of nationalism.

For example, in his 1953 *Nationalism and Social Communication*, Karl Deutsch[15] argued that "the essential aspect of a unity of a people . . .

is the complimentarity or relative efficiency of communication among individuals, something that is in some way similar to mutual rapport, but on a larger scale."[16] Deutsch's focus on the role of communication in national identity formation, which involved explicating quantitative measures and developing predictions of large-scale social forces, was intended to answer the puzzle of why nationalist ideas meet with strong responses in some times and places but not in others. His answer is that nationalist ideas meet a stronger response when there is denser social communication.[17] Denser social communication, he finds, tends to increase with modernization, and that is precisely why, according to him, nationalist movements have met with stronger responses in modernizing locations. This classic piece of social scientific analysis has added significant insight into the nature and timing of nationalist movements.

However, in the roughly fifty years since he published his pioneering work, scholars from many other disciplines (and from multidisciplinary corners) have contributed questions that challenge the ability to study nationalism from this perspective alone. By examining some implicit and explicit responses to Deutsch's mode of examination, I do not mean to suggest that political scientists look only to Deutsch for guidance about nationalism. Instead, I am merely using him as one among many possible examples of how fields can be disciplined to ask only certain kinds of questions. By using Deutsch as an example, then, I do not intend to criticize him per se, but to open up questions that he himself might not have asked for various reasons. Deutsch's suitability for my argument also derives from the legacy of his project. His work contributed to redefining the field of political science *not* principally in terms of studying nationalism; rather, his attention to and argument for a focus on measurability and covering laws have had a decisive impact on the field of political science as a whole, perhaps even more than his study of nationalism.

Two other important scholars of nationalism help articulate the promise and the pitfalls of Deutsch's work. Ernest Gellner and Tom Nairn, both philosophers by training but advocates of a historical approach to the study of nationalism, have argued that Deutsch's understanding of nationalism as increasing with modernization is but one element of a much larger story.[18] They suggest, through careful attention to the dynamic between industrialization and nationalism, that it is the structural handicaps that result from the *uneven* imposition of industrialization that in fact produce nationalist movements.[19] Gellner argues that nationalism is a functional requirement of the modern industrial state and that nationalist doctrine can be explained as fulfilling a need for the rationalization of culture and politics. In this way it is "inherent in a certain set of conditions."[20] It is the way in which we moderns make sense of our world. Nairn's focus is on how nationalism is the work of enterprising intellectuals, an insight that Kedourie had already articulated in a theory of nationalism as the frustrated expression and intellectual underemployment of "marginal men."[21] As Eley and Suny point out, these theories make nationalism more of a historical contingency, "linked to political intervention, new ideologies, and cultural change, and expressing a transformation of social identity, initially on the part of individuals, but eventually for whole populations."[22]

Both Nairn and Gellner, though different in very important respects, have shown what looking at social-historical processes can bring to the study of nationalism by showing exactly how it is linked to industrialization and modernization more empirically through history. Dispensing with Deutsch's social communication theory, they focus on modernization and offer historical explanations of why nationalism has tended to accompany it. Other scholars such as Hroch and Hobsbawm have also situated nationalism in the context of social history using some version of a developmental schema to show that the historicized category of "nation" has been a foundation for the emergence of nationalist movements.[23]

In these sociohistorical approaches to the study of nationalism, national culture is understood very consciously as constituted and contingent. That is, culture has been made by human agency. The impact of anthropology (and more particularly, ethnographic method) reminds budding scholars of nationalism that culture is not simply made by political entrepreneurs ex nihilo, but draws on a somewhat limited set of preexisting symbols and histories. One important insight into culture from the tradition of nationalist thinking argues that "each people, each society, each ethnic group, and each linguistic community—[can] be distinguished by a 'whole way of life.'"[24] The identification that a group known as "the people" is not essentially so (an observation from the social-historians, among others) is crucial to deconstructing the myth that nations are biological. However, this insight does not explain why it is or even how it is that this "whole way of life" is experienced. In other words, simply saying that nations are historical constructions, and placing nationalist movements in their proper historical moments, does not, in itself, explain how ordinary people throughout history have seen themselves as bearers of this constructed identity. Though we can argue against nationalists that this national identity is not awakened or discovered but created by the labors of intellectuals, ethnographic study (ironically) shows us that there does indeed exist some form of culture that is prior to the construction of a nationalist one (which itself is also not essentially so, but rather is the result of a particular history).

Anderson's observation (which I regard as a literary-anthropological one) that we should look not at the falsity/genuineness of nations but at the style in which they are imagined, recognizes that the possibility for self-identification among people changed as various certainties about the world declined. His concern, though, is with the cultural conditions that render possible the subjective experience of a national community and in that sense, though he focuses on communication (print capitalism is one important aspect) like Deutsch, his project has different goals and questions. While Deutsch wanted to know why nationalist movements emerged in some cases but not others, Anderson wants to look at the various cultural conditions that allow ordinary people to experience the nation as such, bearing in mind its abstract nature and intangibility.

While the historical analyses of nationalism represented by Nairn and Gellner can be easily narrated in connection with Deutsch's original research question, a focus on the way in which the nation is represented,[25] how it is authorized as such,[26] and how its historical origins have been narrated[27] in many ways is outside the scope of comparative political inquiry as we often conceive of it. These philosophical-literary contributions ask a different kind of question and make different kinds of assumptions than do most comparative politics researchers. This is simply a difference in the choice of research object that calls into question larger issues of evidence within a discipline. The search for generalities, covering laws, or regularities of some sort tends to characterize contemporary political examination. Evidence, though it can exist at many different levels of analysis, is always assumed to be *true* or at least not *self-consciously fictional*. The main offshoot of this is that political science (here comparative politics more specifically), even when looking at history in order to historicize a given phenomenon, tends not to look for evidence in works of fiction. A focus on the way in which a nation is represented does precisely that, for it would be incomplete to assume that the nation is only represented through political speeches, policy, and law. This introduction of new kinds of texts to the analysis also includes looking at certain kinds of texts in new ways.

For example, there is a piece by literary theorist Jacques Derrida that systematically goes through the U.S. Declaration of Independence and shows how, rhetorically, the authorization of the new nation is articulated. One of the things that this piece does is show how taking the Declaration within its historical moment allows us to see that, although it is now ostensibly obvious to us that the United States is a nation, at that time it was being created rhetorically while at the same time it (the nation) was making reference to a "people," the "American people," as a transhistorical category. That is, Derrida shows how the ambiguity of the Declaration both constituted and recalled the idea of an "American" all in the same instance. More importantly, he points to how it still functions as a nationalist symbol and continues to *authorize* (that is, literally, write) the nation as such. Homi Bhabha's contribution continues this line of questioning, focusing on the ambiguities surrounding the narration of the nation and how confused over (and in) time it becomes. He observes that "historians transfixed on the event and origins of the nation never ask, and political theorists possessed of the 'modern' totalities of the nation—'homogeneity, literacy and anonymity are the key traits'—never pose, the essential question of the representation of the nation as a temporal process."[28] Bhabha calls into question notions of progress and rationality and shows how the narrating of the nation always both performs nationalism and teaches it by design. That is, the act of narrating, telling the story of the nation (in a variety of textual forms), neither enacts the nation nor shows what it once was, but always already does both.

Beyond showing the comparative political scientist that texts such as literary works, school pamphlets, declarations of independence, constitutions, and so on can provide evidence for the study of nationalism, the contribution of literary studies and philosophy can be seen as confrontational to the very premise of social scientific inquiry which is that observable phenomena can best be explained in generalities that transcend particularities. It can also question the uneasy marriage of nation to state. Lisa Lowe and David Lloyd have remarked that "the nationalism articulated in Western state formations posits a historical continuity between the emergence of a people and the development of the state that represents its political sovereignty."[29] Their point is that the great irony of anticolonial nationalism is that nationalists tend to fight for the very institutions (state) that have oppressed them for so long.[30] In other words, the idea of a nationalist movement that is not fighting for the control of the state and wishes not to articulate some kind of primordial traditionalism is left without a language to do so.[31] The assumption that Lowe and Lloyd are attacking is that the self-determination of a people (however understood) is necessarily articulated through the state and therefore may or may not have as its goal the capture of state institutions. All of these ways in which other disciplines can aid the comparative political scientist are in some form or another hard to operationalize within commonly accepted comparative methods. Thinking back to Deutsch's original research question in light of other work on nationalism, one can see that much of what has been learned could never have been arrived at by Deutsch simply because his research question didn't ask certain questions. In part this is because he was self-consciously trying to create quantitative measures that could travel.

Race and American Exceptionalism: The Pitfalls and Promise of Comparative Analysis

White supremacy and explicit notions of inclusion and exclusion based on perceived racial biology and the assertive superiority of whiteness have been a part of more than one state-building process. Anticolonial nationalisms and other nationalisms in response to white supremacy, as a result, have also necessarily taken on a racial dimension. It has not always been the case that whiteness is an indication of belonging for other people who might be or come to be considered "white." That is, the "white nation" is historically contingent, and who counts as "white" has changed over time. This observation comes from a direct engagement with United States and South African history.[32] Both countries have had a long history of racial segregation, though it has not always been clear who counted as "white" for purposes of this segregation. In the United States, for example, popular slang for Irish immigrants overlapped extensively with popular slang for African Americans. At that time what counted as "black" in "white" popular culture included a group now clearly a part of the imagined "white nation"—the Irish.[33] Upon arrival in South Africa, the British colonists regarded the (now "white") Afrikaners as primitive. In these cases, and in others, race is not a variable that can help explain nationalism but is, rather, a worthy object of study in itself—because it defines the entire political landscape. Race is not just something that *impacts* nationalism, but rather, has been the idiom *through which* the nation is subjectively experienced.

Anthony Marx argues that in both the United States and South Africa, ruling elites *legalized* race as a way to consolidate the nation and give previously divided white communities a shared identity in discrimination against "blacks."[34] His cross-national study, which also includes Brazil (as the negative case where racism was not legalized), isolates the period following the Civil War in the United States and the period following the Anglo-Boer War in South Africa as pivotal moments. It was following these wars that elites in both countries concluded that an alliance with ex-confederates and Afrikaners, respectively, would ensure governmental authority vis-à-vis blacks. Thus, the nation-building was self-conscious and self-consciously white.

Methodologically, Marx's study should help illuminate the two points I am raising in this chapter: how interdisciplinarity can be crucial, and why comparative analysis is significant for the study of race and nationalism in the U.S. context. Rather than looking at the book as a whole, I am going to focus on the article "Race-Making and the Nation State" in *World Politics* that preceded the book by two years but that essentially lays out the argument. The article tries to answer the question as to how and why "social distinctions and conflicts come to be projected in terms of physical differences of color or purported race in the first place."[35] In order to answer this question he chooses to look at the United States, South Africa, and Brazil because they are "the most prominent cases in which European settlers dominated indigenous and slave populations of African origin."[36] He begins with the conditions of similarity that allow for the possibility of comparison. In all three cases there was racial discrimination prevalent during "early history" that then "faced extended 'moments' of relative indeterminacy and an unhappy repertoire of possible racial configurations in the aftermath of slavery, at the time of emerging state consolidation."[37] Yet, despite this similarity in "moments," South Africa and the United States implemented official racial doctrines with imposed categories of segregation, while Brazil did not. This *legal* discrimination has only recently been dismantled. Brazil avoided legal distinctions based on race and instead promoted an image of "racial democracy." Marx does not suggest that discrimination did not exist in Brazil, but points out that there was no necessity to institutionalize racism as public policy or to consolidate it as a procedural device in the nationalist project.

The puzzle for Marx is to explain these differing outcomes. The United States and South Africa institutionalized categories of race into law, while Brazil did not. Much work has been done comparing these three cases, yet Marx cannot accept any of the standard explanations that have been offered.[38] Most of the article is spent explaining why the Brazilian case cannot be accounted for simply based on differences of slavery, culture, colonial rule, miscegenation, or economic development. Instead, he argues that, "official post-abolition racial domination or the absence of it was prominently connected to the impetus for building the nation-state."[39] In some sense, and he seems to accept this, Marx's argument subsumes all previous explanations under the heading "nation-building"; everything from slavery to economic development comes to a head during the consolidation of the new nation. In South Africa and the United States, domestic peace was accomplished by giving divided white communities a legally superior standing, while Brazil didn't need legal racism because the whites were already unified. Marx shows that "agreement on a racially defined 'other' as a common enemy defined and encouraged white unity."[40]

In order for Marx's argument to "prove robust," he reasons that it should "also help explain variations of resulting mobilization and conflict; that is, social construction of explicit racial domination and social movements by the victims of such domination should logically be connected."[41] So, he argues that the legalized racism of South Africa and the United States encouraged black solidarity while the "racial democracy" of Brazil elicited more lackluster racial identity and mobilization. In all three cases, forms of protest reflected changes in how the state ruled, though militant protest and separatism never made an appearance in Brazil even in the absence of or reversal of reform measures by the government (the impetus for militancy in the other two cases). In this sense, Marx argues that "the previous dependent variable of official racism can be reconfigured into an independent variable to explain such emergence and various forms of mobilization."[42] Step one of his argument seeks to explain differing outcomes (official categories or not) in racism while step two uses this racism to explain forms of mobilization. Methodologically, Marx's move here is important because though he is interested in whether racial categories were legalized or not, it does not follow for him that the lack of legal categories in any way implies a lack of racism and, therefore, a lack of resistance to racism.

Unfortunately, Marx's method is indistinct. He talks neither of interviews, nor statistics, nor even self-consciously of history, and one does not get a real sense of how "testable" his hypothesis is. Regardless, one can easily deduce his implicit methodological assumptions from the argument made. His method is historically based, yet his argument aims to be causal and not merely descriptive; he wants to explain what caused *legalized* racism in some situations. Marx chose his cases because they are the three "most prominent cases in which European settlers dominated indigenous and slave populations of African origin."[43] For this reason Marx may or may not be guilty of selection on the dependent variable.[44] What this means for Marx is not that his study is not an interesting and useful one, but that his ability to generalize is limited because he did not choose from the entire universe of cases. Indeed, he seems not to have conceived of the entire universe of cases at all. In this sense, Marx's theory has not been tested at all and does not "contribute to the accumulation of theoretical knowledge" in the sense in which a "scientific" study of politics should.[45] In other words, even granting the accuracy of Marx's analysis, that Brazil did not develop legalized racism because there was no intrawhite fighting when nation-building occurred, we cannot generalize to say that whenever intrawhite fighting coincides with a moment of nation-building we will always get legalized racism. We also cannot say that when there is a lack of intrawhite fighting during nation-building there will not be legalized racism. This is simply because Marx did not even mention other cases of racism in his study of areas with European settlers that dominated indigenous or slave populations of African origin. Had he looked at other cases (such as Haiti, Rhodesia/Zimbabwe, Mozambique, Kenya, and so on) his answer to what explains legalized racism might have been different.

Marx's cases are selected using a vague and unsatisfactory "prominence" mechanism. It is unclear what significance the fact that all three of the cases are "prominent" has on the research design. Exactly what constitutes "prominence?" Does Marx mean to say that they are all powerful countries? Or does he mean to say that they are well studied? Indeed, all three countries dominated indigenous and slave populations of African origins, but so did Haiti, San Domingo, and Kenya to name other "prominent" cases. Marx suggests that legal racism occurs when there is intrawhite conflict during a crucial "moment" in state-building. In this sense he aims to generalize beyond the cases that he presents. In order for this to be a valid exercise of generalizability, he would need to have a more representative sample of cases. It is also unclear to me why focusing on communities where European settlers dominated indigenous and slave populations of *African* origin is a valid move for someone who is calling into question the very categories of race that he is studying.

I am suggesting that Marx's focus on "white" on "black" racism does a disservice to the implicit ideological subtext of his argument; he is reinforcing the very categories of separation that he is trying to historicize. Had he defined his universe of cases as those places where European settlers dominated indigenous or slave populations, without reference to the "African origin" of those populations, he would have had a much more robust study. His assumption seems to be that there is something about black populations ("of African origin") that makes it more likely that they will be the "other" against which whites define themselves in the crucial moment of nation-building. While this seems intuitively right (to social scientists in the United States), there would be much gained by including, for example, India or Australia in the analysis.

One other related charge that Marx cannot deflect is that of truncated variation. Because Marx suggests that what he is interested in is either the existence of or nonexistence of legal racism, he ignores the variation within each of the two extremes that is likely to offer some illumination. Although he looks specifically at the institution of racial categories in the law, his suggestion in the work is that he is interested in a binary outcome, whether it existed or not. Obviously, there are other mechanisms of domination employed such as informal housing policies not explicitly based on *legal* racial categories that also help explain the question of why race becomes salient at all. Although Marx is careful to avoid assuming race as a preexisting category, he neglects to identify the various ways in which race is made.[46] By focusing on only one way (the legalized institution of racial categories) he seems to suggest that the system of norms and identities that emerged in Brazil is somehow less "racist" than the legal forms that prompted social movement activity in the other two countries. This is a point that Brazilian history doesn't seem to support. Far from celebrating African culture and racial democracy, the republican state trumpeted doctrines of white supremacy that, although not grounded in the legal discourse at the time, looked much like those expressed in the United States and South Africa. One wonders if there is something about Brazilian history that Marx doesn't tell us. Namely, one wonders what Brazilian racism *did* look like.[47]

Is Marx's project a failure? No. Would I do it differently? Yes. I propose that there are a number of methodological problems with the scientific study of race. I support Marx's claim that it is important to make the shift from using race as a "tool of analysis" to considering it as an "object of analysis."[48] Yet, how race becomes an object of analysis is a vexed question.

Race operates in official discourse but also in unofficial discourse and at the level of the unconscious. Marx's isolation of official implementation of racial categories seems to me to be a good start at being able to ask an empirical question about the emergence of racism that is potentially useful for the development of theoretical knowledge. While Marx's story makes it sound as if racial categories emerged in the law during the time of nation-building, the "histories" of his cases do not support this insofar as they suggest a more detailed story. For example, in the cases of both South Africa and the United States, racial categories were used for at least forty years as official policy, though the categories were not explicitly stated in national law. In South Africa this was because the nation qua nation did not exist (until 1910 with the creation of the Union of South Africa) and in the United States this was because the dominant legal interpretation was that race was implied in the nonracially specific Constitution. It seems to me that Marx's isolation of the period of nation-building in each case was selected precisely because of the implementation of racial categories and that the long process of nation-building, though certainly affected by intrawhite conflict, cannot be reduced to this one issue.

Taking Marx's own research question, I would suggest a different method. I would operationalize race as the object of inquiry by studying the implementation, or lack thereof, of official categories of race. However, I would include all countries with a substantial white settler population instead of just those "prominent" examples involving populations of African origin. Not only would the universe of cases be larger, but the question itself would change from one that assumes the "racial makeup" of the population to one that does not. Taking a cue from Marx, I would test his hypothesis (which he does not present as a "hypothesis" at all). This would be done first by assessing the long-term rise and fall of intrawhite conflict based on the dominant interpretations of history. Mapped onto this analysis would be the introduction, if any, of official categories of racial difference, including dominant economic and planning activities and, of course, legal constructions. I would suggest that there is likely a correlation between intrawhite conflict and the legal implementation of racial ideology, but that it may be too simple to develop a monocausal theory of the rise of official categories of race. I would also suggest that the best way to test his theory would be to begin by using quantitative analysis to examine the entire universe of cases to determine whether there is some correlation between intrawhite conflict and the time of implementation of legal categories of racism. This alone would constitute a contribution to theory-building because it would provide data that would allow qualitative researchers to try to explain why, in individual cases, legalized racism did or did not exist and how and if it fits the general model developed by the quantitative research.

In this sense I think that Marx's project was simply too ambitious. I support his question, but I question his case selection. The mechanism by which he selected his cases seems arbitrary on the one hand but biased on the other. Given that he claims to account for the rise of legal categories of separation generally, his methodology is incomplete. Marx universalizes race from the specificity of the three cases that he chose. The impulse to universalize race as a category, given how differently it operates in different settings, runs counter to his underlying political project of a critique of racial categories as constructed, though it is certainly in the tradition of methodological approach pioneered by, among others, Karl Deutsch. As social scientists we have the power not only to call social categories constructed but also to use them as such. The idea that racism against people of African origin is something qualitatively different than racism against other populations not only reinforces the idea that "African populations" is still a valid term of reference (a point that many African intellectuals launch against African American and Afro-European intellectuals) despite its continued grounding *only in* ascription. It also marginalizes the experiences of racial domination of other populations the world over that do not fit the "black/white" paradigm. Thus it is that Japanese categories for Koreans, European categories for Gypsies or Jews, and degrees of varying lightness or darkness in India, to name a few examples, become marginal to the larger assumption that "white" racism is directed primarily at "black" people. White and black are merely shorthand for a system of power relations based on ascriptions.

A larger universe of cases to study, even a universe that isolates European populations as the dominating group, goes a long way toward recognizing the extreme complexity of operationalizing race, not as a variable, but as the object of study. Race can look like a more general phenomenon that transcends national borders at the same time that the particularities of each example of the implementation of power based on ideologies of skin color can be salvaged. In this sense, the implications of the study can be about mobilization against racial categories more generally and explaining the rise of solidarity based on the appropriation of imposed racial categories instead of (as Marx would have it) the ability to explain black solidarity and social movements as dependent on the fact of legalized racial categories or not. That is, the implications of Marx's study are decidedly political. With some of his conclusions, people fighting against racism can gain practical, strategic knowledge about how race and nationalism work. The study also has the potential for a more robust analysis insofar as it allows for the possibility of explaining why "white" people might engage in protest activity against legal categories despite their privilege within the system of categorization. This seems particularly important given that both the South African and the United States cases have a history of "nonblack" participation in struggle against racial categories.

Conclusion: Approaches to U.S. Identity as Racialized

Residents and citizens of the United States have long called into question the relationship between racial ascriptions (identifications concurrently and often ambiguously originating in the other and the self) and national identity. This is perhaps easy to forget because such interrogations have been remarkably easy for many people to overlook and have not always been taken as seriously as they should, both in academic disciplines and in the culture at large. The Frederick Douglass excerpt at the start of this chapter is to me the most potent articulation of an ostensibly peculiar "American" national identity that purports unity while at the same time is experienced as exclusionary. In many ways, Douglass's remarks on the occasion of the United States' most nationalistic celebration anticipates W. E. B. Du Bois's enunciation of "double consciousness" in *The Souls of Black Folk* that has probably induced more lasting scrutiny by scholars. In conversation with others—ranging from Ida B. Wells to Alain Locke to C. L. R. James—these thinkers and the secondary works that consider them are certainly among the most invaluable tools in historically and theoretically contextualizing the present moment in U.S. national identity. Their persistent perceived status as "marginal," however, can be understood in myriad ways.

Producing and analyzing work from "the margins" has fittingly been the focus of some of the most meaningful work on U.S. nationalism, especially as it relates to differently conceptualized racial ascriptions. This is because thinking and writing "from the margins" can subvert assumptions of homogeneity and appropriately points to how racial construction and exclusion have accompanied the U.S. national project since its inception. While scholars of race and/or nationalism in a variety of disciplines have been increasingly successful at writing and thinking from "the margins," there is a methodological dilemma in the numerous literatures that touch either race or nationalism. Although academic disciplines can impose rigor and maintain standards of excellence, they can also consign to the dustbin modes of inquiry that allow us to see concepts, theories, and actual events and persons in a new light. It is my view that in the study of race and nationalism, disciplinary norms have often prevented scholars from producing nuanced and politically relevant material. Through the use of interdisciplinarity, on the other hand, scholars have been able to tackle questions and approaches that from disciplinary perspectives may seem inappropriate, nonrigorous, or more likely "marginal."

Any interdisciplinary investigation into U.S. identity and the role of race faces considerable difficulties in terms of literatures to take into account. This is because there is widespread disagreement over the relevant terminology to employ when talking about race especially and there is significant silo-activity in terms of scholars working on related concepts but using different terms to do so and never encountering each other's work. It is my view that to appreciate relationships between race and U.S. national identity one needs to study interconnected ways of getting at conceptual and practical concerns such as immigration, citizenship, assimilation, patriotism, borders, empire, globalization, and the role of aliens and foreigners in political discourse. Some of the richest places for investigating the intersection of race and nationalism in the United States have employed differing terms and potentially incongruous approaches to do so. In order to explain this point and to reinforce the point that the study of race and nationalism not only often is but *should be* interdisciplinary, I proposed a modest reading of how to view the contributions of different kinds of disciplinary approaches. My implicit assumption is that no single disciplinary way of viewing nationalism and race is alone sufficient, and though there are scholars working on various important aspects of the intersection, that contribution across disciplines makes for richer insight. Moreover, scholars also committed to dismantling racially coded systems of oppression may find interdisciplinarity particularly important in properly narrating a shifting terrain of meanings. This means being very cautious in using universalizing methodologies because of the assumptions that methodologies can unintentionally hide and/or naturalize.

Notes

1. Benedict Anderson, *Imagined Communities* (New York: Verso, 1983).

2. Matthew Frye Jacobson's *Barbarian Virtues: The United States Encounters Foreign Peoples at Home and Abroad, 1876–1917* (New York: Hill and Wang, 2000) situates the national project as simultaneously responding to immigration fears and internal racism, suggesting that any historical or theoretical examination of the role of race in American nationalism should be conterminously examining how "foreign peoples" are perceived. David W. Noble's *Death of a Nation: Culture and the End of Exceptionalism* (Minneapolis: University of Minnesota Press, 2002) somewhat deceptively argues that the notion of American exceptionalism has not ended but rather has morphed forms. As a critique of canonical figures in the history of race and nation, Noble's book offers an important look at attempts to challenge the exceptionalism thesis.

3. In his "Beyond Tocqueville, Myrdal and Hartz: The Multiple Traditions in America," *American Political Science Review* 87, no. 3 (September 1993), 549–566, Smith explains that historians and political scientists interested in citizenship have underrecognized the role that inegalitarian ideologies have played in American political culture over time. This work, along with his "The American Creed and American Identity:

The Limits of Liberal Citizenship in the United States," *Western Political Quarterly* 41, no. 2 (June 1988), 225–251, and *Civic Ideals: Conflicting Visions of Citizenship in U.S. History* (New Haven, CT: Yale University Press, 1997) recast the meaning of American citizenship as a project with significant variance in its objects and effects.

4. Eric Foner's work, including *Nothing but Freedom: Emancipation and Its Legacy* (Baton Rouge: Louisiana State Press, 1983), *Free Soil, Free Labor, Free Men: The Ideology of the Republican Party before the Civil War* (New York: Oxford University Press, 1970), *Reconstruction: America's Unfinished Revolution, 1863–1877* (New York: Harper and Row, 1988), and *Forever Free: The Story of Emancipation and Reconstruction* (New York: Knopf, 2005) links the history of slavery and emancipation to American identity. The landmark history of postslavery identity formation in the United States is Michael Omi and Howard Winant's *Racial Formation in the United States: From the 1960s to the 1980s* (New York: Routledge and Kegan Paul, 1986).

5. An early formulation of this project can be found in Peggy McIntosh's "White Privilege: Unpacking the Invisible Knapsack" (Wellesley, MA: Wellesley College Center for Research on Women, 1988) but has also been linked to such journals as *Race Traitor*, which is meant to continue in the abolitionist tradition. This essay was also published in *Race, Class, and Gender in the United States: An Integrated Study*, 5th ed., ed. Paula S. Rothenberg (New York: Worth, 2001), 163–168.

6. Arthur M. Schlesinger, *The Disuniting of America: Reflections on a Multicultural Society* (New York: Norton, 1992).

7. Samuel P. Huntington, "The Hispanic Challenge," *Foreign Policy* 140 (March–April 2004): 30–45.

8. Iris Marion Young, *Justice and the Politics of Difference* (Princeton, NJ: Princeton University Press, 1990).

9. Will Kymlicka, *Multicultural Citizenship* (Oxford, UK: Oxford University Press, 1995).

10. Paul Gilroy, *The Black Atlantic: Modernity and Double Consciousness* (London: Verso, 1993).

11. Charles Mills, *The Racial Contract* (Ithaca, NY: Cornell University Press, 1997).

12. Emmanuel Chukwudi Eze, "The Color of Reason," in *Postcolonial African Philosophy*, ed. E. C. Eze (Cambridge: Blackwell, 1997), 103–140.

13. Bonnie Honig's *Democracy and the Foreigner* (Princeton, NJ: Princeton University Press, 2001) examines the symbolic politics of foreignness and Jürgen Habermas's *The Inclusion of the Other* (Cambridge, MA: MIT Press, 1998) explores the themes of national identity and the need for public reason in order to include "others." Linda Bosniak's *The Citizen and the Alien: Dilemmas of Contemporary Membership*

(Princeton, NJ: Princeton University Press, 2006) is a new and welcome work on the problem of inclusion and exclusion from a legal theorist who makes excellent links to philosophical traditions.

14. Barbara Geddes, "How the Cases You Choose Affect the Answers You Get: Selection Bias in Comparative Politics," *Political Analysis* 2, no. 1 (1990): 131–150.

15. Karl Deutsch immigrated to the United States from Germany in the early twentieth century. His work has been instrumental in the rise of the use of modeling to study the political and he was present at the San Francisco conference in 1951 that resulted in the Treaty of Peace with Japan. He taught at MIT, Yale, and Harvard before his death in 1992.

16. Karl Deutsch, *Nationalism and Social Communication* (Cambridge, MA: MIT Press, 1953), 188.

17. Ibid., v.

18. For Nairn it is not modernization but industrialization that can help us understand the rise of nationalist movements.

19. Tom Nairn, "Scotland and Europe," in *Becoming National*, ed. Geoff Eley and Ronald Grigor Suny (New York: Oxford University Press, 1996). See also Ernest Gellner, *Nations and Nationalism* (Oxford, UK: Blackwell, 1983).

20. Gellner, *Nations and Nationalism*, 125. For critiques of Gellner's functionalism, see Anthony Giddens, *Studies in Social and Political Theory* (New York: Basic Books, 1977) and Gerry Cohen, "Functional Explanation, Consequence Explanation, and Marxism," *Inquiry* 25 (1981): 27–56.

21. Elie Kedourie, *Nationalism* (London: Hutcheson, 1960).

22. Geoff Eley and Ronald Grigor Suny, introduction to *Becoming National*, ed. Geoff Eley and Ronald Grigor Suny (New York: Oxford University Press, 1996), 6.

23. See Miroslav Hroch, *Social Preconditions of National Revival in Europe* (Cambridge: Cambridge University Press, 1985) and Eric Hobsbawm, *Nations and Nationalism since 1870: Programme, Myth, Reality* (Cambridge: Cambridge University Press, 1990). Hroch agrees with Deutsch that the process of modernization impacting nationalism is mediated by social communication, but like Hobsbawm historicizes the concept "nation."

24. Glenn Jordan and Chris Weedon, *Cultural Politics: Class, Gender, Race and the Postmodern World* (Oxford, UK: Blackwell, 1995), 565. Jordon and Weedon are here referring to Johann Herder.

25. Anderson, *Imagined Communities*.

26. Jacques Derrida, "Declarations of Independence," *New Political Science* 15 (1986): 7–15. See also Bonnie Honig, "Declarations of Independence: Arendt and Derrida on the Problem of Founding a Republic," *American Political Science Review* 85, no. 1 (1991): 97–113.

27. Homi Bhabha, *The Location of Culture* (London: Routledge, 1994),139–170.

28. Ibid., 142 (quoting Gellner).

29. Lisa Lowe and David Lloyd, introduction to *The Politics of Culture in the Shadow of Capital*, ed. Lisa Lowe and David Lloyd (Durham, NC: Duke University Press, 1997), 7.

30. Frantz Fanon made this point in *The Wretched of the Earth* (New York: Grove Weidenfeld, 1963). See especially the chapter on "National Culture" where he explicates the importance of the colonized creating their own, new institutions that can genuinely be called national. His use of the dialectic makes clear that the drive to true self-determination (and national identity) is always in tension with the dominance of colonial conceptions, not only in terms of institutions, but in terms of the lens through which the world is seen. Lowe and Lloyd maintain a kind of optimism for postcolonial nationalist projects that Fanon did not share.

31. I see this dynamic as one that theorists of new social movements are trying to capture. See, for example, Alberto Melucci, "The New Social Movements: A Theoretical Approach," *Social Science Information* 19, no. 2 (1980): 199–226.

32. See George Fredrickson, *White Supremacy: A Comparative Study in American and South African History* (Oxford, UK: Oxford University Press, 1981), Stanley Greenberg, *Race and State in Capitalist Development* (New Haven, CT: Yale University Press, 1980), and John Cell, *The Highest Stage of White Supremacy* (Cambridge: Cambridge University Press, 1982).

33. David Roediger, *The Wages of Whiteness* (London: Verso, 1991).

34. Anthony Marx, *Making Race and Nation* (Cambridge: Cambridge University Press, 1998).

35. Anthony Marx, "Race-Making and the Nation-State," *World Politics* 48, no. 2 (1996): 181.

36. Ibid.

37. Ibid.

38. In addition to Greenberg, Cell, and Fredrickson, see Carl Degler, *Neither White nor Black: Slavery and Race-Relations in Brazil and the United States* (New York: Macmillan, 1971).

39. Marx, "Race-Making," 200.

40. Ibid., 182.

41. Ibid., 200.

42. Ibid., 201.

43. Ibid., 181.

44. See Gary King, Robert O. Keohane, and Sidney Verba, *Designing Social Inquiry: Scientific Inference in Qualitative Research* (Princeton, NJ: Princeton University Press, 1994). The charge is unwarranted by King,

Keohane, and Verba's definition because Marx's selection "mechanism" allows for the possibility of variation on the dependent variable. Indeed, the variance in dependent variables is precisely Marx's puzzle; why Brazil did not have legal discrimination in the same way that South Africa and the United States did. Consequently, if this is what "selection of the dependent variable" means, Marx is in the clear. On the other hand if we look at Geddes's critique of Theda Skocpol's *States and Social Revolutions* (Cambridge: Cambridge University Press, 1979), the selection problem appears to actually be something different. In fact, Geddes's point is a slightly different one, though it goes by the same name. She argues that in order to test a hypothesis, there needs to first be a universe of cases to which the hypothesis should apply. Once the universe is explicated (which it is not in Marx's article) the task is to find a sample that is "selected from the universe in such a way as to insure that the criteria for selecting cases are uncorrelated with the placement of cases on the dependent variable" (Geddes, "How the Cases You Choose Affect the Answers You Get," 135). In King, Keohane and Verba's analysis, Marx would not be guilty of selection bias precisely because the question that he asks is based fundamentally on the fact of variation in the dependent variable (racism as either legally constructed or not). Yet Geddes's understanding of the same phenomenon would suggest that he is guilty of something exactly because he uses the fact of legalized racism (or not) as the mechanism by which cases are chosen. The implication to Geddes's criticism is that even by choosing cases because of the dependent variable (whether you choose them based on the same score of the variable or not) one biases the conclusion.

45. Geddes, "How the Cases You Choose Affect the Answers You Get," 149.

46. Marx, "Race-Making," 180.

47. Similarly, Marx seems to be interested in legalized racism that has as its object those people of African origin, yet makes no qualitative distinction between the Brazilian and American cases where Africans were not considered indigenous and South Africa where they are. In all three cases, slaves dominated by Europeans generally came from West Africa, yet in South Africa most Africans were not slaves. Certainly Marx, a scholar whose first book was about South Africa, knows this. Yet why do the three cases offer sufficient similarity to each other and difference from others to warrant comparison? In order to answer this it is important to remember that for Marx Brazil is the anomaly. Unlike the violent intrawhite tension of the American South and between British and Afrikaner South Africans, Brazil, according to Marx, provides an essential comparison, because of the lack of comparably violent ethnic or regional conflict to impede the consolidation of the state. Brazilian nation-building did not require formal discrimination and instead the state's ideological project

was one of "racial democracy." Marx dismisses the possibility that Portuguese colonialism as "humanitarian slavery" can explain this difference and similarly rejects the idea that Brazil's higher levels of miscegenation would have made it more difficult to impose racial categories by arguing that both South Africa and the United States created such categories for those sects of the population known as mixed. Although he recognizes the importance of economic factors, he also rejects an economic explanation of the variation as well. In this way Marx seems to be attempting Mills's method of difference with his incomplete sample by systematically going through possible causes and seeing how they measure up in each of the cases. See Charles Ragin, *The Comparative Method: Moving Beyond Qualitative and Quantitative Strategies* (Berkeley and Los Angeles: University of California Press, 1987), 39. Marx rejects competing hypotheses by showing that there is an absence of both the cause and effect in one case; yet he makes not even a passing note suggesting that he has called into question the histories from whence he gets his data. Marx's study seems to suggest that legalized racism is the norm of nation-building with the lack of such measures in Brazil being the anomaly to be explained. Not only does Marx not sample from the entire universe of nations qua cases, he also does not give sufficient time to the multiple histories of each case that allows him to support his historical claims.

48. Marx, "Race-Making," 180.

7

Citizenship and Political Friendship

Two Hearts, One Passport

Eduardo Mendieta

Passports are badges of privilege, backed by both "soft" and "hard" power, as well as centuries of colonialism, imperialism, and "globalization." While I was born in Colombia, South America, I grew up in the United States. I had a Colombian passport, used to travel to the United States, which is no longer valid. I have only one passport, and the United States of America issues it. I have never been tempted by, or even considered, the possibility of petitioning for a Colombian passport, though I have heard from friends that Colombia now grants dual citizenship, which would allow me to have two passports. Except for my first trip to the United States, I have always and only traveled with an "American" passport. Most of the time I think this was my mother's gift to me: a "passport" to a future never imaginable for her or my siblings in Colombia. Many, I know, think of an "American" passport as a gift, if not a blessing. The fact is that when I go through customs, and the invariably "person of color" stamps my passport and more often than not says "Welcome home," I get a metaphysical ache in my heart. It is unsettling to have a stranger say to you "Welcome home"! It is stranger yet when those words come from an African American, Latino, Asian American, or Italian American. Many times I have wondered, however, whether the Department of Customs and Border Protection has a very strict affirmative action recruitment policy. In one of my latest entries back into the United States, I had a young man of Middle Eastern background, and a very obvious Middle Eastern last name, stamp my passport. It is certainly wonderful, and this is the metaphysical pain that I unfailingly feel when I get my passport stamped, to be welcomed by such a racially, ethnically, and gendered diverse group of citizens. Sometimes, only sometimes, I think that "racial justice" is a "homeland" a *patria*, a fatherland, a motherland, to which we return when we have gone abroad.

Yet, while I travel under one passport, my heart is torn asunder. My heart is torn because I know very palpably, and I only need to go through customs to be reminded of this, that my country is not one of racial justice. People like me are derided in this country that issued my passport. I have been shamed by racial slurs, and I have been shamed by public racism toward others. As an educator I have been witness to the lasting and crippling effects of institutional racism toward my students. I can't read minds, and I can't do personality profiles, but I know that educational success builds and accrues. It takes years to educate a successful student, and it begins in grade school. Semester to semester I am reminded of the meaning of "institutional racism." It is also a fact that "my country" does not let me forget the "race question." Not only because it is palpable and visible in our everyday existences, but also because there is a very respected and worthy tradition of racial critique that has shaped my understanding of citizenship, patriotism, and belonging.

The metaphysical ache I feel is undoubtedly rooted in my having grown up in Central Jersey and Manhattan looking up to justice heroes such as Martin Luther King Jr., Malcolm X, Cesar Chavez, James H. Cone, Cornel West, and bell hooks, and later being nurtured by mentors such as Richard Bernstein, Seyla Benhabib, Steve Bronner, Agnes Heller, and Douglass Kellner. I am shamed, disappointed, deeply saddened, even pessimistic, about the possibility of achieving racial justice in my country, which has invested so much institutional power to ensure racial and class privilege. On the other hand, I know that much has changed, and that there have been many, many citizens, teachers, and priests who have devoted their lives, in many cases putting their own lives on the line, to push forward the quest for racial justice. Without question a large part of the greatness of the United States, real as well as imaginary, derives from the history of the quest for racial justice that is integral to its identity. The struggle for racial justice is doubtless integral to the narrative through which people imagine the United States. For this reason, at times the United States of America is a metonym for what Dominican public intellectual and man of letters Pedro Henriquez Ureña called *patria de la justicia*.[1] It is indeed an honor to be a citizen of a country that has that kind of history. But it is one that also condemns many of its citizens to live with torn hearts, two hearts, but one passport.

There is another sense in which the "two hearts" in the subtitle of my chapter can be taken, and I am partly alluding to it. This is the sense that Arjun Appadurai developed in a wonderful, if little-known, essay "Patriotism and Its Futures."[2] In this essay Appadurai explores the consequences of the emergence of the "postnational" on citizenship and its attendant forms of loyalty and patriotism. Citizenship, and the nation-states within which it is embedded, are "products of the collective imagination." "[C]itizens *imagine* themselves to belong to a national society."[3] During the nineteenth and twentieth centuries, the narratives go, nation-states mobilized both race and ethnicity in order to produce the kind of narratives and "imagined communities" necessary to produce a national identity. These racial and ethnic nationalisms turned genocidal, at worst, or gave rise to regimes of racial privilege, caste stratification, obdurate segregation, and apartheid, at best. In Habermas's terms, "the postnational constellation," has given birth to a postnationalistic order in which the loyalties of citizens are differentiated, split, equivocal, and not easily sequestered by nationalistic projects. According to Appadurai, the postnational condition manifests itself in divided, fragmented loyalties, biculturalisms, and triple-hyphenated, transnational identities. Postnational identities are thus not just beyond the nation-state, but also beyond the types of nationalisms that spawned so much of the violence of the nineteenth and twentieth centuries. Postnational and transnational converge in a heart that has many allegiances and loyalties, and which therefore may not be easily sequestered in or locked in step with xenophobic nationalism. It is not difficult to appreciate the correctness of Appadurai's analysis. The globalization of mass media, the revolution in the means of telecommunication, as well as the growth and ease in the intercontinental and transcontinental flight industry, has given rise to a global condition that is indeed postnational and postethnic. How we imagine ourselves as citizens in this new postnational context, however, is Appadurai's central concern in this essay. In fact, Appadurai notes:

> My own complexion and its role in "minority" politics, as well as in street encounters with racial hatred, prompt me to reopen the links between America and the United States, between biculturalism and patriotism, between diasporic identities and the (in)stabilities provided by passport and green cards. Postnational *loyalties* are not irrelevant to the problem of diversity in the United States. If, indeed, a postnational order is in the making, an Americanness changes its meanings, the whole problem of diversity in American life will have to be rethought.[4]

Appadurai touches on two themes here that are central to what I want to accomplish in this chapter. First, there is the issue of loyalty, surely one of the most important civic virtues, which is generally distorted by and conflated with patriotism.[5] Civic loyalty, or a citizen's loyalty to a national project and identity are indispensable for the continuation of a nation. The second issue is already implied in the notion of loyalty, and it has to do with the meaning of "Americanness." National identity is that which commands a citizen's loyalty. As citizens we feel loyal toward that which defines us. There is an inevitable circularity here. As citizens we imagine ourselves part of a nation if it possesses the kind of identity that can command our loyalty. We grant our loyalty to a national identity with which we can identify. We cease to bestow our loyalty on that which has betrayed us and that, instead of making us proud and honoring us, has humiliated and degraded us. Loyalty is related to honor, self-respect, and dignity. What commands our loyalty discloses our own self-regard. Conversely, the intensity and breadth of citizens' loyalty confirms the dignity and integrity of that national identity that commands their solicitude and deference.

Loyalty, which manifests itself as allegiance, is a civic virtue that elucidates brilliantly the dependence of citizenship on affect. Loyalty is a form of love and faithfulness that cannot be elicited by a list of rights.[6] A catalog of rights and duties is part of the fabric of citizenship. Yet, these are meaningless without a prior affective and emotive commitment to them from citizens. Respect for the rights of citizens does not flow from the rights themselves, but rather from the loyalty and allegiance that we confer on the nation that grants us those rights. Those rights stand for our national identity. Citizenship is an emblem of that national identity; it is posterior to it and is never exhausted by it. To be an "American" means more than simply being an American citizen. In the following I want to study the relationship between citizenship, trust, loyalty, and political friendship in terms of what I call a public somatology. The goal is to establish a conceptual bridge between civic affect and political friendship. This bridge, it is my contention, offers a more sturdy and lasting venue to a newly imagined postnational "American" identity that is attentive to its history of racial injustice and inequity but that nonetheless profiles for us a project that may command our loyalty, a loyalty that does not require of us our humiliation and dishonor.

In the following, I want to approach the centrality of trust to citizenship in terms of political friendship, for it is in the latter form that trust is best expressed among citizens and within a polity. Trust is uncoerced and gratuitous, and in this it resembles friendship, which is at its best when it is most noninstrumental and solicitous. But before arriving at this family relationship between trust and friendship, a short historical detour is necessary. I want to illustrate the centrality of trust and friendship in citizenship by looking at the role of affect in the process of citizenship development. I will look at *Brown v. Board of Education*, with a half century of hindsight, in order to gauge what I call the motivational deficit of citizenship when only looked at through the litigious lens of the law and political machinations. *Brown* offers us the perfect exemplar of the insidious entwinement of law with affect that results in the recrudesce and further entrenchment of racism. Then, I will turn to Aristotle, Cicero, and Kant, to argue that political friendship is not just moral excellence, but also, and perhaps most centrally, the highest actualization of the political nature of the human being. In and through political friendship we exhibit the excellence of civic virtue. In the fourth and last part, I turn toward the link between political friendship, trust, solidarity, and the practice of freedom.

Another preliminary remark is in order here at the outset. This text was conceptualized and written in the aftermath of 9/11, the terrorist attacks of 2001. My reflections here are conditioned by these traumatic events, and they are partly an attempt to comprehend not why they happened but what we, as U.S. citizens, should do in the so-called shadow of the vanished towers, and the death of many postnational U.S. citizens. Yet, I have deliberately stayed away from discussing directly these events for the simple reason that too much has been written that will become obsolete as soon as the waves of another Washington scandal wash away the sands of public memory. Perhaps it may suffice to note that in an early version of this text I began with a note on a pad of paper that said "terrorism: attack on quotidian existence by means of the quotidian, and betrayal of trust, the trust that makes the everyday life of citizens possible." Terrorism is parasitic on a web of relations and institutions that are nurtured and sustained by trust. Terrorism is so profoundly disorienting because it is a betrayal of what we give and expect on a continuous basis when we interact with each other. Betrayal by compatriots and cocitizens is perhaps the most devastating form of disloyalty, and this is why treason is perhaps the worst crime a citizen can commit against his or her nation. Yet, terrorism is exceptional and the exception. A hermeneutics of failure, à la Heidegger, flashes brightly over the web of mutuality, trust, loyalty, respect, in two words, political friendship, that sustains the innocuous and presupposed public life of citizens. After 9/11 we have once again resorted to the imperial ethos that urges us to think and feel as we are that evil is besieging us from without, while also inviting us to avert our public gaze from the acts of betrayal, and even treason, we ourselves have committed. Terrorism, theirs and ours, should make us think about whether we have been honorable and self-respecting citizens, and whether our public expression of affect or extension of political friendship is strengthening our polity, or corroding it.

Public Somatology, Trust, and Political Friendship

Citizenship is a political category that binds public affect, or public somatology, to a legal order. Citizenship is a bundle of rights and duties, but it is also a bundle of emotions, passions, desires, in short, affect. A public somatology is matched or accompanied by a moral psychology of citizenship, for certain ways of feeling enable certain moral attitudes, certain moral attitudes in turn command certain affect or emotional responses. At the core of the bundle of passions and emotions that make up a civic somatology and moral psychology of citizenship is trust. Trust, curiously, is both an affective response and a moral attitude. Trust exhibits most lucidly the entwinement between affect and a moral sanction that is fundamental to citizenship.

Law may guarantee our status as citizens, but it is a form of trust, or rather, political friendship, as I will show, that moves us to feel as citizens, to be engaged, invested, committed to a certain notion of citizenship. Trust, thus, is not just an interpersonal affect that takes place between two, but it is also an affective response among many, and between individuals and strangers with whom they share the ascription of citizenship. Citizenship is the routinization of trust, as well as the expansion of its horizon of reach. We trust our cocitizens, above any other strangers. Nationalism and patriotism are surely some of the ways in which trust is both mobilized against strangers, sometimes for nefarious uses, and instigated in order to expand our loyalties and make them more enduring, with ennobling and edifying consequences. But it is through political friendship that citizenship expands and takes root in the hearts of citizens.

At the phenomenological level, trust is a form of vulnerability in which subjects open themselves to the solicitous care of another, the other in whom one trusts. Trust, therefore, is also dialogical, reciprocal if not symmetrical, but always a form of vulnerability and powerlessness. For this reason, trust also entails loyalty, fidelity, solicitude, and gratuitous generosity. Trust, like generosity, is without condition, to use a Derridian formulation. Trust, solicitude, loyalty, and solidarity, in fact, are some of the virtues that make true citizens, good citizens, noble citizens.[7] This catalog of virtues is indispensable for the efficacy of citizenship, but it also constitutes the bundle of passions that make up what I call civic or public affect, or a public somatology. By public somatology I mean also things like civic politeness, civic solidarity, civic loyalty that conforms to a certain modus vivendi that involves, mobilizes, and educates the entire spectrum of passions and emotions. We are not born citizens. We become citizens. We become citizens by being educated into a public somatology that varies from nation to nation, from country to country, from ethnic group within nations to ethnic group.

Our citizenship is guaranteed by a legal matrix, one that has surely evolved and expanded not solely because of the internal unfolding of the law, but mostly because of the affective investment of citizens who have sought the inclusion of new rights to citizens, thus expanding our concept of citizenship, or the guarantee of respect of rights suspended or abrogated to a derogated and marginalized group of citizens. It is the legal matrix of citizenship that assures citizens the right to the state, that is, the right to participate in self-legislation, as well as rights from the state, that is the right to the noninterference of the state in the pursuit of our happiness. While it is the legal matrix that makes us citizens de jure, or nominally, it is public affect that makes us citizens de facto, and substantively. Another way of saying this is to claim that citizenship, if seen solely or merely as a legal-political structure and category, would suffer from a motivation deficit. When law is the only guarantee of citizenship, then that polity is already lost.

Racial Malice and Legal Fortuity

May 17, 2004, marked the fiftieth anniversary of *Brown v. Board of Education*, unquestionably one of the most important decisions reached by the Supreme Court of the United States. *Brown v. Board of Education* is as famous as *Dred Scott v. Sandford* and *Plessy v. Ferguson* are infamous. Just as most citizens celebrate one, the other two are vehemently reviled by most. While the latter two decisions established the legal foundations for a racial polity, one by withdrawing citizenship from blacks, the other by establishing a stratified racial order, the former reconsecrated and reaffirmed the Declaration of Independence's proclamation of the equality of all before and under the law. With half a century of perspective we can perhaps derive a modicum of insight into the potentially positive effects of law on social transformation, but we may also be able to have an insight into the relationship between affect and citizenship, public somatology and constitutional interpretation, that is, the law of the land. In 2004 a spate of books was published that sought to provide assessments of the importance and efficacy of *Brown v. Board of Education*. In a recent publication, I have engaged the works of Richard Kluger and Michael J. Klarman on *Brown*.[8] Both authors produced very important historical assessments of this momentous decision. Here, I want to focus on two civil rights lawyers, who also published in 2004 assessments and reflections on the meaning of *Brown* after a half century of its announcement by Chief Justice Earl Warren. First, I will consider Charles J. Ogletree Jr.'s distinctly autobiographical *All Deliberate Speed: Reflections on the First Half-Century of Brown v. Board of Education*.[9] Then I will turn to a brief discussion of Derrick Bell's *Silent Covenants: Brown v. Board of Education and the Unfulfilled Hopes for Racial Reform*.[10]

Ogletree's book is guided by three explicit goals. First, it aims to explain the import of *Brown* during a time of extreme racial segregation in the United States. It underscores the clear and unambiguous language in which the Court rejected the doctrine of "separate but equal," and called for the end of legalized inequality in the United States. At the same time, Ogletree discusses the eviscerating role that *Brown II* had on *Brown I*, the original decision calling for the end of segregation. *Brown II* came as a consequence of litigants claiming they could not fulfill the requirements of *Brown I*. The Court allowed for desegregation to take place with "all deliberate speed," which in most cases meant no speed at all. *Brown II* undermined the force of *Brown I*, rendering it almost moot, and calling for another decade of litigation that would end in the Civil Right Acts of 1964 and the Voting Rights Act of 1965. In Ogletree's analysis, the compromise also loudly announced with *Brown II* rendered the decision flawed from the beginning. Second, Ogletree's work discusses very closely the efforts that many civil rights lawyers and Supreme Court justices committed to achieving racial justice. Third, and finally, and this is what makes Ogletree's book distinctive and particularly useful, is that it aims to offer an individualized portrait of the substantive effects of *Brown* on black Americans by chronicling Ogletree's own biography. The book weaves a personal story of how Ogletree himself was a beneficiary of *Brown*, and how he contributed personally as a lawyer in the struggle for racial justice.

Ogletree offers two important reflections on the meaning of *Brown* that I want to highlight, as they contribute to establishing my main points about the relationship between citizenship and affect. Ogletree dismisses critics of *Brown* who belittle the decision on the grounds that it did not achieve what it was supposed to achieve, namely, integration. On that reading, in fact, *Brown* has been miserably ineffective, and some may say has even been irrelevant. In fact, if we look at the racial composition of most schools today we will discover a disquieting pattern of resegregation. For Ogletree, *Brown* was not primarily or solely about integration. It was about reaffirming the country's commitment to racial equality, as it has been proclaimed in the Declaration of Independence, and had been reconfirmed with the postbellum civil rights amendments to the Constitution. *Brown* was also about changing the way citizens addressed and viewed each other. Ogletree writes, "The challenge of *Brown* was not only to achieve integration but also to recognize that once integrated, all of us are diverse: we have all given up something to gain something more. Integration does not simply place people side by side in various institutional settings; rather, it remakes America, creating a new community founded on a new form of respect and tolerance."[11] This hopeful reading of *Brown*, however, is tempered by the sanguine, bitter, and sad conclusion that *Brown* in fact has left us with a "tragic" lesson about the role of law and racism in American society:

> Whereas *Brown I* made possible the institutional equality first promised in 1776 with the Declaration of Independence ("All men are created equal") and again in 1865 with the ratification of the Thirteenth and Fourteenth Amendments, *Brown II* created the

> method and manner in which America would resist the mandate of the equality ideal. If *Brown I* made integration a legal imperative, *Brown II*, with its decision to proceed "with all deliberate speed" ensured that the imperative was not implemented as a social imperative.[12]

The resonating and profoundly symbolic renunciation of unconstitutional legal separation was muted and nullified by the Court's timidity before and deference to racial malice. *Brown* was crippled from its inception because it was born of an obsequious obeisance toward white segregationists' sensibilities and their own distinctive form of racial affect.

Derrick Bell has been a friendly, albeit skeptical, critic of *Brown* at least since 1976 when he published a law review article entitled "Serving Two Masters: Integration Ideals and Client Interest in School Desegregation Litigation,"[13] in which he argued that it was counterproductive to seek racial balance in a school's student body population. Instead, educational equity should have been the aim. In 1980 in an equally important article entitled "*Brown v. Board of Education* and the Interest-Convergence Dilemma,"[14] Bell articulated his idea of legal fortuity, which argues that gains in civil rights were fortuitous and thus were bound to be impermanent and fleeting. Those gains would be swept away as soon as it was thought that they in any way hurt, penalized, or burden white Americans. According to Bell, *Brown* was decided not primarily because it aimed to redress the injustices done to black Americans, but because in the mid-1950s, at the height of the cold war, it was of great importance that the United States present to the world a different face than it was presenting: one disfigured by racial caste, intransigence, and hateful racial violence. The interests of blacks converged momentarily with those of white Americans, and thus there arose the legal fortuity of *Brown*. As a fortuitous decision, *Brown* did not seek to follow legal precedent, or to address what was necessary, logical, consequent, and expectable from the Supreme Court. *Brown* was a contingent legal solution to a glaring problem, but barely a prophylactic to address a century of Jim Crow and two hundred years of slavery. The courts, as well as the other branches of the U.S. government, have more often than not abandoned and even sacrificed black American causes than sought to address them seriously and permanently. If there have been any gains for black Americans, argues Bell, it has been due to what he calls "interest convergence," that is, when the interest of Americans are furthered, first, and those of black Americans are served too but only as a bonus. When these two sets of interests do not converge, then there is no possibility of either redress or advancement.

Many of the key arguments about the failures of *Brown* by Bell had been reheard already in various forms in different law articles, but they are refined and presented in a new and eloquent way in his 2004 book *Silent Covenants: Brown v. Board of Education and the Unfulfilled Hopes for Racial Reform*. For instance, chapter 3, "*Brown* Reconceived: An Alternative Scenario," had an earlier form, namely, as a longer chapter contribution to a book published in 2001 entitled *What Brown v. Board of Education Should have Said: The Nation's Top Legal Experts Rewrite America's Landmark Civil Rights Decision.*[15] Both texts are versions of Bell's own *Brown* decision, as he would have written it back in 1954, had he been a justice of the Supreme Court. What is interesting is that the 2001 version is articulated as a dissenting opinion, whereas the 2004 book version is articulated as the plurality decision. There are a couple of passages from Bell's *Brown* rewrite that demand attention.

In the 2001 version, Bell writes, "I dissent today from the majority's decision in these cases because the detestable segregation in the public schools that the majority find unconstitutional is a manifestation of the evil of racism the depths and pervasiveness of which this Court fails even to acknowledge, much less address and attempt to correct."[16] What Bell refers to as "the evil of racism" here is what I call "racial malice." Ogletree also refers to the evils of racism, and he agrees with Bell that the Supreme Court failed in 1954, as well as throughout most of its history, to see this evil as an evil. Evil, however, makes us think of a noun, some metaphysical presence that guides and determines as if from without. Malice, instead, keeps us within the realm of the moral and legal, this side of the human and, most importantly, in the mode of the verb and subjects that are tethered to verbs: some one, some others, have malice, or are malicious. Bell continues: "The Court's long-overdue findings that Negroes are harmed by racial segregation is, regrettably, unaccompanied by an understanding of the economic, political, and psychological advantages whites gain because of that harm."[17] In the 2004 version, this passage is rendered differently, "Rather, we suggest that segregation perpetuates the sense of white children that their privileged status as whites is deserved rather than bestowed by law and tradition. We hold that racial segregation afflicts children with a lifelong mental and emotional handicap that is as destructive to whites as the required strictures of segregation are to Negroes."[18] Indeed, Bell has brilliantly put his hermeneutical finger on a major conceptual problem with Warren's *Brown* decision, namely, that it articulates its constitutional rejection of "separate but equal" only in terms of the harm to black children, but fails absolutely to see, or even fathom, the ways in which racism endures precisely because whites derive not just substantive economic but also psychic and emotional benefits from the harm caused to blacks. This is what I call racial malice. By failing to address the enduring stability and the psychic investment of the racial polity of the United States in racism, the Court already called forth the resistance to *Brown* that it would be met with. "By its silent assumption that segregation is an obsolete artifact of a bygone age, the Court set the stage not for compliance, but for levels of defiance that will prove the antithesis of the equal educational opportunity the petitioner's seek."[19] This silence merely dismisses the odious doctrine of "separate but equal" established with *Plessy*, whereas the aim should have been of dismantling it by unambiguously targeting the odious institutions that benefit whites at the expense of black segregation and exclusion.

I want to conclude my discussion of Bell by quoting from the conclusion of his imaginary plurality *Brown* decision:

> Imagining racism as a fixable aberration, moreover, obfuscates the way in which racism functions as an ideological lens through which Americans perceive themselves, their nation, and their nation's other. Second, the vision of racism as an unhappy accident of history immunizes "the law" (as a logical system) from antiracist critique. That is to say, the Court would position the law as that which fixes racism rather than that which participates in its consolidation. By dismissing *Plessy* without dismantling it, the Court might unintentionally predict if not underwrite eventual failure. Negroes, who, despite all, are perhaps the nation's most faithful citizens, deserve better.[20]

This is surely a moving and perspicacious conclusion to an eloquent plea. There are three elements that I want to draw out that are central to my argument. First, racism is imagined, imaginary, and imaginable, but it is central to the way Americans see themselves. Here we have echoes of Appadurai's notion of citizenship as a collective act of imagination. In this case, U.S. citizenship is imagined through a racial lens. Second, law is seen as not the only and sole remedy for enduring racism. Law is itself complicit, engaged, invested, tainted by the racism that suffused its polity and against which it fights too feebly and without conviction. It is to be noted that U.S. jurisprudence and juridification has a longer history of investment in racism than fighting against it. Third, and finally, Bell touches on the Ariadne's threat of this text, namely, on the "faithfulness" of black citizens. Faithfulness, love, loyalty are forms of affect that grant us the fortitude to remain steadfast in a struggle or project even when we face repeated defeats and the malice and enmity of our cocitizens.

Political Friendship and Moral Excellence

The concept of political friendship is eloquently and deliberately formulated for the first time by Aristotle in his *Nicomachean Ethics*, yet he was able to do so because he already had at his disposal a substantive corpus of reflection and thinking on the concept.[21] Homer's *Odyssey* is an exploration of both male friendship and conjugal love. The *Iliad* is a study in martial courage, but also male friendship and love.[22] Nonetheless, it was Plato who gave us some of the most elaborate and extensive reflections on the relationship among friendship and the search for wisdom, moral excellence, and civic virtue. Plato deals with friendship in many of his most important dialogues, such as *Lysis, Symposium*, and *Alcibiadies*. Yet, it is in the *Gorgias* that Plato comes closest to articulating the concept of political friendship, for it is in that dialogue that Plato links the vocation of philosophy to moral happiness, and justice. For Plato, philosophy, the quest for truth, is a dialogic vocation, that is, a pursuit that is best done with and through friends. Indeed, philosophy is a form of friendship, or love, namely, the friendship of those who seek wisdom and the love of it. In the *Gorgias*, most clearly, but also in the *Protagoras* and the *Republic*, Plato binds justice to wisdom as it is disclosed through and by philosophy. Justice for Plato is thus a love of wisdom, the good, and the beautiful. Kallipolis, the beautiful city, is the city in which justice, truth, and moral happiness, or *eudaimonia*, are conjoined through the love of wisdom. Love of wisdom is the highest form of friendship. Yet, it was Plato's student and *philos*, Aristotle, who took Plato's binding of justice, truth, and moral happiness and articulated the concept of political friendship.

Books VIII and IX of the *Nicomachean Ethics* are devoted to the analysis of friendship, and they are the de rigeur points of reference for any reflection on friendship, love, amity, and civic concord or unanimity. Friendship was already singled out in chapter IV, section 6, as one of the moral virtues that has to do with "social intercourse." In chapter IV, interestingly, Aristotle notes that "friendliness" is the mean between the extremes of flattery or obsequiousness and churlishness or contentiousness. This mean, however, does not have a proper name (1126b), or rather the virtue that is between these extremes is "without a name." Chapter VIII, on the other hand, affirms at the outset that friendship is either a virtue, or implies virtue, and furthermore, it is the type of virtue that is most essential to the human being, for without it, or its benefits, no one would choose to live. Friendship is the expression of human nature, and without it, humans would not actualize their potential. Already at the outset, additionally, Aristotle links the virtue of friendship to the virtue of justice, in the following way:

> Moreover, friendship would seem to hold cities together, and legislators would seem to be more concerned about it than about justice. For concord would seem to be similar to friendship and they aim at concord among all, while they try above all to expel civic conflict, which is enmity. Further, if people are friends, they have no need of

justice, but if they are just they need friendship in addition; and the justice that is most just seems to belong to friendship.[23]

This is a pivotal passage in the introduction to the first chapter on friendship, for here we have several core ideas or tenets of political friendship. First, Aristotle is affirming that friendship, rather than law, is what holds together a polity. Even if law is necessary, it is not as indispensable and fundamental as friendship. Concord or unanimity, or in other words civic peace, is a product of friendship, or more precisely political friendship. And this is why rulers aim at promoting civic friendship rather than juridification and litigation. Second, friendship is prior to justice, for justice is a by-product of friendship. This is an extremely important claim, for it affirms that justice, and its dispensation, are motivated by friendship or friendliness. Even if we have justice, in the form of a legal matrix, or a legal tradition, we still require the disposition of friendship for this justice to have enough effect or impact. Third, the "truest" or "highest" form of justice is considered a friendly quality, that is, the extension of friendship toward those being taken care of by justice. To achieve the highest and truest form of justice, friendship and friendliness are indispensable. We could say that friendship is both necessary and sufficient for a well-ordered polity, while justice is merely, if even that, sufficient. Fourth, here Aristotle is already anticipating an argument that he only makes explicit much letter, in section 9 of chapter VIII (1160), where he addresses the reach or horizon of efficacy of both friendship and justice. In the first section to section 9, chapter VIII, Aristotle argues: "Friendship and justice seem, as we have said at the outset of our discussion, to be concerned with the same objects and exhibited between the same persons." Friendship and justice are addressed to the same group of entities, and furthermore, both have the same extension, or reach (see 1160a 6–10). Aristotle scholar Paul Schollmeier summarizes Aristotle's linking friendship and justice in the following way: "We see thus that political friendship of the good kind includes kingship, aristocracy, and polity. We see also that kingship and aristocracy are altruistic constitutions that are more difficult to attain. For kingship and aristocracy aim at intellectual virtue and its activity. But polity is an altruistic constitution which is easier to attain, for polity aims at the activity of moral virtue."[24]

The next step in the philosophical exploration of friendship is to discuss with whom can we obtain the most noble friendships, and given that there are always differences among the types of human we interact with, the question arises whether we can be friends with unequals. Indeed, it is the inequality among friends that leads Aristotle to explore the different kinds of friendships that are to be had. He distinguishes among three kinds, equal in kind to those entities that are the object of our loving or friendliness. There are those whom we love because of their utility, and those whom we love because we derive from them some pleasure. Both forms of friendship are pursued not in virtue of what the other person has in themselves, or is in themselves, but in virtue of what they provide to me: either utility or pleasure, both of which are measured by my own interests and desires. These two forms of friendship are therefore considered by Aristotle to be incidental, that is, contingent, ephemeral, circumstantial, and pragmatic. They are bound to dissolve as soon as our interests and utility have been satisfied, and our pleasure has been satiated or dissolved. As against these forms of friendship, Aristotle delineates a third type, which he calls perfect friendship. This friendship is among men who are good and equal in virtue. Perfect friends are good in themselves. They are our friends for themselves, not because of what they provide to me. These friendships are permanent, but they are also rare, for men who are virtuous, and good in themselves, are rare. Perfect friendship, which is permanent, is only possible among equals in virtue and goodness.

If perfect and enduring friendship is only possible among good and virtuous men, why would they need it when it is their very goodness that would make them the object of friendship, rather than the seeker or subject of friendship? Perfectly virtuous men seem to be self-sufficient, and thus have no need of others, who are potentially inferior, and a moral liability. Aristotle affirms, "It is also disputed whether the happy man will need friends or not." The question had arisen whether perfectly virtuous men, who as such are therefore happy, need friends at all. Virtue and goodness are components of eudaimonia, moral happiness or virtuous happiness. The happy man, then, is the supreme exemplar of justice, goodness, and virtue. Why would they need friends? According to Aristotle, friendship and friends are among the greatest of external goods. It would seem strange, ponders Aristotle, not to also assign friendship and friends to the completely virtuous man. This leads him to argue:

> Surely it is strange, too, to make the supremely happy man a solitary; for no one would choose the whole world on condition of being alone, since man is a political creature and one whose nature is to live with others. Therefore the happy man lives with others; for he has the things that are by nature good. And plainly it is better to spend his days with friends and good men than with strangers or any chance person. Therefore the happy man needs friends.[25]

Thus, the epitome of human excellence is by nature a friend and someone who needs friends, for by nature the human being is a political creature, a creature of sociality and social discourse. Chapter IX, in fact, concludes that the essence of friendship is living together. Thus, friendship is indispensable not just to the political community, for all communities are components of the political community, and in this way, friendship is indispensable to social amity and concord, but also to the very actualization of the human being. As a scholar put, "The entire free citizenry of the *polis* was held to be related in the manner of a friendship. Politics came thus to be seen as the means for the exercise of friendship."[26]

Cicero in his extremely important small treatise *De Amicitia* addresses directly the question of the relationship between the need for friends and friendship, and human nature.[27] Cicero asks, "Does the fact that people need friendship mean there is some weakness and deficiency in themselves?"[28] If friendship was indeed an expression of weakness or a deficiency then we would pursue them only for instrumental reason. They would be fettered to a quid pro quo. Cicero admits that friendships and friendship in general fulfills some utility and pragmatic needs, but these are aleatory and not essential to both friendship and human nature. For Cicero, friendship is expression of something natural and profoundly important to the human being. He writes, "As for its origins, do these not, rather, lie in something altogether more primeval and noble, something emanating more directly from the actual process of nature? For goodwill is established by love, quite independently of any calculation of profit: and it is from love, *amor*, that the word friendship, *amicitia*, is derived."[29] Friendship arises from an "inclination of the heart." Just as Aristotle believes that friendship is the actualization of a human potentiality, so does Cicero believe that to remove human from the sociality of friendship would be to deprive them of that which makes them complete, or through which they obtain moral perfection. Like Aristotle, furthermore, Cicero also believes that friendship is the expression of moral goodness. For Cicero, friendship arises from "goodness of character." And it is from this goodness of character that all "harmony, and permanence, and fidelity, come." When friendship is present, and "reveals its brilliant light, and perceives and recognizes the same illumination in another person, it is impelled in his direction and receives its beams."[30]

Immanuel Kant, who on most registers is usually juxtaposed to Aristotle and the ancients tout court, held on to the moral relevance of friendship. Friendship was a recurring theme of his lectures on ethics, and not just because he considered it to be the "hobby-horse of all poetical moralists" where they sought "nectar and ambrosia."[31] In his lectures Kant approaches the question of friendship in terms of what motivates humans to action. On the one side we have the motive of self-love, or that which arises from within. The other motive is external, or from without, and this is the motive of duty. Friendship arises when these two motives enter into conflict, and in Kant's view, it is the resolution between inner and outer compulsion. For the pursuit of one's own inner compulsion is the pursuit of one's own happiness, while the pursuit of outer or external motives is the pursuit of someone else's happiness. Friendship is the means by which my happiness and the happiness of others is reconciled. "It looks as if a man loses, when he cares for other people's happiness; but if they, in turn, are caring for his, then he loses nothing. In that case the happiness of each would be promoted by the generosity of others, and this is the Idea of friendship, where self-love is swallowed up in the idea of generous mutual love."[32] When we take the other side of the equation, namely, when we pursue our own happiness without regard for that of others, this is certainly morally permissible, but there is no moral "merit" in it. We are not forced to be friendly, so long as we do not impose obstacles in other people's pursuit of their happiness. Faced with the choice of whether to pursue friendship or self-love, Kant argues that we should choose friendship on "moral grounds." But, for practical ends or reason, we are likely to choose self-love. Yet, there is no moral merit in the pursuit of one's happiness, alone, while there is moral approbation and worth in our choosing friendship.

Even in Kant's discussion of friendship we find Aristotle's differentiation between incidental and perfect friendship. Kant makes a similar distinction, namely, between friendships undertaken for need, pleasure and taste, and disposition. The perfect friendship, which is enduring and radiant, is moral friendship, which arises from disposition and not from either need or taste. Moral friendship arises from respect to the moral law, which coerces us with a nonviolent force. While egoism and narcissism are not morally proscribed, they do not have moral worth. Friendship, benevolence, and generosity do have moral worth, for they are done out of regard for the moral integrity of others. Moral friendship is the expression of the moral integrity and worth of humans when they treat each other as ends and never as means.

There is another issue on which Aristotle and Kant agree, namely, on the fact that friendship is an expression of human sociality. For Aristotle, the human being is a political animal, a creature of companionship, whose moral happiness is directly related to their social intercourse. For Kant, our moral worth and merit, which we earn by acting out of respect for the moral law and that is thus exhibited in our acting from duty, is expressed also in friendship. Kant puts it thusly in *The Metaphysics of Morals*:

> The human being is a being meant for society (though he is also an unsociable one), and in cultivating the social state he feels strongly the need to *reveal* himself to others (even with no ulterior purpose). But on the other hand, hemmed in and cautioned by fear of the misuse others may make of his disclosing his thoughts, he finds himself constrained *to lock up* in himself a good part of his judgments (especially those about other people).[33]

In this formulation, however, Kant departs from Aristotle, for here not only is friendship an expression of humanity essential sociality, but friendship is pursued for the sake of the "self-disclosure" of the human being. Such "revealing" and "self-disclosure" are essential to the pursuit of moral clarity, honesty, and transparency. If our actions only have moral merit and moral worth because they are done from pure respect for the moral law, then we must be vigilant that our intentions are always without question, without doubt, without calculation, without machination. Here, Kant converges with Plutarch, who in late antiquity was the first one to make friendship a moral mirror. In his "How to Distinguish a Flatterer from a Friend," Plutarch departs from both Aristotle and Cicero in seeing friendship as an expression of human nature and also as an indispensable means for the obtainment of moral excellence. Reading closely Aristotle, Plutarch realizes that friendship and friendliness is the mean between the extremes of flattery and insult, encomium and frankness. But in contrast to Aristotle, and perhaps anticipating Kant, Plutarch sets out to demonstrate that friendship indirectly contributes to our self-knowledge, inasmuch as they always put us on guard as to what is a proper level of praise, and when frankness and criticism turn into something like schadenfreude. Friendship is a path, if not the privileged path, to moral excellence, because loyal friendship leads us to engage our vigilance against falling for the false praise of false friends, or being hurt by the invidious and jealous censure of those whom we take to be friends. Plutarch does not take it for granted that friends are always paragons of moral excellence; instead, he assumed that friends may become morally praiseworthy through friendship, so long as they are always ready not to conflate fatuous flattery, hurtful candor, and honest censure. And in this way, friendship becomes also central in the moral pedagogy of individuals, as well as in the exercise of political freedom.

Conclusion: Pride, Loyalty, Self-Respect

I began this chapter with a discussion about passports, imagined identities, loyalty, and citizenship. I talked about my own torn heart, the two-ness at the center of my emotional being, and the metaphysical pain of coming home, a home that commands my faithfulness and loyalty. I confessed that I feel like I have two hearts, but travel under one passport, out of a sense of loyalty. The heart is the seat of our passions, the place where we gather our loyalties. I reflected on what rends asunder and tears in half my civic loyalties, namely, racism and its persistence in this United States. I took a detour through the work of Charles Ogletree and Derrick Bell in order to reflect on *Brown* as a way to gauge the influence of affect and what I called a public somatology on law and vice versa. *Brown* has become the synecdoche of judicial enlightenment, and the beacon of racial justice projected by an impartial, dispassionate, and rational Court. Yet, with half a century behind them, neither Ogletree nor Bell, very intimate participants in the civil rights struggles that sought to make *Brown* a social reality, have concluded optimistically about its overall efficacy and enduring stability. In Bell's words, *Brown*'s half-light is already fading and is all but eclipsed by the enduring racial enmity and malice of a citizenship that is neither interested in nor moved by the appellations for racial justice of black citizens. This detour sought to establish that citizenship presupposes the education of public affect, a form of public somatology, in which how we feel about our cocitizens is far more important than whether there is a specific list of rights to which they are entitled and by means of which they may litigate. A nation, as Arjun Appadurai noted, is the product of a collective act of imagination, and affect inflects, distorts, shapes, and directs that imaginary identity. Evidently, law regulates civic affect as well, and nothing illustrates more forcefully this direction of influence than the way *Plessy* legislated that blacks should be held at bay and apart, and the way the numerous miscegenation laws have regulated intimacy among different races in the polity. *Brown*, in reverse, also demonstrated the way law and public affect determine each other. *Brown* was read by many, and mostly Southern whites, as an intrusion of the Court on the intimacy of their lives. By allegedly forcing their white children to sit next to black children, the Court had violently imposed itself on their private racially untainted lives.[34] The insight I want to garner from this discussion is that law may have a "salutary civilizing" effect on the nation, but this effect will be null or negligible if it is not priorly and concurrently accompanied with a pedagogy of civic affect. We have to be educated as citizens to feel not just tolerance, but especially solidarity, empathy, pride, and loyalty toward our cocitizens, who both share in our burdens and contribute to our collective well-being.

Richard Rorty articulated eloquently the relationship between affect and citizenship when he argued that "national pride is to countries what self-respect is to individuals: a necessary condition for self-improvement."[35] For Rorty self-respect is a means, not an end. The end here is self-improvement. Self-respect and national pride are the means through which we "made ourselves better than we were in the past." Both are indispensable in the Deweyan and Emersonian projects that see the country as something to be achieved, and one in which we are able to "envisage our nation-state as both a self-creating poet and self-created poem."[36] This country, whose moral identity is yet to be achieved rather than having to be preserved, cannot "contain castes or classes, because the kind of self-respect which is needed for free participation in democratic deliberation is incompatible with social divisions."[37] These are surely some of the most heartfelt and moving sentences Rorty may have written. For him, the racial past and endurance of racism were blemishes in the country's self-regard and self-respect.[38] There cannot be self-improvement of the nation unless we come to terms with both class and racial caste and divisions. What is noteworthy in Rorty's discussion is the way in which he links national pride to self-regard: they are analogous, and mirror each other, but it is clear that Rorty also means that we cannot feel national pride if this nation does not allow for self-respect. National pride and self-respect are codependent.

I want to conclude by arguing that national pride and self-respect are mediated by political friendship. In fact, I want to argue something stronger, namely, that there is no possibility of national pride without the kind of political friendship that makes it possible for citizens to overcome any kind of humiliation, abjection, derogation that undermines, diminishes, and destroys self-respect and self-regard. The law does not make us integral. It only protects and preserves the moral and psychic integrity that is nurtured in enabling political friendship and regarding public affect. Disobedience and disloyalty are inevitable when a nation makes it impossible for citizens to retain their self-respect and honor, some of the most enduring fruits of political friendship. If a nation's legitimacy is measured by its treatment of dissenters, it is also measured by the way in which its builds up the self-respect of its citizens. A nation loses not just the allegiance and loyalty of the citizens it derogates, but it also may command their disobedience and disloyalty. In other words, a legitimate nation, one that can and should claim the unwavering loyalty of its citizens, in such a way that they may feel national pride, in Rorty's sense of the kind of pride that is indispensable for self-improvement, is one that is a "decent society," to use that propitious phrase by Avishai Margalit.[39]

A decent society is one that does not humiliate its citizens. Humiliation is the injury to a person's self-respect; it is an attack on the moral integrity and self-regard of a person. While a decent society may be negatively characterized as the kind of society that does not humiliate its members, it can also be positively characterized as a society "that accords respect through its institutions to people under its authority."[40] There is an even stronger positive characterization of the decent society, "A decent society is one that fights conditions which constitute a justification for its dependents to consider themselves humiliated. A society is decent if its institutions do not act in ways that give people under authority sound reason to consider themselves humiliated."[41] Margalit's definition of a decent society emphasizes the active dimension of humiliation and its opposite, self-respect. Both are products of actions, activities, and deliberate practices. Concurrently, it is not just individuals who either humiliate or respect each other, but most importantly institutions. A decent society is not just made of decent citizens; it is made primarily of institutions that do not by either action or inaction humiliate, but rather actively seek to abolish those conditions that demean and diminish the self-respect of its members.

National pride is proportional to the decency of one's nation, for one cannot have pride in a nation whose institutions actively, or by malignant inertia, humiliate not just many of its citizens, but also the citizens of other nations. A nation that labors intently on humiliating many of its most "faithful citizens"—in Bell's phrasing—calls forth not just their skepticism, but even their disloyalty. A society in which neither self-respect nor national pride are possible cannot possibly improve itself, cannot think of itself as a country yet to be achieved, and whose moral character is to be forged rather than to be preserved. But I am reminded of all the times I have come through customs and a multiethnic "American" has welcomed me home. A decent society is one made up of decent institutions, but this society is produced by the enduring and ceaseless labor of political friendship. Political friendship, as I have shown, is gratuitous and based on intimacy, the solicitude and deference of mutually respecting citizens. Political friendship is "a relationship based on freedom and is, at the same time, a guarantor of freedom," to paraphrase an astute analyst of friendship.[42] I think this is what Derrida meant when he wrote, "When will we be ready for an experience of freedom and equality that is capable of respectfully experiencing that friendship, which would at last be just, just beyond the law, and measured up against its measurelessness?"[43] Indeed, political friendship is the practice of our freedom, but it is also the practice of trust in our cocitizens, for friendship is also a form of vulnerability, reaching beyond the law, that which is measureless in friendship. We cannot become a better nation than we were nor can we gain the self-respect indispensable for self-improvement if we do not practice our freedom in the intimacy of a trusting and ennobling polity. "O my democratic friends."[44]

Notes

I would like to thank Robert Crease, who invited me to give a Templeton lecture "On Trust" at Stony Brook University. This first lecture became the foundation of this text. I later had the opportunity to present a more developed version of this chapter at Albright College, where Fouad Kalouche hosted me. I benefited from all the critical and positive response from the faculty and students.

1. Pedro Henriquez Ureña, "Patria de la justicia," *La Utopia de America* (Caracas, Venezuela: Biblioteca de Ayachucho, 1978), 8–11.
2. Arjun Appadurai, "Patriotism and Its Futures," *Public Culture* 5 (1993): 411–429.

3. Ibid., 414.

4. Ibid., 422; emphasis added.

5. I have tried to disaggregate patriotism as a civic virtue, from jingoistic nationalism that is deaf and blind to the horrors a nation may commit. See Eduardo Mendieta, "Anti-Americanism and Patriotism," *Peace Review* 15, no. 4 (December 2003): 435–442. On the relevance of patriotism, see the important monograph by Jonathan M. Hansen, *The Lost Promise of Patriotism: Debating American Identity, 1890–1920* (Chicago: University of Chicago Press, 2003). See also Maurizio Viroli, *For Love of Country: An Essay on Patriotism and Nationalism* (New York: Oxford University Press, 1995).

6. See the outstanding discussion on loyalty by George P. Fletcher, *Loyalty: An Essay on the Morality of Relationships* (New York: Oxford University Press, 1993). One of the still valuable and generative points of reference on questions of loyalty is Josiah Royce, *The Philosophy of Loyalty* (New York: Macmillan, 1908).

7. See David Batstone and Eduardo Mendieta, *The Good Citizen* (New York: Routledge, 1998) and Michael Schudson, *The Good Citizen: A History of American Civic Life* (New York: Free Press, 1998).

8. Eduardo Mendieta, "Racial Justice, Latinos, and the Supreme Court" in *Race or Ethnicity? On Black and Latino Identity*, ed. Jorge J. E. Gracia (Ithaca, NY: Cornell University Press, 2007), 206–224.

9. Charles J. Ogletree, *All Deliberate Speed: Reflections on the First Half-Century of Brown v. Board of Education* (New York: Norton, 2005 [2004]). The paperback edition from 2005 has a new afterword in which Ogletree considers the future of the court in light of Justice Sandra Day O'Connor's retirement and the appointment of John G. Roberts Jr. as chief justice.

10. Derrick Bell, *Silent Covenants: Brown v. Board of Education and the Unfulfilled Hopes for Racial Reform* (Oxford, UK: Oxford University Press, 2004).

11. Ibid., 301.

12. Ibid., 311.

13. Derrick Bell, "Serving Two Masters: Integration Ideals and Client Interest in School Desegregation Litigation," 85 Yale L. J. 470 (1976).

14. Derrick Bell, "*Brown v. Board of Education* and the Interest-Convergence Dilemma," 93 Harvard L. Rev. 518 (1980).

15. Jack M. Balkin, ed., *What Brown v. Board of Education Should have Said: The Nation's Top Legal Experts Rewrite America's Landmark Civil Rights Decision* (New York: New York University Press, 2001).

16. Derrick Bell, "Dissenting" in *What Brown v. Board of Education Should Have Said*, ed. Jack M. Balkin (New York: New York University Press, 2001), 185.

17. Ibid., 185.

18. Bell, *Silent Covenant*, 23.

19. Bell, "Dissenting," 186.

20. Ibid., 27.

21. I have benefited greatly from the synoptic article by James V. Schall, "Friendship and Political Philosophy," *Review of Metaphysics* 50 (Summer 1996): 121–141, and Pat Easterling, "Friendship and the Greeks," in *The Dialectics of Friendship*, ed. Roy Porter and Sylvana Tomaselli (London: Routledge, 1989), 11–25.

22. See David Konstan, *Friendship in the Classical World* (Cambridge: Cambridge University Press, 1996), chap. 1, the section entitled "The World of Homer," 24 ff.

23. Aristotle, *Nichomachean Ethics*, chap. VIII, sec. 1, p. 1155.

24. Paul Schollmeier, *Other Selves: Aristotle on Personal and Political Friendship* (Albany: State University of New York Press, 1993), 96. This is an outstanding study of the role of friendship in Aristotle's ethical and political writings. See also the condensed discussion in Lorraine Smith Pangle, "Friendship and Self-Love in Aristotle's *Nichomachean Ethics*," in *Action and Contemplation: Studies in the Moral and Political Thought of Aristotle*, ed. Robert C. Bartlett and Susan D. Collins (Albany: State University of New York Press, 1999), 171–202.

25. Aristole, *Nichomachean Ethics*, chap. IX, sec. 9, p. 1169a.

26. H. Hutter, *Politics as Friendship: The Origins of Classical Notions of Politics in the Theory and Practice of Friendship* (Walterloo, ON: Wilfrid Lauriel University Press, 1978), 25.

27. Cicero, "Laelius: On Friendship," in *On the Good Life*, trans. with intro. Michael Grant (New York: Penguin Books, 1971), 175–227.

28. Ibid., 191.

29. Ibid.

30. Ibid., 225–226.

31. Immanuel Kant, *Lectures on Ethics*, trans. Peter Heath (Cambridge: Cambridge University Press, 1996), 184.

32. Ibid.

33. Immanuel Kant, *The Metaphysics of Morals*, in *Practical Philosophy* (Cambridge: Cambridge University Press, 1996), § 47, p. 586.

34. For this analysis see my discussion of *Brown* in Mendieta, "Racial Justice."

35. Richard Rorty, *Achieving Our Country: Leftist Thought in Twentieth-Century America* (Cambridge, MA: Harvard University Press, 1998), 3.

36. Ibid., 28 and 29, respectively, and in that order.

37. Ibid., 30.

38. See my interviews on racism and reparation with Rorty in Richard Rorty, *Take Care of Freedom and Truth Will Take Care of Itself: Interviews with Richard Rorty*, ed. and intro. Eduardo Mendieta (Stanford, CA: Stanford University Press, 2006).

39. Avishai Margalit, *The Decent Society*, trans. Naomi Goldblum (Cambridge, MA: Harvard University Press, 1996).

40. Ibid., 5.

41. Ibid., 10–11.

42. Ray Pahl, *On Friendship* (Cambridge, UK: Polity, 2000), 163.

43. Jacques Derrida, *Politics of Friendship*, trans. George Collins (London: Verso, 1997), 306.

44. Ibid., 306.

Part 3
Homeland

8

On the Limits of Postcolonial Identity Politics

Namita Goswami

Every year since 1947, the National Turkey Federation presents the US president with a turkey for Thanksgiving. Every year, in a show of ceremonial magnanimity, the president spares that particular bird (and eats another one). After receiving the presidential pardon, the chosen one is sent to Frying Pan Park in Virginia to live out its natural life. The rest of the fifty million turkeys raised for Thanksgiving are slaughtered . . . ConAgra Foods . . . says it trains the lucky birds to be sociable, to interact with dignitaries, school children and the press. . . . That's how New Racism in the corporate era works. A few carefully bred turkeys . . . are given absolution and a pass to Frying Pan Park. . . . Some of them even work for the IMF and the WTO—so who can accuse those organizations of being anti-turkey? Some serve as board members on the turkey choosing committee—so who can say turkeys are against Thanksgiving? . . . Who can say the poor are anti-corporate globalization? There's a stampede to get into Frying Pan Park. So what if most perish on the way?

—Arundhati Roy, *An Ordinary Person's Guide to Empire*

Somewhere between Altar and Phoenix, new Americans are being forged in a burning desert. No one is really counting the people, no one is really recording their journeys. Soon, they and their descendants will number 30 million. And this vast silence is likely to be the savage part of their repressed history.

—Charles Bowden, "Exodus: Border-Crossers Forge a New America"

On June 19, 2003, Stanley Kurtz, research fellow at the Hoover Institution (Stanford University) with a degree in social anthropology, expressed his horror before the U.S. Congress as it deliberated over Title VI of the Higher Education Act.[1] According to Dr. Kurtz,

> [The] ruling intellectual paradigm in academic area studies (especially Middle Eastern Studies) is called "post-colonial theory." Post-colonial theory was founded by Columbia University professor of comparative literature, Edward Said. . . . [The] core premise of post-colonial theory is that it is immoral for a scholar to put his [*sic*] knowledge of foreign languages and cultures at the service of American power. . . . For at least a decade the African-, Latin American-, and Middle East Studies Associations have sponsored a boycott against NSEP [National Security Education Program[2]]. . . . Shamefully, a mere two months after September 11, Title VI African Studies Center directors voted unanimously to sustain their boycott of military intelligence related funding, including the NSEP. . . . [S]cholars who study the Middle East (and other areas of the world) . . . tend to purvey extreme and one-sided criticisms of American foreign policy.

Kurtz's native informancy generated considerable academic and activist uproar.[3] In addition to the use of classic anthropological tropes, such as individual (United States) versus community (the rest of the planet), knowledge (by the United States) versus information retrieval (of the rest of the planet), and the definition of "American" (the United States) as ontologically a potential victim of terrorism (by the rest of the planet), Kurtz's post–9/11 nationalistic fervor posits a nativist genealogy for postcolonial theory: he claims that it was "founded" at an elite institution, Columbia University, by an equally elite Palestinian American scholar, in the very city where the World Trade Center attacks took place. The location of New York City as simultaneously the point of origin of postcolonial theory and as the point of its logical conclusion (the destruction of the United States, which ostensibly enabled postcolonial theory to be "founded" in the first place) demonstrates the fraught relationship of the nation-state with its heterogeneous constituencies. Indeed, "foreign policy" becomes a litmus test with which to determine the "foreign" in our midst, a test that the late Dr. Edward Said, in spite of having been, in many ways, the consummate New Yorker, fails.

While Kurtz posits U.S.-centric migration as postcolonial theory's "founding" condition of possibility, where it subsequently fails to become properly indigenized through enabling U.S. foreign policy, Arif Dirlik particularizes this migratory history. According to Dirlik, postcolonial theory seems not to begin with negotiated independence in the colonies but with the large-scale migration of South Asian (Indian) scholars to the United States.[4] In fact, Indian scholars are also the particular class of migrants singled out by African American feminists such as Ann DuCille, Carol Davies, and bell hooks as representative of postcolonial theory in the U.S. academy. Kurtz's nativist genealogy and the problematic conflation of postcolonial theory with Indian Americans, however, may be heuristically useful to glean whether postcolonial theory and Indian Americans do *not* put their "knowledge of foreign languages and cultures at the service of American power."[5]

Although many immigrants experience poverty and are a part of the low-wage, exploited classes, the selectively self-represented Indian American community, or "model minority,"[6] on one hand, seeks identification with the racial underclass by placing itself in an analogical position as victims of U.S. racism. On the other hand, the Indian American community attains the "American Dream" by reinforcing U.S. nationalism and foreign policy, premised on U.S. exceptionalism, in opposition to and often as exploiters of older racialized immigrants and indigenous disenfranchised populations, such as Latin, African, and Native Americans,[7] who become, by implication, "nonmodel" minorities.[8]

Similarly, postcolonial theorists claim racism like "nonmodel" minority academics but also academic prestige as a Eurocentric "model minority" creating a Eurocentric "model minority" discourse.[9] Eurocentrism privileges European colonialism at the expense of U.S. internal and external colonialism thereby reinforcing U.S. exceptionalism, as Donald Pease argues. Eurocentrism also displaces and appropriates U.S.-centric "nonmodel" minority discourses. Gayatri Spivak's critique of postcolonial reason emphasizes that U.S-centric migrancy for aspirational class advancement allows Indian American scholars to represent the "postcolonial" while simultaneously serving as "native informants" of their ostensibly original homeland for U.S. neocolonialism.[10] Spivak, however, along with other postcolonial scholars who contest the notion of postcolonialism and the moniker postcolonial,[11] excludes the United States from postcoloniality because of neocolonial domination.

This chapter argues that neocolonial domination *is* U.S. postcoloniality and U.S-centric migrancy and U.S.-centric identity politics for aspirational class advancement *are* neoimperialistic. Indian American migrancy *is* postcolonialism because it is made possible by neocolonialism and *is* neocolonial in its bid for aspirational class advancement.[12] Postcolonial neoimperialism and concomitant identity politics enable a particular class of migrants to assume that they are the proper postcolonials. These proper postcolonials, who are also the consumptive middle and upper classes at "home" and the upwardly mobile in the United States,[13] become the proper representatives of the nation, in a process that Arundhati Roy terms "vertical secession."[14] Aspirational class advancement constitutes exemplary citizenship in the nation and the nation itself is a vehicle for this class advancement via neoimperialism.[15] How is colonialism, therefore, a passage into postcolonialism such that postcoloniality is an entrance and a passage into neocolonialism?

I continue the aforementioned conflation of U.S. postcolonial theory with Indian migrants and the Indian American community only to foreground that postcolonial scholars of Indian "origin" are intrinsically a part of the selectively self-represented Indian American community through a common migrant history: "hope of justice under capitalism."[16] The fact that postcolonial migrancy occurs as a result of neocolonial economic structures fractures and undermines any claim that the migrancy in question is *inherently* progressive and oppositional to U.S. nationalism and "foreign policy" by virtue of being postcolonial. Indian American migrants, *as* "Americans," however, can disrupt the mutually reinforcing continuity between neocolonialism and U.S.-centric migrancy, assumed to be the case by Kurtz, by becoming "native informants" of their homeland, not *of* an imagined India *for* the neoimperialistic postcolonial United States but *of* the neoimperialistic postcolonial United States *for* anti-imperialism.

If U.S. internal and external colonialism and neoimperialism are posited *as its postcoloniality*, and therefore our own, we can broaden our understanding of postcolonialism, since neoimperialism, as Spivak has repeatedly argued, is the condition of postcoloniality par excellence.[17] In other words, U.S.-centric migration as class advancement aligns "illegal" immigrants and "law-abiding" elites, such as Dinesh D'Souza[18] and CNN's Dr. Sanjay Gupta, insofar as it demonstrates the mechanisms through which neoimperialistic structures are able to reinforce and reify themselves. This alignment holds even though the much-publicized "illegality" and "criminality" of those desperately struggling to survive, often immigrants from the very nations the United States has no problem entering or interfering with "criminally" and "illegally," allows others to class advance.

In the first section, I analyze how postcolonial migrancy for aspirational class advancement enables, as Donald Pease argues, one of the most fundamental tropes of U.S. nationalism and "foreign policy"—the belief in U.S. exceptionalism. The second section examines how academic postcolonialism, the source of Kurtz's latent and manifest anxieties, furthers the ethnically cleansed Anglocentrism and Eurocentrism of the U.S. academy, at the expense of the United States' other indigenous traditions of African, Native, and Latin American scholarship, which render "America" and "American" *eo ipso* hyphenated and fractured. The third section addresses some of the specific ways in which postcolonial theory, by internalizing and accepting this migrant history of U.S.-centric aspirational class advancement, can disrupt the mutually reinforcing continuity between U.S.-centric migrancy and neocolonialism.

I do not intend to be reductive of the complexity and heterogeneity of diverse disciplines, nation-states, and their immigrant communities. I speak in broad strokes only to foreground how the racialized politics of U.S. nationalism and "foreign policy," to use Kurtz's dissembling umbrella term, are often mirrored in the identity politics of the U.S. academy, which are often as base and simplistic as the disciplines and their scholars are subtle and complex. At issue, therefore, is not that we should have all stayed "home" and thereby prevented this complicity, as if this were even possible, but how we as migrants can disrupt the continuity that Kurtz assumes between immigration to the United States and adherence to U.S. nationalism and "foreign policy." Rather than excluding the United States from postcoloniality, another one of postcolonial theory's founding gestures, because it is not the right color (legitimizing the United States as "white"), or because it is powerful and dominant, how can neoimperialistic postcolonial migrancy *to* the neoimperial United States qua U.S. postcoloniality constitute, uncannily, a reversing and recoding of tracks, a journey, if you will, into the heart of darkness?

The Other Postcolonialism

Donald Pease argues that by "restricting the referentiality of the term 'postcolonial' to the political settlements that took place after the decolonization of former european [*sic*] colonies, postcolonial theory has constructed the most recent of the variations on the theme of US [*sic*] exceptionalism."[19] U.S. exceptionalism, "as a normative presupposition, as an historical paradigm, and as a national narrative,"[20] not only naturalizes U.S. dominance but also naturalizes U.S. innocence because it provides the alibi with which explicitly colonial practices can be cast as exceptions, including those practices targeted at groups whose relationship to the state is as exceptions. Postcolonial theory, according to Pease, repeats the "negative reference" of internal and external colonialism by exempting the United States from postcoloniality through exceptionalism.[21]

If postcolonial theory began in the United States, by a Palestinian American scholar, and exempts the United States from postcoloniality, thereby acquiescing to U.S. exceptionalism, then what form of (founding) exceptionalism does this allow postcolonial theory to grant itself? Postcolonial theory, by remaining Eurocentric, furthers U.S. exceptionalism because it effaces U.S. colonialism. By effacing U.S. colonialism it neglects how U.S. colonialism as U.S. postcoloniality succeeds in transcoding colonial practices as global dominance without colonies.[22] By negating U.S. colonialism as U.S. postcoloniality, postcolonial theory also negates the constitutive role of these practices for the relay, to use Spivak's term,[23] from colonialism to neocolonialism, that is, U.S. postcoloniality.

The effacement of U.S. colonialism, made possible by U.S. exceptionalism ("global dominance without colonies"), which also determines U.S. nationalism, and therefore of U.S. postcoloniality, erases the constitutive conditions of U.S.-centric migrancy by postcolonial scholars. The disavowal of these constitutive conditions of postcolonial migrancy, from postcolonial qua passage to neocolonial India to neoimperialistic postcolonial United States, and their further erasure in postcolonial theory's Eurocentrism, enables the U.S.-centric postcolonial migrant to assume the mantle of the postcolonial per se if postcolonial theory is assumed to begin, as Kurtz suggests, in the United States. Postcolonial theory begins in the United States even as the United States is exempt from postcoloniality; the United States' exemption from postcoloniality determines postcolonial theory as a repetition of nationalist U.S. exceptionalism. As a repetition of U.S. exceptionalism, postcolonial theory disavows precisely the neoimperialistic *postcoloniality* that is its condition of possibility. This disavowal of neoimperialistic postcolonial migrancy for aspirational class advancement to the neoimperialistic United States qua U.S. postcolonialism prevents analysis of how academic postcolonialism may repeat U.S. exceptionalism precisely because of its Eurocentrism, which renders postcolonial theorists a "model minority." If the selectively self-represented Indian American community positions itself as a "model minority" against (by implication) "nonmodel" minorities, then postcolonial theorists position themselves as a "model minority" not only through class advancement as members of the U.S. academy but also through the Eurocentrism constitutive of their very discipline. Postcolonial theory's founding exceptionalism, which is the exclusion of the United States from postcoloniality even as postcolonial theory originates in the United States, per Kurtz's nativist genealogy, the denial of the relay from colonialism to neoimperialism as the U.S.'s postcoloniality, and the disavowal of this relay as precisely the conditions of possibility for postcolonial migrancy, enables claims of exclusion and marginalization analogous to African, Latin, and Native American scholarship but also the reinforcement and reification of precisely the Eurocentrism that excludes and marginalizes African, Latin, and Native American scholarship in the first place.

As Deepika Bahri points out, however, postcolonial literature and theory in the United States could not have been possible had African American studies, African and black diaspora studies, queer studies, Latin American studies, and women's studies not already waged the requisite battles on academic and activist fronts.[24] Similarly, Ann DuCille argues that "postcoloniality takes its current preeminence . . . from the very resistance narratives it seems to threaten: black studies and women's studies."[25]

Jenny Sharpe emphasizes that postcolonial theory and literature, unlike African American, African and black diaspora studies, and women's studies, "did not emerge in response to student demands or a political activism that spilled over onto college campuses."[26] The "model minority" status of postcolonial theorists and postcolonial theory, however, has insidious consequences, especially given that "faculty in higher education remains 90.4 percent white, a figure that has not changed since 1989."[27]

"Nonmodel" Model Minorities[28]

The Eurocentrism of postcolonial theory leads bell hooks and Ann DuCille to regard the postcolonial theorist as the middle person/passage between homegrown, unruly, and troubling *blackness* and more global, learned, and sober *whiteness*. As hooks puts it, "Third World nationals often assume the role of mediator or interpreter, explaining the 'bad' black people to their white colleagues or helping the 'naïve' black people to understand whiteness."[29] The privileging of postcolonial theory constitutes, for hooks, objectification and diffusion of opposition through a "benevolent hierarchy . . . where power-over becomes the occasion for the assertion of a generosity."[30] Ann DuCille writes that the "study of power relations between colonizer and colonized" is not new and argues against the displacement brought on by postcolonial theory: "once again foreigners have taken over *our* field" and the "interest of outsiders" serves to "legitimize a discourse," which did not have respect "when it was dominated by diasporic blacks."[31]

DuCille, furthermore, creates a binary: if Eurocentric postcoloniality is "discourse—an exotic foreign field whose time has come in the U.S. academy—Afrocentricity is 'dat course'—local color (homeboy and homegirls) whose time has come and gone, if indeed it ever was."[32] If the "critique from African American studies and the alternative worldview from Afrocentricity cut uncomfortably close to home," then "postcoloniality seems to pose its opposition from a distance."[33] If in its "insistence on a local place," African American studies "implicates" the United States, then "postcoloniality, for the most part, lets [it] off the imperialist hook."[34] Postcolonial theory, through "academic merchandising of *different* difference,"[35] can be used to "affirm the European or Anglo-American center."[36] Indeed, hooks reminds us that "many Third World nationals bring to this country the same kind of contempt and disrespect for blackness that is most frequently associated with white imperialism."[37]

The privileging of postcolonial theory because of its Eurocentrism feigns a global discourse that renders black women, as Carol Davies argues, "automatically interpellated in ideologies of posting or postponing."[38] In other words, "post-coloniality can only have meaning if we accept postmodernism as the only current legitimizing narrative."[39] Indeed, postmodernism refers to "post-European modernism" and not internal colonization in the United States or in the formerly colonized, ostensibly decolonizing nations, for example.[40] Similar to Barbara Christian, Davies contests this form of periodization, because Eurocentrism attributes "rather arrogantly, a certain alreadyness" such that "current formulations wanting to be identified as theoretically current have to construct themselves within the context of this alreadyness or afterness, or even done-by-Europeanness."[41] Although the moniker "postcolonial," like "poststructuralist" or "postmodernist," assumes the aura of political opposition by virtue of an axiological prefix, it renders the *difference* of African, Latin, and Native American scholarship political *plus*: the untheoretical raw material—experiential knowledge—to be transformed and sold as patented theory with major cultural value.[42]

African, Latin, and Native American scholarship, long-standing traditions predating the arrival of postcolonial theory, poststructuralism, and postmodernism in the U.S. academy, which were just gaining ground in the post–civil rights U.S. academy, are read as if they are particular *examples* of these broader forms of reading, writing, and theorizing. Or, they are considered to be relevant only when the *difference* of "race" or "ethnicity," for example, is to be examined. Such periodization, as Barbara Christian argues, leads to a false genealogy of African , Latin , and Native American scholarship, even as these traditions are still in the process of recuperating and revitalizing their (fractured) genealogies.[43] Hazel Carby asks, therefore, "at what point do theories of 'difference,' as they inform academic practices become totally compatible with—rather than a threat to—rigid frameworks of segregation and ghettoization at work throughout our society?"[44] For example, the 1996 anthology, *Contemporary Postcolonial Theory: A Reader*, includes Barbara Christian's 1987 essay "The Race for Theory" in its section entitled "Disciplining Knowledge" alongside Spivak, Anthony Appiah, and Arun Mukherjee. The editor, Padmini Mongia, "introduces" Christian by stating that in "a related, if albeit different, vein" she addresses the impact of hegemonic theorizing because it "silences black, feminist voices."[45] Christian, however, is the only African American feminist scholar included in this volume, whose "related, if albeit different" theorizing elicits no further comment as to not only its specific content but why it is placed in a volume on contemporary postcolonial theory.

In another example, Spivak deploys Toni Morrison's 1987 *Beloved* in her 1999 *A Critique of Postcolonial Reason* as the "figuring ('places') of an 'Africa'" that is, the "pre-history of Afro-America or New World African—to be strictly distinguished from the named contemporary continent—in the undeconstructible experience of the impossible."[46] She also dedicates her chapter on translation in *Outside in the Teaching Machine*

(1993) to Morrison as she analyzes the lack of contemporaneity attributed to the slave, the "roar" of the slave that does not "*make it across*" to the "master marks" that a slave must use to "put together a history."[47] Similarly, Homi Bhabha's discussion of *Beloved* in his 1994 *The Location of Culture* transcends the specificity of black female slavery to announce that the "'middle passage' of contemporary culture, *as with slavery itself*, is a process of displacement and disjunction that does not totalize experience."[48] Yet, even though Spivak vociferously criticizes the manner in which Indian American postcolonial theorists claim an analogical relation with the racial underclass as victims of U.S. racism, and this chapter follows her incisive, unwavering, and invaluable lead, her Eurocentric methodology prevents her from engaging even a *single* African American feminist scholar in her discussions of *Beloved*. Bhabha's Eurocentrism, because he is a scholar of Indian "origin" in the United Kingdom, for the purposes of my critique, is even more interesting. Bhabha's discussion of the African American experience of slavery, that is, the "American" experience of slavery through *Beloved*, like Spivak's, does not engage a *single* African American feminist text, even though he is discussing a text written by an African American woman. Instead, Bhabha uses Elizabeth Fox-Genovese's *Within the Plantation Household: Black and White Women of the Old South*.[49] A text written by a white woman becomes representative not only of U.S. feminist scholarship but also of scholarship on U.S. slavery and its impact on African American women. A Eurocentric methodology grants historical and epistemological priority to Anglo- and Euro-American U.S. feminist scholarship and canonical philosophy, of which African American feminist thought becomes a different subset.

The question, however, is why *Beloved* becomes the paradigmatic postcolonial/deconstructive text par excellence, the reading of which does not seem to require an encounter with African American feminist thought.[50] Why is *Beloved* shorthand for and indeed often interchangeable with U.S. blackness/femaleness in these texts? Why are Bhabha and Spivak able to read formidable figures such as Derrida, Hegel, Heidegger, Lacan, Freud, de Man, Kristeva, Levinas, and Irigaray, yet fail to include African American feminist thought? What, moreover, allows for the appropriateness of canonical philosophical paradigms and Anglo- and Euro-American feminist theory to understand slave experience without reference to not only *contemporaneous* African American feminist theory but also to a centuries-old tradition of African American feminist theory?[51] What form of colonial–postcolonial neocolonial symbiosis between the United States and the United Kingdom, reinforced and reified by neocolonial postcolonial U.S.-centric and U.K.-centric migrancy, allows canonical postcolonial scholarship's Eurocentric methodology to appropriate African American women's writing while excluding African American feminist scholarship? What kind of Anglocentrism and Eurocentrism is being further entrenched when Bhabha, a postcolonial migrant of Indian "origin" to the United Kingdom, is given greater critical currency to understand United States slavery than African American women? The very fact that postcolonial scholarship produced in the United Kingdom receives greater academic prestige than African American feminist thought by U.S. postcolonial scholars, even if it ignores African American feminist scholarship precisely when speaking about African American women, demonstrates a peculiar kind of nativism by U.S. postcolonial theorists because they privilege fellow neocolonial migrants. Anglocentrism and Eurocentrism not only serves status advancement and tenure but also furthers a form of academic nativism that renders Anglo- and Euro-American scholars the proper representatives of the U.S. academy.[52]

Who Speaks for Postcolonialism?

In this chapter, I began with Spivak's call that postcolonial theorists, in particular Indian Americans, recognize postcolonial migration for aspirational class advancement as neocolonial. Indian Americans, instead, as mentioned earlier, attempt to have it both ways: success as a "model minority" but oppression and marginalization analogous to (by implication) "nonmodel" minorities. By accepting and internalizing this history, postcolonial theory can discern and thereby disrupt the connections between U.S.-centric migration for class advancement and U.S. nationalism ("U.S. exceptionalism"), an assimilation-based continuum that Kurtz assumes.

The presumed continuity between U.S.-centric migration for class advancement and U.S. nationalism can be disrupted in three specific ways: First, academic postcolonialism can bridge the cleavage between an assumed and "inherent radicalism by virtue of category alone"[53] and the conservative nativism often demonstrated by those in its ranks as well as by the selectively self-represented Indian American community toward older migrants, indigenous communities, the poorest in its own ranks, and non-Hindu Indian Americans.[54] Postcoloniality is not eo ipso oppositional and progressive; postcoloniality also includes U.S.-centric migrancy for aspirational class advancement, itself made possible by neoimperialism. Numerous scholars, such as Chandra Mohanty and Inderpal Grewal, have addressed precisely this form of complicity with the racialized politics that constitute the "American Dream."

Thus, postcolonial theorists can examine not only how neoimperialism enables postcolonial migration for aspirational class advancement but also how this neoimperialistic postcolonial migration further entrenches internal colonialism in the United States. Postcolonial theory can question precisely the conditions of possibility for the "American" Dream, the colonial practices (internal and external), as Donald Pease argues, that not only borrowed from European orientalism,[55] but also constitute U.S. orientalism,[56] disavowed by a nationalism founded on the premise of exceptionalism: unlike Europe, the United States became a "dominant global power without colonies."[57] How does postcolonial U.S.-centric migration for class advancement reinforce U.S. exceptionalism and thus U.S. nationalism by disavowing precisely the neoimperialism ("foreign policy") made possible by U.S. colonialism that allows that migrancy to take place?

Second, by accepting and internalizing U.S.-centric migration for aspirational class advancement as one of the "founding" conditions of possibility for postcolonial theory in the U.S. academy, postcolonial theory can address the ethnically cleansed Anglocentrism and Eurocentrism of the U.S. academy, and thus its ethnically cleansed Americentrism, that allows for its co-option as a species of postmodernism[58] and poststructuralism and deconstruction,[59] as opposed to, for example, an examination of how poststructuralism and deconstruction may in fact be a species of Eurocentric European postcolonialism, or rather neocolonialism. Postcolonial theory could examine how by being co-opted as postmodernism it functions as a species of Eurocentric and U.S.-centric spectralization/dissimulation of postcolonial neocolonialism[60] if it keeps the economic "under erasure"[61] and neglects "transnational literacy."[62]

This form of postmodern postcolonial theory may also function as a doctrine of equivalence, and thereby further spectralization/dissimulation of postcolonial neocolonialism, because by describing "local" negotiations and resistances (the first world is rarely considered "local") it either prevents things from seeming as bad as they really are, and permits easy self-congratulation (see, we didn't destroy them completely and now they are hybrid global subjects!), or it simply represents what is a banal fact of human history, one that should in fact be a presupposition in any scholarly endeavor, that human beings have *always* resisted and negotiated. Postcolonial theory is complicit in this process of its own co-option as it often seeks, like U.S. poststructuralism and deconstruction, derivative academic prestige from European affiliation, as filiation for postcolonial theorists is not possible, or is disavowed, and for U.S. poststructuralists recedes further into generational distance.[63]

Postcolonial theorists, as argued earlier, can confront how postcolonial theory and the notion of postcolonialism co-opts and displaces, as Ann DuCille, bell hooks, and Carol Davies argue, indigenous and long-standing scholarly traditions, such as African, Latin, and Native American, which predate the arrival of postcolonial theory in the U.S. academy, and had barely gained much ground in the U.S. academy. If postcolonial theory began with Edward Said's 1978 *Orientalism*, then how, Aijaz Ahmad asks, has its consolidation, including that of postmodernism, poststructuralism, and deconstruction in the subsequent years, been heavily subsidized by the retrograde white supremacist tribalism of the Ronald Reagan and George H. W. Bush presidencies?[64]

Third, postcolonial theorists and Indian Americans can problematize how the "nation-state they still call culture"[65] becomes "a species of 'retrospective hallucination'" as it is manufactured not only as a "national identity" prepped for inclusion in the "ethnic composition of the population" but also as a product ready to be disseminated by a "well-prepared investigator" and "native informant"[66] in the academic marketplace or in the "cultural diversity" of the United States. Rather than assuming that by virtue of being a postcolonial production, this "national identity" is inherently progressive and oppositional, how does this "national identity," in its bid for inclusion, pit itself against other identities? How does this "national identity," created as part of what Hazel Carby terms the multicultural wars of U.S. identity politics, become representative of the Indian nation itself? What role do postcolonial theorists/Indian American immigrants play, as Spivak repeatedly asks, as the exceptional (by definition) native informants who are available in metropolitan space and thereby save the anthropologist his or her trip to the periphery?[67]

What culturalist accounts of postcolonial nation-space are being created, which often serve a self-consolidating function for postcolonial theorists and Indian American migrants who can not only present themselves as privy to that culture but also as those who managed to escape its preternatural qualities? Peripheral nation-space, now oversaturated with culture, allows the U.S.-centric migrant to not only reinforce U.S. nation-space as the possibility for objectivity (and as proper culture per se) but also posits postcolonial nation-space, as Spivak emphasizes, a space simply to be read and not as a space that produces knowledge, neither of itself, nor, more significantly, of the West.[68] Indeed, disavowing neocolonialism as the condition of possibility of U.S.-centric migration as well as for class advancement puts the economic "under erasure" and renders "transnational literacy" simply inclusion of one's "national identity" in U.S. multicultural identity politics. The very presence of postcolonial migrants, moreover, allows a dissimulation of postmodernity, that is, the passage from modern colonialism to postmodern neocolonialism, as if it has "a kind of built-in critical moment"; rather, postcolonial migrancy is a part of postmodern neoimperialism.[69]

The selectively self-represented Indian American community often readily, in the relay from imperialism to national/energy security, or empire to commercial interests, either puts its "knowledge of foreign languages and cultures at the service of American power"[70] or seeks inclusion on the basis of a "national identity" without transnational literacy, such that the postcolonial nation becomes synonymous with an excessive but overreached-via-migrancy culture; however, postcolonial knowledge production made possible by neoimperialistic U.S.-centric migrancy for aspirational class advancement cannot assume inherent oppositional and progressive politics, and therefore, in that sense, cannot even assume *postcoloniality*.

Conclusion

Obviously, it is not the case that postcolonial theory does not address U.S. neoimperialism ("foreign policy," "energy security," "commercial interests"); postcolonial scholarship, in particular transnational feminism, which also has a remarkable African, Latin, and Native American genealogy predating the fashionable academic coinage of the term "transnational," presents some of the most vociferous and astute criticisms of U.S. "foreign policy," as did, we know, Dr. Edward Said. Rather, postcolonial theorists who are part of the Indian American community have often not thought through the conditions of possibility for their own migrant history, including the consolidation of that migrant history and U.S.-centric identity politics as postcolonialism. In that sense, as Spivak states, the "world is squeezed into migrancy in the metropolis."[71]

Postcolonial theory, a "model minority" discourse practiced by a "model minority" community of scholars, assimilates by virtue of a neoimperialistic turn of the screw, that is, its *postcoloniality*, and thereby reinforces, through its denial of *neoimperialistic* postcolonial migrancy, on par with the selectively self-represented "model minority" Indian American community, the neoimperialism that is its constitutive condition of possibility. It creates the United States as simultaneously its point of origin, following Kurtz's testimony, and as its point of return even as it vacates precisely *this* place from postcoloniality. In terms of U.S. exceptionalism, "model minority" status not only denies the relay from colonialism to neocolonialism that is U.S. postcoloniality but also how the racialized mechanisms of class advancement reinforced and reified in U.S. society are replicated and further reinforced in the U.S. academy through the privileging of postcolonial theory and its scholars over and against African, Native, and Latin American scholarship and their scholars because of its Anglocentrism and Eurocentrism.

Postcolonial theory and postcolonial theorists, therefore, perpetuate a kind of "blackening" of "blacks," even as they assimilate indigenous oppositional knowledges that not only speak about internal colonialism but also refute a belief in U.S. exceptionalism. By refuting U.S. exceptionalism, these indigenous knowledges undermine U.S. nationalism and thereby face the charge of anti- or un-"American," just as the "model minority" status perpetuates a belief in African, Latin, and Native American populations as "nonmodel" minorities. As Ann DuCille notes, the elision of "cultural and geopolitical difference" allows institutions to hire postcolonial scholars to fulfill diversity requirements and who constitute a nonthreatening "'black' presence" unlike "Spivak's 'black blacks.'"[72] Both Afrocentricity and postcoloniality rely on an academic "skin trade" that propagates an "alterity" that is also simultaneously "intellectually denied."[73] Such an approach homogenizes the concept of race by rendering it synonymous with blackness. Thus, although race signifies "irreducible difference" it becomes in fact "a sign of reducible *sameness*."[74]

If postcolonial migrants do not examine their ventriloquist functions in neocolonialism, they render themselves synonymous with *postcoloniality* and come to *stand in* for decolonization as such.[75] Spivak, therefore, asks why postcolonial theorists attempt to obfuscate the fact that they are also "agents of domination" by defining themselves as "victims of First World knowledge factories."[76] She goes further, however, and emphasizes that postcolonial theorists must acknowledge that they are Americans and migrated "to be Americans," which does not necessarily mean "to be an 'Anglo-clone.'"[77] As opposed to assimilation, postcolonial migrants should regard themselves as "American, hyphenated." Indeed, "American *is* hyphenated."[78]

Spivak argues against the spectral identitarian collectivities that allegorize capitalism, because the postcolonial migrant, standing in for and speaking as the ostensibly postcolonial nation, constructs an identity dependent on the vicissitudes of U.S. postcoloniality. This identity also fails to disrupt the particular logics deployed by "indigenous elite nationalists, by way of the culture of imperialism"[79] because it is bound, just like the imperial-nationalist dialectic, by the dynamics of neoimperialism qua aspirational class advancement. Indeed, in neoimperial postcolonial migrancy, *Indian* nationalism seems to be successful class advancement in the United States, mirrored by the consumptive and much-publicized upper and middle classes at home.

Thus, when Spivak states that Indian migrants should regard themselves as "Americans," she speaks precisely to the reinforcement and reification of "American" as neoimperialistic class advancement. This "position of *agency*" would allow the recognition, "for example, that Article 301 and Super 301 in the General Agreement on Tariffs and Trade thwarts social redistribution in our countries of origin" and the debates surrounding "intellectual capital" would reveal that aspirational class advancement in the United States requires the "manipulation of our countries of origin."[80] By refusing to speak simply about themselves, or refusing to speak *as* themselves, and thereby refusing to claim the whole agency of capitalism only for themselves, postcolonial migrants could become "more conventionally political,"[81] perhaps political *plus*.

Stanley Kurtz's native informancy, as he tells tall tales about a prodigal academic postcolonialism, betrays precisely this desire, that postcolonial migrants refuse agency in/by neocolonialism and become, instead, the repositories of instrumental information about their "areas": the native informant is now conveniently located in the United States but does not create or write back "home" with knowledge and information about the United States, or that knowledge about the United States is not produced elsewhere and by others.[82] Spivak's critique of postcolonial reason is a refusal of ventriloquism based on postcolonial theory's and the Indian American migrants' class-based interests. She recognizes, however, that much work remains to be done in terms of its race-based interests in racialized politics of nationalist U.S. exceptionalism.

Postcolonial reason finds itself in relation, therefore, to internal colonization. For example, "African American society in the United States is an example of the gains and vicissitudes of postcoloniality."[83] Any perceived solidarity between postcolonial migrants and African Americans must prioritize "investigation of the institution of the so-called origins of the white-supremacist United States"[84] and "negotiated independence" for African Americans.[85] In addition, postcolonial theory must examine the "incredible and slow increase in racist rage and backlash" and the "failures in decolonization" critiqued by African American scholars and activists.[86] I argue that Spivak does not appropriate African American experience and scholarship to further bolster postcolonial theory's ostensible ability to speak for marginality and oppression on a global scale. Instead, African American postcoloniality speaks precisely of U.S. postcoloniality and, in so doing, reminds us, as does Spivak, "American *is* hyphenated." Thus, when Spivak emphasizes that postcolonial migrants must consider themselves "US colonialists, rather than post-colonials in the United States,"[87] a position that also opposes the moniker "model minority," she is asking for a postcolonialism worthy of its proper name.

Notes

This chapter is dedicated to the young African American woman at Chicago's Midway Airport who, when stopped by me for cutting the line to board our flight, responded by asking if I had a box cutter and if she and the other passengers should watch their backs. In the gains and vicissitudes of postcoloniality, we travel together.

1. "Although 9/11 brought broad public and political attention to global integration and national security needs, the Federal government has long recognized this need. . . . Title VI and Fulbright-Hays programs form the vital infrastructure of the . . . international service pipeline. . . . [In] 1958 . . . Title VI was introduced as a part of the National Defense Education Act (NDEA) . . . [as] the 'Language Development' section . . . National

Resource Centers (NRCs), Foreign Language and Area Studies Fellowships (FLAS), and International Research and Studies (IRS) remain central programs in the Title VI array, evolving and expanding their foci in reaction to and in anticipation of global trends and security needs" ("Title VI Programs: Building a U.S. International Education Infrastructure," Department of Education, available at http://www.ed.gov/about/offices/list/ope/iegps/title-six.html).

2. The NSEP serves "U.S. national security and national competitiveness" through "language learning and international education" initiatives with "progressively minded partners throughout the U.S. education community" (http://wwwndu.edu/nsep).

3. Sources on Title VI, H.R. 509 (formerly H.R. 3077) can be found at http://programs.ssrc.org/mena/MES_Opinions/ (Social Science Research Council) and at http://www.mesa.arizona.edu/aff/af_other_readings.htm (Middle East Studies Association).

4. Arif Dirlik, "The Postcolonial Aura: Third World Criticism in the Age of Global Capitalism," *Critical Inquiry* 20 (Winter 1994): 329.

5. I focus on the Indian American community because I belong to this community. I have lived in the United States since 1990—first as a student and then as an H-1B "high-skilled" employment visa holder. My application for permanent residency is pending at the time of this writing.

6. President Lyndon B. Johnson signed into law the Immigration and Nationality Act amendments (1965) that undid national-origin quotas in place since 1924 which favored Western European immigrants. India witnessed a massive "brain drain" of highly educated and technologically trained citizenry who became racialized as "model minorities." See "Lyndon B. Johnson: Special Message to the Congress on Immigration," available at http://www.presidency.ucsb.edu/ws/index.php?pid=26830; Jennifer Ludden's, "1965 Immigration Law Changed the Face of America," May 9, 2006, available at http://www.npr.org/templates/story/story.php?storyId=5391395; Jasbir K. Puar and Amit S. Rai's, "The Remaking of a Model Minority: Perverse Projectiles Under the Threat of (Counter) Terrorism" in *Social Text* 80, 22, no. 3 (Fall 2004): 75–104.

7. Gayatri Spivak, *A Critique of Postcolonial Reason: Toward a History of the Vanishing Present* (Cambridge, MA: Harvard University Press, 1999), 360–361.

8. According to Spivak, "metropolitan multiculturalism" often "pre-comprehends U.S. manifest destiny as transformed asylum for the rest of the world." See her "Foreword: Upon Reading the *Companion to Postcolonial Studies*," in *A Companion to Postcolonial Studies*, ed. Henry Schwarz and Sangeeta Ray (Malden, MA: Blackwell, 2000), xvi. The "new-immigration-in-capitalism" and assimilation "followed the pattern of Anglocentrism first, and a graduated *Euro*centrism next." See Spivak,

"Teaching for the Times," *Journal of the Midwest Modern Language Association* 25, no. 1 (Spring 1992): 5, 10. Postcolonial discourse emerged "haphazardly" as a "response to a felt need among minority groups." Its "focus" and "grounding pre-suppositions" are "metropolitan," and its "language skills are rudimentary, though full of subcultural affect." See Spivak, "The New Subaltern: A Silent Interview," in *Mapping Subaltern Studies and the Postcolonial*, ed. Vinayak Chaturvedi (London: Verso, 2000), 331.

9. Indian Americans are often obliged to represent an easily digestible "India": simultaneously glorious ("ancient culture") and spectacularly abject ("widow-burning"). Fredric Jameson, for example, reduces "third world" literature to national allegory in "Third World Literature in the Era of Multinational Capitalism," *Social Text* 15 (1986): 65–88. Deepika Bahri argues against using postcolonial literature for information retrieval in *Native Intelligence: Aesthetics, Politics, and Postcolonial Literature* (Minneapolis: University of Minnesota Press, 2003).

10. See Spivak, *A Critique of Postcolonial Reason*, ix; see also Spivak, "How to Teach a Culturally Different Book," *The Spivak Reader: Selected Works of Gayatri Chakravorty Spivak*, ed. Donna Landry and Gerald Maclean (New York: Routledge, 1996), 239.

11. See, for example, Kwame Anthony Appiah, "Is the Post- in Postmodernism the Post- in Postcolonial?," *Critical Inquiry* 17 (Winter 1991): 336–357; Douglas Barbour, "Postcolonial Theorizing Achieves Academic Acceptance," *Mosaic: A Journal for the Interdisciplinary Study of Literature* 29, no. 3 (1996): 129–139; Anne McClintock, "The Angel of Progress: Pitfalls of the Term 'Post-Colonialism'," *Social Text* 10, no. 31–32 (1992): 84–98; Benita Parry, "The Postcolonial: Conceptual Category or Chimera?," *Yearbook of English Studies* 27 (1997): 3–21; Gyan Prakash, "Who's Afraid of Postcoloniality?" *Social Text* 14, no. 4 (1996): 187–203.

12. See Amrijit Singh's "African Americans and the New Immigrants," in *Between the Lines: South Asians and Postcoloniality*, ed. Deepika Bahri and Mary Vasudeva (Philadelphia: Temple University Press, 1996), 93–110, for an analysis of pre-1965 migration and for postcolonial theory's relation to multiculturalism and civil rights.

13. On June 26, 2006, the cover of *Time* magazine featured a bejeweled South Indian female dancer's face with headset and microphone. The logo "India Inc.," awash in saffron and white, two colors of the Indian flag (the third, green, noticeably missing), celebrates democracy/the nation/postcoloniality as consumptive modernity ("economic superpower" is in the color of Hindu communalism, saffron) and gendering is its vehicle. Yet, "81% of [India's] population lives on $2 a day or less" (Alex Perry, "Bombay's Boom," 40). The article does not mention land, water, and electricity agreements made by transnational corporations with

the Indian government or remuneration rates of the Indian staff at outsouced locations, such as call centers.

14. See Arundhati Roy, "On India's Growing Violence: 'It's Outright War and Both Sides are Choosing Their Weapons,'" *Tehelka*, March 25, 2007. Available at http://www.tehelka.com/story_main28.asp?filename=Ne310307Its_outright_CS.asp.

15. Globalization has replaced "exceptionalism" as the alibi for U.S. imperialism. See Donald Pease, "US Imperialism: Global Dominance without Colonies," in *A Companion to Postcolonial Studies*, ed. Henry Schwarz and Sangeeta Ray (Malden, MA: Blackwell, 2000), 219.

16. Spivak, "Teaching for the Times," 3.

17. The Anglo American corporation (unhyphenated) is a symbol of colonial-postcolonial symbiosis. Margaret Thatcher and Ronald Reagan welcomed profits obtained from apartheid. See Pauline Baker, *The United States and South Africa: The Reagan Years* (New York: Ford Foundation, 1989); Linda Freeman, "All But One: Britain, the Commonwealth and Sanctions," in *Sanctions Against South Africa*, ed. Mark Orkin (Cape Town, South Africa: David Philip, 1989), 142–156. CNN's Web site ranks Anglo American 196th in the Fortune 500 for 2006.

18. The title of D'Souza's book, *The Enemy At Home: The Cultural Left and Its Responsibility for 9/11* (New York: Doubleday, 2007), speaks for itself.

19. Donald Pease, "US Imperialism," 208.

20. Ibid., 209. Historians' separate slavery, "overseas colonialism," and "exploitation of refugees" from the "*realpolitik* of the international arena." Immigration laws institutionalize colonial stereotypes and foreign policy openly violates "democratic ideals." Asian, Hispanic, and Native American struggles demonstrate the relationship between the "domestic" and the "foreign" disavowed by U.S. exceptionalism (205–206).

21. Ibid., 208.

22. Ibid., 203.

23. Gayatri Spivak, "Transnationality and Multiculturalist Ideology: An Interview with Gayatri Spivak," in *Between the Lines: South Asians and Postcoloniality*, ed. Deepika Bahri and Mary Vasudeva (Philadelphia: Temple University Press, 1996), 71.

24. Bahri, *Native Intelligence*, 38.

25. Ann DuCille, *Skin Trade* (Cambridge, MA: Harvard University Press, 1996), 126.

26. Jenny Sharpe, "Postcolonial Studies in the House of US Multiculturalism," in *A Companion to Postcolonial Studies*, ed. Henry Schwarz and Sangeeta Ray (Malden, MA: Blackwell, 2000), 116.

27. Naomi Zack, *Inclusive Feminism: A Third Wave Theory of Women's Commonality* (Lanham, MD: Rowman and Littlefield, 2005), 3.

28. Portions of this section and the conclusion have been published in Namita Goswami, "The Second Sex: Philosophy, Feminism, Postcolonialism, and the Race for Theory," *Angelaki: Journal of Theoretical Humanities*, 13, no. 2 (August 2008): 73–91.

29. bell hooks, *Yearning: Race, Gender, and Cultural Politics* (Cambridge, MA: South End Press, 1990), 94.

30. Ibid., 95.

31. DuCille, *Skin Trade*, 124–125.

32. Ibid., 123.

33. Ibid., 127.

34. Ibid., 134.

35. Ibid., 123.

36. Ibid., 134.

37. hooks, *Yearning*, 93.

38. Carol Davies, *Black Women, Writing, and Identity: Migrations of the Subject* (London: Routledge, 1994), 83.

39. Ibid., 86.

40. Ibid.

41. Ibid., 83.

42. According to Hortense J. Spillers, names for African American women, such as "Brown Sugar" and "Sapphire," are examples of "signifying property *plus*" (384). See her "Mama's Baby, Papa's Maybe: An American Grammar Book," in *Feminisms: An Anthology of Literary Theory and Criticism*, edited by Robyn R. Warhol and Diane Price Herndl (Brunswick, NJ: Rutgers University Press, 1991), 384–405. I term this visibility/invisibility political *plus*: being excessively political, that is, prepolitical ("ground zero"), yet not really figuring ("invisibility").

43. Barbara Christian, "The Race for Theory," *Cultural Critique* 6: 51–63, esp. 55 and 57. See also Patricia Hill Collins, *Black Feminist Thought: Knowledge, Consciousness, and the Politics of Empowerment* (New York: Routledge, 1990).

44. Hazel Carby, "The Multicultural Wars," *Radical History Review* 54 (1992): 12.

45. Padmini Mongia, ed., *Contemporary Postcolonial Theory: A Reader* (New York: Oxford University Press, 1996), 9.

46. Spivak, *A Critique of Postcolonial Reason*, 430.

47. Gayatri Spivak, *Outside in the Teaching Machine* (New York: Routledge, 1993), 200; emphasis added.

48. Homi Bhabha, *The Location of Culture* (New York: Routledge, 1994), 5; emphasis added.

49. Elizabeth Fox-Genovese, *Within the Plantation Household: Black and White Women of the Old South* (Chapel Hill: University of North Carolina Press, 1988).

50. Fictional texts and "fantasized black female and male subjects" substitute for "sustained social or political relationships with black people" (Carby, "Multicultural Wars," 12). Pedagogy focuses on the "complexity of response in the (white) reader" and not on "relations of power and domination" (12) or the "political activity of desegregation (16)."

51. See Beverly Guy-Sheftall, *Words of Fire: An Anthology of African-American Feminist Thought* (New York: New Press, 1995).

52. See Ann DuCille's "The Occult of True Black Womanhood: Critical Demeanor and Black Feminist Studies," *SIGNS: Journal of Women in Culture, and Society* (Spring 1994): 591–629.

53. Bahri, *Native Intelligence*, 7.

54. Dr. Akshay Desai of the Indian American Republican Council regards Indians as "natural allies" of the Republican Party due to "traditional" family values, education, and faith. Sunil Adam, "Indian Republicans in Florida Wield Their Clout in National Politics," November 8, 2004, *India West*, available at http://www.indiawest.com. Hillary Clinton's campaign received contributions from four thousand Indian Institute of Technology alumni. Indeed, "Indian Americans have the highest income, on average, of any racial or national origin group." The median household income in 2005 was $73,575, "59% above the national average." These "wealthy kids" model the American Jewish Committee due to their common "concern" with "Islamic fundamentalism and terrorism." George W. Bush hired more Indian Americans than any other president. See Josh Gerstein, "Clinton Taps Newly Active Indian Donors," *New York Sun*, June 12, 2007, available at http://www.nysun.com/article/56332. Muslims and the poor are absent in the Indian and U.S. (inter)nationalist imaginary.

55. Pease, "US Imperialism," 215.

56. See Ella Shohat, "American Orientalism," *Suitcase: A Journal of Transcultural Traffic* 2 (1997): 56–62.

57. Pease, "US Imperialism," 218.

58. See Rey Chow, "Postmodern Automatons," in *Writing Diaspora: Tactics of Intervention in Contemporary Cultural Studies (Art and Politics of the Everyday)* (Bloomington: Indiana University Press, 1993), 55–72. For Spivak, if "colonialism was modernization/ism," then "postcolonialism is resistance to postmodernism; *or*, the 'true' postmodernism; now, only the postmodern postcolonialist is the triumphant self-declared hybrid" (*A Critique of Postcolonial Reason*, 361).

59. In decolonized space, for Spivak, "urgent" political claims of nationhood, citizenship, democracy, socialism, and secularism are "regulative political concepts the authoritative narrative of whose production was written elsewhere, in the metropolis" (*Outside in the Teaching Machine*, 213). If a "concept-metaphor without an adequate referent is a catachresis,"

then "claims to catachreses as foundations also make postcoloniality a deconstructive case" (281). Zillah Eisenstein's *Against Empire Feminisms, Racism, and the West* (New York: Zed Books, 2004) criticizes the assumed European/Western provenance of these regulative political concepts.

60. For Spivak, conflating Eurocentric migrancy with postcolonialism neglects the failure of decolonization: "Who decolonizes?" See Mahasweta Devi, *Imaginary Maps*, trans. Gayatri Spivak (Calcutta: Thema, 2001), appendix (by Spivak), 207. This conflation furthers the "spectralization of the rural" through its "conversion . . . into a database for pharmaceutical dumping, chemical fertilizers, patenting of indigenous knowledge, big dam building." The "material wretchedness of [rural] normality" is not analyzed as the "remote depredations of capitalist exploitation without capitalist social productivity." See Gayatri Spivak, *Death of a Discipline* (New York: Columbia University Press, 2003), 92–93.

61. Spivak, *A Critique of Postcolonial Reason*, 266.

62. Transnational literacy is "a sense of the political, economic, *and* cultural position of the various national origin places in the financialization of the globe." See Gayatri Spivak, "Subaltern Talk: Interview with the Editors," *The Spivak Reader: Selected Works of Gayatri Chakravorty Spivak*, ed. Donna Landry and Gerald Maclean (New York: Routledge, 1996), 295.

63. According to Crystal Bartolovich, U.S. postcolonial studies would not exist without decolonization and diaspora; "ditto for identity politics and poststructuralism." See her "Global Capital and Transnationalism," in *A Companion to Postcolonial Studies*, ed. Henry Schwarz and Sangeeta Ray (Malden, MA: Blackwell, 2000), 130. Spivak's translation of Derrida's *Of Grammatology* (Baltimore: Johns Hopkins University Press, 1976) binds the postcolonial migrant and deconstruction irrevocably in the U.S. academy.

64. Aijaz Ahmad, *In Theory: Nations, Classes, Literatures* (New York: Verso, 1994), 5. Mark Sanders discusses *Of Grammatology* as a postcolonial text in his "Theory in Translation," *Gayatri Chakravorty Spivak: Live Theory* (New York: Continuum, 2006), 30–53.

65. Spivak, *A Critique of Postcolonial Reason*, 357.

66. Ibid., 360–361.

67. See Spivak, A *Critique of Postcolonial Reason*, xii; see also Spivak's translator's preface in Devi, *Imaginary Maps*, xvii–xviii.

68. Judy Burns and Jill Mac Dougall, with Catherine Benamou, Avanthi Meduri, Peggy Phelan, and Susan Slymovics, "An Interview with Gayatri Spivak," *Women and Performance: A Journal of Feminist Theory* 5, no. 1 [9] (1990): 82.

69. Spivak, *A Critique of Postcolonial Reason*, 361.

70. Kurtz, 2003, from www.campuswatch.org. For example, the nonprofit Immigration Voice states that the unreformed employment based

immigration system would create "a *reverse brain drain*" and "exacerbate the effects of *overseas outsourcing* on economy [*sic*]." "High-skilled legal immigrants" enable "American technological superiority." Quotations are available at http://immigrationvoice.org. According to Jay Pradhan, a computer programmer, reform should benefit those "who have worked so hard and followed all Laws." see "Despite Claims, Immigration Reform Bill Does Not Help High Skilled Legal Immigrants," May 29, 2007, availableat http://www.prlog.org/10018492-immigration-reform-punishes-legal-high-skilled-immigrants-says-immigration-voice.html. See also Jonathan Stein, "Immigration Bill Point System: More Indian Engineers, Fewer Hispanic Families," Mother Jones, June 5, 2007, available at http://www.motherjones.com/mojoblog/archives/2007/06/4578_immigration_bil_1.html.

71. See Tani E. Barlow, "Not a Properly Intellectual Response: An Interview with Gayatri Spivak," *positions* 12, no. 1 (2004): 139–163, 157.

72. DuCille, *Skin Trade*, 129.

73. Ibid.

74. Ibid.

75. Spivak, *A Critique of Postcolonial Reason*, 18, 33.

76. Spivak, *Between the Lines*, 75; emphasis in original.

77. Ibid., 84

78. Ibid.

79. Spivak, *A Critique of Postcolonial Reason*, 60.

80. Spivak, "Subaltern Talk," 295.

81. Spivak, "The New Subaltern," 331.

82. Kurtz's degree is in social anthropology and he cites anthropologist Jane Guyer. See Edward Said's "Representing the Colonized: Anthropology's Interlocutors," *Critical Inquiry* 15 (Winter 1989): 205–225.

83. Spivak, "Subaltern Talk," 294.

84. Spivak, "Teaching for the Times," 12.

85. Spivak, *Between the Lines*, 71.

86. Ibid.

87. Gayatri Spivak, "Culture Alive," *Australian Feminist Law Journal*, 5 (August 1995): 11.

9

Theorizing the Aesthetic Homeland

Racialized Aesthetic Nationalism in Daily Life and the Art World

Monique Roelofs

THE EXPERIENCE OF race and of nation pervasively engages the aesthetic. Aesthetic modes of signification are fundamental participants in the structures of inclusion and exclusion that assist in the organization of the art world and the sustenance of a sense of the quotidian. Subjects of aesthetic desire, we play out our attachments and disassociations on aesthetic territory. Aesthetic habits help delineate formations of difference and identity. Disciplines of race and nation must therefore be understood in their aesthetic functioning. Structures of collectivity—the institutionalized bonds and distances that connect humans to one another and keep them apart—owe their iterability, coherence, discontinuities, and liability to change, in part, to the workings of the aesthetic, which itself amounts to a collective phenomenon, putting into play registers of the local, the regional, the national, and the transnational. Accordingly, in order to comprehend the workings of race and nation it is necessary to clarify the workings of aesthetic relationality—that is, the web of aesthetically mediated and mediating relationships we entertain with one another and the material world.[1] Among the densely imbricated constellations of aesthetic relationality are the operations of what I call "racialized aesthetic nationalism." By this I mean the modes of address and embodiment that enlist aesthetic forms, meanings, and experiences in the service of racialized, nationalist conceptions and attitudes.[2] This chapter investigates the interpretive elisions and appropriations, the modes of owning and disowning that help shape racialized aesthetic nationalism.

Racialized aesthetic nationalism arises in the history of aesthetic theory, and reappears as a strategy of cultural homogenization in the post–9/11 U.S. social landscape. As instances of this at the level of quotidian existence, I consider rhetorical means of cultural surveillance in the aftermath of 9/11, government injunctions to go shopping, and newspaper vignettes commemorating individual victims of the attacks.[3] These forms protect an ethnocentric, homogeneous notion of what I call the "aesthetic homeland." At the level of the art world, I examine art critics Rosalind Krauss's and Arthur Danto's remarks on the work of Colombian artist Fernando Botero, and especially Danto's review of the series of paintings and drawings with which Botero responded, from 2004 to 2006, to the news reports and photographs exposing the torture of Iraqi prisoners by U.S. military forces in Abu Ghraib.[4] Danto's conceptual framework imports racialized, aesthetically nationalist elements into his interpretation of Botero's art, eliding Botero's critical body policies and shielding against the visual critique that this work levies at the system of justice and punishment instituted by the United States in Iraq and at the operative regimes of spectacularized terrorization. Danto's flattened reading creates a sanitized sense of artistic and aesthetic culture that guards a racist and nationalist construal of the aesthetic homeland. Philosophy faces the need to free aesthetic epistemologies from tendencies toward racialized aesthetic nationalism, not only at the level of the quotidian or the artistic but also in the highly condensed places where these registers meet.

Culture as Property: Racialized Aesthetic Nationalism in Everyday Life

Racialized aesthetic nationalism has deep roots in the history of aesthetic theory and criticism. It concerns a privileging of the culture that is ascribed to a given nation or ethnic group over cultures that are attributed to other nations or ethnic groups. An example is the disposition to seek out preferred qualities such as purity, order, or formal novelty in artworks by white Europeans and Anglo-Americans, coupled with the tendency to read for devalued or ambivalently valorized features such as embodied rhythms, sexualized passions, and fantastic contents in the works of black diasporic, Latin American, and latino/a artists.

Historically, racialized aesthetic nationalism yields judgments as to what kind of art, artistic activities, and artists ought to be included in or excluded from a given national culture. A prominent advocate of an explicitly racialized form of aesthetic nationalism is David Hume, who tied the phenomenon of taste closely to the social, economic, and political well-being of the nation-state. Hume enlisted aesthetic elements in support of racialized, nationalist stances by configuring both taste and nation in explicitly ethnocentric terms through cross-cultural comparisons (for instance, between Britain's and France's level of civilization and that of other countries) and by contrasting genuine taste with a range of inferior ones (those of Indians, women, and blacks). Hume's racialized, aesthetically nationalist position is quite common. Shaftesbury preceded him in this regard. Kant's *Observations* followed suit.[5] The phenomenon, moreover, continues to constitute an influential register of everyday aesthetic experience to this date.

Explicit judgment, however, represents only the surface of the phenomenon. At issue are schemes of interpretation, experience, and address that underlie our everyday aesthetic lives. Racialized aesthetic nationalism is a matter of embodied, relational existence. It resides in our orientations toward others and the material world, and in the ways we read and experience human beings, actions, things, artifacts (and expect to be read and experienced ourselves) against cultural horizons informed by entwined racial, aesthetic, and national forms, norms, and hierarchies. These horizons need not typically be consciously endorsed but produce their systemic effects as constituents of the modalities of signification and sociality we inhabit. While racialized, aesthetically nationalist modes of address and embodiment rely on habitual and unconscious interpretive and experiential molds,[6] they also deploy aesthetic modalities that reside in vigilant discipline, consuming passions, carefully distilled choices, deliberately experimental manipulations of materials and forms, meticulously formulated judgments, cherished imaginaries, sharply regimented consumptive palates, aggressively reiterated icons, and attractions toward ever-changing flows of images, sounds, and tastes. The structures of address that harbor these modes make up uneven textures of signification connecting (and disconnecting) subjects, objects, environments, and aesthetic epochs and traditions. Interlaced racial, national, and aesthetic formations resist analysis in terms of habitual dispositions because of their material heterogeneity, the ongoing labor of their design and upkeep, their mobilization of mutant, accidental forms of collectivity, and the vitality they extort from frictions and confluences with market structures and daily politics. This multiplicity can congeal into horizons that condition experience. However, as an aesthetic stance, racialized nationalism must also be read in the fragmentary yet systemic inscriptions of culture that not only give this position its contours but that it attempts to organize and control.

At the level of everyday existence, a racialized, nationalist aesthetic tends to engage proprietary registers of experience. Filtering the objects of aesthetic perception through the intersecting categories of race, class, gender, ethnicity, nationality, and sexuality that underwrite the meanings that social identities hold for us, our aesthetic experiences often encode these objects as belonging to "us" or "them," indexing them through perceptions of suitability and meaningfulness (or a lack thereof) to cultural groups. As shaped through the mediation of identity categories, the aesthetic lifeworld partially derives its organization and substance from suppositions about the capacities and entitlements that we take to normatively mark specific, culturally situated individuals and populations. Such conceptions, which introduce interlocking aesthetic, racial, and national norms into our aesthetic interactions, are implicit in our ordinary, embodied understandings of social identities and differences.

Proprietary registers of experience make up a fundamental part of daily aesthetic existence. We find various degrees of sustenance in the experience of being at home in *our* streets, city blocks, collectives, institutions, countries, and cultures. Ambivalent as our feelings about home may be, they are rarely indifferent. For many, the idea of home represents states of trust and belonging, even if it also connotes reliable rhythms of pain, sadness, and, perhaps, agony. The experience and aesthetic imagination of what is sensed as "home" significantly feed our interactions with others, both internal and external to the boundaries of that home, and are also produced by way of such interactions. Racialized aesthetic nationalism is a dimension of, among other things, the feeling that one is among one's own people, in a territory one can legitimately call one's own. This sense is coupled with the differentially compelling idea, not ordinarily conscious, that being present in one's own culture constitutes something desirable, a good one is entitled to and may part with only at inevitable cost—psychic, epistemic, or aesthetic.

Racialized aesthetic nationalism represents powerful currents of aesthetic desire and passion at the heart of individuals' daily aesthetic lifeworlds. As noted earlier, this form of nationalism has a firm grounding in the history of aesthetics. Hume and Kant explicitly associate the possession of good taste with class-inflected, racialized, and gendered forms of participation in a civilized national culture. They profoundly interweave taste with the construction of nation. The connections between taste and nation, in their accounts, run both ways, to mutually enhancing effects. The aesthetic is enlisted in a nation-building project of racialization and class and gender formation. At the same time, processes of racialization and class and gender formation advance a nation-building project of aestheticization. Taste and racialized nationhood reinforce one another.

A consideration of racialized aesthetic nationalism at the level of ordinary existence alerts us to its hitherto unrecognized symptoms in the history of aesthetics, a history that must be read for its condensation of logics of race and nation. A case in point is Joseph Addison's association of the aesthetic with a kind of "property" found in what is seen:

"[Aesthetic contemplation] gives [the Man of a Polite Imagination] . . . a kind of Property in every thing he sees, and makes the most rude uncultivated Parts of Nature administer to his Pleasures."[7] Addison's analogy imports a conception of social, economic, and political relationships into the notion of aesthetic contemplation. If seeing is in some sense analogous to the claiming of property, then this experience would seem to be deserving of protection, and, more generally, to constitute a basis for rights and entitlements. The idea that aesthetic contemplation distills pleasure from "rude uncultivated Parts of Nature" understands aesthetic attention as a form of disciplinary control over its object. If vision implies a form of reciprocity, owing to the spectator's embodied, spatial presence among objects of perception, as Maurice Merleau-Ponty argued, then Addison's notion of proprietary seeing locates visual agency primarily in the originator of the gaze and, to a lesser extent, in the perceived environment. In receiving and administering over what arrives at him in a mode of contemplation, Addison's spectator occupies a position of integrity within the visual field, a centered location, from which he is able to regulate the environmental impulses that reach him. This positioning of the spectator has significant consequences for constructions of everyday aesthetic and artistic embodiment, on which aesthetic traditions, both mainstream and avant garde, have capitalized uncritically.[8] The spectator's supposed measure of control renders unlikely the possibility that he would be enveloped in an unruly corporeal world, lose his bearings under a barrage of visual influx, or initiate a gently improvised exchange between his own bodily movements and shifting perceptual contents or the motions of other people's bodies. Underscoring the analogy of property, Addison emphasizes individualized perceptual agency over a more diffuse, collaboratively achieved, interactive communal sharing of what is seen.

The economic analogy inscribes a disciplinary regimen into the act of aesthetic contemplation, alongside the social hierarchies that enable and ensue from individual property ownership. Addison's picture of the spectator juxtaposes politeness (refinement) with the realm of rude and uncultivated otherness, marking aesthetic contemplation by rigorous class, gender, racial, and colonial connotations. As he finds ownership in what is seen, the spectator selectively abjects what stands in the way of pleasure, disowning the rude and the uncivilized. The achievement of pleasure in seeing thus emphatically demands also a nonseeing, a distancing of those parts of the seen that inhibit the pleasure. Such abjection, for Addison, is the correlative of pleasurable visual sensations.

When viewed through contemporary theoretical lenses, the notion of a kind of property the spectator expropriates from *everything* he sees articulates a proprietary conception of visual culture, and, given the omnipresence of technologies of the image today, of culture and embodied agency generally. This expansive notion of aesthetic ownership requires correspondingly far-reaching procedures of disowning.

The concept of a proprietary aesthetic forces the long-standing theoretical controversy on disinterestedness to address configurations of racial and national identity. Adopting the terminology of disinterestedness, we can posit that racialized aesthetic nationalism attaches a form of interest to a (supposedly) disinterested form of contemplation, namely, the good that accrues to the sense of being at home in one's cultural environment. This aesthetic stance introduces a set of *racialized and racializing* effects to the interests it guards, that is, to the interests it finds in allegedly disinterested attention. Attention to sensory elements for their own sake (as demanded by ideals of disinterestedness[9]) can effectively *be curtailed, made possible, organized, and motivated* by an overarching (even if in some respects distanced) *proprietary intent*, namely, the desire to inhabit an environment that is experienced as "ours," and differentiated from spaces marked as racially and ethnically other, which are disowned. This proprietary consciousness and its attendant procedures of abjection are then able to lend structure and give meaning to the sensory world experienced by culturally situated subjects. As a form of comportment and address directed at self, others, and the material environment, a racialized nationalist aesthetic constitutes a rich resource of proprietary experiences of culture. An embodied orientation that takes place across the senses and is discursively mediated, this form of nationalism allows culture to be experienced and produced as property by enlisting the aesthetic in the service of racially and ethnically coded affective, political, and socioeconomic needs and desires. Where these interests are felt to be tampered with, the feeling of proprietariness and the sense of being at home are in danger of slipping away. An everyday racialized, nationalist construal of the aesthetic, accordingly, safeguards such interests. In this capacity, it endows ordinary aesthetic life with a crucial set of differentially available rewards.

In the years following 9/11, influential U.S. institutions embarked on a revitalization of proprietary cultural passions. Intensified strategies of cultural surveillance conjoined with a renewed emphasis on a sharply circumscribed register of cultural and aesthetic citizenship known as "patriotism," which was cashed out, among other things, in terms of appropriate levels of consumption, and policed, in part, by way of the USA PATRIOT Act, which allowed for the monitoring of, for example, library loans. We can recognize in this cultural construal of citizenship a rearticulation of what may be called the "*aesthetic* homeland," that is, the culture we are imagined to own and foster through suitable aesthetic behaviors such as appropriate reading habits and other consumption patterns (or that, correlatively, we threaten to undermine through inappropriate aesthetic conduct, such as, say, wearing an antiwar T-shirt while shopping at a mall[10]). Disciplinary measures restricting civil rights attempted to mobilize everyday aesthetic energies in support of a culture that was understood in a racialized, nationalist proprietary sense.

Racialized, aesthetically nationalist strategies of culture formation stand in relations of mutual indebtedness to rhetorical figures. "A terrorist attack on American soil," for example, deploys a metaphor that sustains a proprietary conception of national culture.[11] The term "American soil" with its sensory, earthy, material overtones is suggestive of U.S. cultural ownership of the land; it contrasts an imagined American-owned culture with a terrorist threat that is connoted as non-American. The juxtaposition of "American soil" and "terrorist attack" masks the fact that the "American soil" is itself a product of the terrorism that has resided in the destruction of indigenous peoples, the deployment of slave labor, continued practices of racial subordination, and the extrajudicial use of force in political conflicts around the world. This historical terrorism is disavowed under the reconstruction of the American land that is invited by the above juxtaposition. Such violence is rendered invisible; it is extirpated from what counts as the U.S. aesthetic homeland. We encounter here a rhetorical appropriation of the land as a realm of white innocence and entitlement. The image of the fresh soil that is ready to bear its fruits to the American nation lends this construction a distinctive aesthetic attractiveness. The aesthetic turns out to be complicit in a shifting and intensified sense of a white, Anglo-European—as opposed to Indian, black, Latino/a, or Asian American—entitlement to ownership and control over "American" cultural property, that is, over the racialized, "American" land or nation, experienced on a model of property.

Racialized aesthetic nationalism is grounded in the daily aesthetic patterns of meaning making and experience we enact while conducting relationships with one another and the environment. It resides in the styles of existence we mold through culinary practices, etiquette, gestural vocabulary, bodily expression, physical, prosthetic, and economic mobility, the spatial and temporal organization of work, leisure, and friendship. Nationalist feelings have a broad aesthetic base. Cell phones, iPods, children's songs, New Year's Eve, the library, bicycles, and trains all have aesthetic dimensions that may or may not contribute to a regulative feeling of presence in our own or other environments.

A proprietary aesthetic investment in the nation was actively encouraged by the economic exhortations Dick Cheney, George W. Bush, and Rudolph W. Giuliani voiced in the weeks immediately following the 9/11 attacks. Americans were urged to go shopping and conduct business as usual. Cheney, as reported by the *Los Angeles Times* on September 17, 2001, promoted shopping as a patriotic duty, remarking that "I would hope the American people would, in effect, stick their thumbs in the eye of the terrorists and say that they've got great confidence in the country, great confidence in our economy, and not let what's happened here in any way throw off their normal level of economic activity."[12] Virtually equating the country with its economy, the vice president compressed the distance between buying stocks and consumption goods and supporting the nation in the war on terror. Addressing a joint session of Congress regarding the subject of terrorism on September 20, 2001, Bush solidified the appeal to the population's vital yet sagging buying and selling instincts: "I ask your continued participation and confidence in the American economy. Terrorists attacked a symbol of American prosperity. They did not touch its source. America is successful because of the hard work and creativity and enterprise of our people. These were the true strengths of our economy before Sept[ember] 11 and they are our strengths today."[13] Attributing the United States' success to the strengths of the people, and equating these with the strengths of the economy, the president's request located the economy, the people, and the country in dazzlingly close proximity to one another. In his radio program on September 21, New York City mayor Giuliani contributed his part to the populace's economic enactment of good citizenship and nationhood by summoning shoppers into the city's stores.[14]

In line with the reductionism characterizing contemporary neoliberalism, ethical and aesthetic consciousness took here the form of market rationality. The injunction that declared economic activity a patriotic calling addressed Americans as individuals, in abstraction from their social and economic position, their race, religion, and ethnicity. The order to shop and do business projected a deceptive unity onto the nation, which was imagined as a collective of entrepreneurial and consuming agents.[15] Focusing on individual participation in the market, the strategy shortcut the ethical and aesthetic question of how the community might respond as a social body, an entity made up of constituencies with divergent economic needs.

Market rationality inevitably enlists aesthetic values and decision-making in its operations. Aesthetic desires must inform the relevant consumptive and financial choices. The urge to buy in support of the nation presupposes an aesthetic impulse to identify with normative levels, modes, and styles of consumption. The American people en masse—though as individuals—were asked to perform this aesthetic identification, that is, to subject themselves as moral and aesthetic agents to the nation's markets. A historical scaffold for liberal individualism, the market is profoundly imbricated with consumerist aesthetics, a toolbox for the realization of social distinction.[16] Under late capitalism, aesthetic subjectivity substantially consists in economic agency. Consumptive (and productive) aesthetic choices help shape our specific cultural, national, and racial identities. To make a long story short, Bush's, Cheney's, and Giuliani's recommendations, which were echoed by many others, drew on influential interlocking structures of economic and aesthetic subject formation.[17] Because the commercial imperative addressed the American people as individuals—replicating the gesture that passes off institutional and governmental realities as the achievements or failures of individual economic and aesthetic agents[18]—it could be mapped with little friction onto the economic project of the war in Iraq, which sought to mobilize the nation as an undivided collective made up of united individuals. Racialized aesthetic nationalist tactics were thus part and parcel of the neoconservative, neoliberal rewriting of civil life in the initial post–9/11 era, as the country moved to enlist the labor and lives of the United States' working classes and poor, and of the population of Iraq, in projects that were to advance the interests of a small economic elite.

A similarly homogenizing vision was achieved through the aesthetic structures of mourning invited by the *New York Times*' "Portraits of Grief," a series of idealized memorials, devoted to the victims left dead in the attacks. Highlighting the specialness of the depicted subjects by citing distinctive anecdotes from their lives and bringing out unique personality traits, this commemorative effort, like the shopping imperative, allowed for a rapid passage from each individual to her or his larger communities, and thereby naturalized the link between the individual and the nation. Nancy Miller comments on the toothpaste one victim, a broker at Cantor Fitzgerald, we are told, used to leave almost every morning for his wife on her toothbrush, before going off to work:

> If this is not a "telling" detail in the narrative universe of the *Times* portraits, what is? For it tells the story of what worked in the marriage, and to the extent that the portraits represent something larger than an individual—and they do—they are crafted to serve as the microcosm of family life, of a valiant, and though wounded, above all, happy America. The domestic detail of the toothbrush comes to stand for the intimacy of the home, and the home for the nation's public life: the home front against the incursions of terrorism. The detail as the index of poignant loss—the toothpaste on the toothbrush, the minute and the familiar—embodies that which we cherish against what is foreign and terrifying, that which protects against the war on terrorism.[19]

The portraits ask the reader to reimagine the aesthetic homeland on the model of familial bonds, while offering her a way to preserve it as an object and source of love. The personalized miniatures reaestheticize the "home front" in the form of a disrupted domesticity, an intimate enclosure destroyed by terrorism. But in the detail's invocation of bereavement, as Miller suggests, and its tapping of grief, the reader is also invited to experience the love that was lost as a source of affective sustenance, to draw nourishment from a capacity it may have to regenerate individual and public life in the face of terror.

Yet, as the portraits have the individual victim stand in for the country as a whole, their narrative structure projects a unified vision of the homeland that evades the question of whose sustaining attachments the aestheticized nation upholds, at the cost of what kinds of terrorization. The intimacy the portraits locate at the heart of American life is the product of an incontrovertible history of constitutive exclusions, the traces of which are blurred in the visual and narrative selections mandated by the operative codes of loving memorialization.

Racialized, aesthetically nationalist regimes of address in the post–9/11 landscape were instrumental in foreclosing ethical, political, and aesthetic inquiries that could reach beyond the demands of victimhood and market rationality. Aesthetic structures assisted in abridging deliberative, affective, and symbolic processes that ought to have galvanized a democratic reevaluation of America's relationships to the global community as well as its own heterogeneous constituencies. Racialized and nationalist aesthetic stratagems helped institutionalize a defensive proprietary stance toward culture, shaping cultural agency on the model of property management and ownership. The regulative presence of proprietary conceptions of culture in aesthetic theories and everyday practices is mirrored by similar dispositions in the art world.

Disruptive Body Politics: Racialized Aesthetic Nationalism in the Art World

When critical interpretations of works of art deploy racialized, aesthetically nationalist concepts, the result is an unjustifiably constricted construal of the art world. Interpretations developed in terms of such conceptions limit the repertoire of reciprocal encounters that take place between the world of art and the aesthetic of the everyday, and shelter cultural sensibilities against aesthetic challenges. Racialized and nationalist interpretations of artworks give rise to a diminished, proprietary sense of aesthetic and artistic possibility. They institute a pattern of cultural appropriation that restricts the realm of culture to what, in a figurative sense, is "ownable," that is, to what privileged subjects can properly, safely, own up to. This section analyzes an example of such a reading and briefly highlights its theoretical implications.

Fernando Botero's paintings and drawings about the torture of Iraqi captives by U.S. military forces in the prison of Abu Ghraib have been exhibited in numerous countries. The Marlborough Gallery in New York displayed a selection of these works in autumn 2006. In a review of the show for *The Nation*, entitled "The Body in Pain," Arthur Danto situates the series against the backdrop of the artist's preceding oeuvre. He considers the new works astonishing. From his philosophical lexicon, they call forth the category "masterpieces of disturbatory art."[20] With his representations of torture, Botero elevates his art from what Danto considers bland and repetitive folksy artifice to, for this painter, unprecedented heights of intensity. About the earlier works, and especially the sculptures, Danto reminisces:

> Colombian artist Fernando Botero is famous for his depictions of blimpy figures that verge on the ludicrous. New Yorkers may recall the outdoor display of Botero's bronze figures, many of them nude, in the central islands of Park Avenue in 1993. Their bodily proportions insured that their nakedness aroused little in the way of public indignation. They were about as sexy as the Macy's balloons, and their seemingly inflated blandness lent them the cheerful and benign look one associates with upscale folk art. The sculptures were a shade less ingratiating, a shade more dangerous than one of Walt Disney's creations, but in no way serious enough to call for critical scrutiny. Though transparently modern, Botero's style is admired mainly by those outside the art world. Inside the art world, critic Rosalind Krauss spoke for many of us when she dismissed Botero as "pathetic."[21]

What in the eyes of Danto and Krauss constitutes Botero's dubious artistic track record poses a challenge for the viewer of his work.[22] If we may believe these critics, to take his paintings seriously is to risk overstepping the boundaries of the art world. According to Danto and Krauss, the viewer who delights in Botero's works courts contamination by art's "others." Beyond the limits of the contemporary art world, these theorists detect the specter of the mass-produced, the commercial, the childlike, the forcibly happy, the popular, the faux-folk, the safely inoffensive, the calculatingly good-natured, love on command, saccharine and farcical. The suggestion is that Botero's pieces threaten to diffuse the viewer's orientation toward vital aesthetic and moral borderlines. Consequently, Danto's and Krauss's comments reinaugurate distinctions that were taken to be in danger of unraveling. Echoing Krauss's verdict of pitiable, somewhat contemptible artistic unworthiness, Danto joins in her judgment, and, in the same gesture, in that of numerous other art world compatriots. Critical convergence runs deep in their remarks. Tropes of cartoonish commodification feature prominently in both Krauss's and Danto's commentaries on Botero's art.[23] So does the mantra of the artist's questionable position in relation to the art world.

The context for Krauss's commentary is a 1998 edition of CBS's *60 Minutes* on Botero's work. Introduced by Steve Kroft, a reporter for the show, as one of the artist's many detractors in the international art world who deem his work of "absolutely no consequence to twentieth-century fine art," Krauss affirms: "In the world from which I come—which is a world of, you know, universities, museums, art magazines, no one talks about Botero. He is simply a non-figure. He's a dark hole. There's no reason to talk about Botero."

This language of reasons, it turns out, is closely affiliated with the concept of the art world, as Danto conceives of it. In his view, reasons hold together the art world: "The art world is the discourse of reasons institutionalized, and to be a member of the art world is, accordingly, to have learned what it means to participate in the discourse of reasons for one's culture."[24] On Danto's theory, a lack of reason to talk about Botero, or the failure of his works to participate in the discourse of reasons institutionalized for the international art world, thus certifies Botero's status as an outsider vis-à-vis the global world of fine art.

I have no doubts about Botero's participation in the relevant kind of art discourse but wish to linger briefly with Krauss's idea, in order to see what a possible argument against Botero's membership in the art world based on the apparent absence of reasons can tell us about the structure of this world and the logic of its boundaries, for this argument generates an instructive paradox. Clearly, the charge is unable to seal Botero's exclusion from the art world, within Danto's theory, if only for the reason that Krauss *did* speak about Botero, indeed, was somehow lured *to find reason* to talk about him. There may have been little art or reason to Krauss's reason, as measured by the standards of the art world or, for that matter, by the criteria of "universities, museums, art magazines." But rather than proving there was in fact no good reason, this merely presses certain expansive questions about the nature of the reasons at issue in Krauss's and Danto's discussions, such as, What constitute the right kinds of reasons for talking about an artist or oeuvre? What does it mean for a relevant reason to belong to a discourse, and more specifically, an institutionalized discourse? And last, what are the conditions for participating in a discourse of reasons?

The hypothetical case against Botero's membership in the art world brings out the instabilities and uncertainties that attach to the project of circumscribing the borders of this world. The argument underscores the malleability that the art world's boundaries, as conceived by Danto, share with the discourse of reasons. One not necessarily very solid reason, of a rather extrinsic nature, gives rise to another reason, which, prior to the advent of the first reason would not have constituted a reason, and certainly not a compelling or seductive one, until reasons suddenly abound. Krauss's found reason, perhaps even owing to her initial lack of a reason, now provides ample reason to talk about Botero, and, in fact, Botero has already ventured to make an entry into the art world merely owing to Krauss's discussion of him.

An especially potent dimension of the art world's malleability lies then in the liability of the discourse of reasons to enlargement through encounters with materials and events of an uncertain art world status. This lends the art world a susceptibility to a centrifugal form of inflation, an internally generative voluminousness that prepares it to set off from its bearings, like a Macy's balloon taking flight during the parade. The art world's inherently generative potential for expansion when in contact with externalized sources constitutes not only an endlessly fecund power but also a risk, an ineluctable vulnerability to infraction on account of which art's boundaries are never secure, irrevocably ambiguous, and resistant to patrolling.[25]

While the spectator of the *60 Minutes* broadcast views footage of Krauss, who looks through books about Botero,[26] the interviewer's voice-over explains that to this particular critic, as well as many others, the artist's distinctive style is a gimmick, designed to pander to wealthy collectors who are ignorant of "serious art." Krauss's voice interjects: "The figures in his work have the quality of Pillsbury Dough Boys or Barney, the stuffed dinosaur. This is pathetic."

Despite the availability of Krauss's critical vocabulary for the articulation of an interpretation of the Abu Ghraib series, Danto will have none of it. To develop a reading of the representations of torture, he resorts to a more traditional language of affect and morality, for which he draws on the European Counter-Reformation.[27] Indeed, Danto accounts for the twenty-first-century prison abuse pieces in terms of their rendering of the suffering of the Iraqi captives. In his view, the voluminous fleshiness of the victims' bodies lends them a specific vulnerability to pain. The viewer internalizes that pain and comes to feel it as her own: "Botero's Abu Ghraib series immerses us in the experience of suffering. The pain of others has seldom felt so close, or so shaming to its perpetrators."[28]

For Danto, accordingly, the visitor of Botero's exhibit participates in the Iraqi prisoners' feelings, vicariously experiencing them as if they were hers. In the ontological plane, the category of "disturbatory art" justifies such imaginative participation.[29] Art of this sort, on Danto's theory, is designed to recreate a magical contact with a disturbing reality. Infracting on the boundaries with life, this kind of art converts the spectator into a participant in a ritual in order to make certain transformative effects.[30]

In the case of sculptures by Richard Serra, for example, the spectator's consciousness of her own embodiment in the flesh, a participatory state of mind, enables her to become aware of "latent structures and forces" of the kind that, in Danto's historical picture of it, art has outgrown.[31] Disturbatory art reaches back to a "primitive" stage of art's development, one that is underwritten, likewise, by a "primitive" relationship between artist and audience.[32] Like a priest conducting "a primitive ritual," the disturbational artist initiates a collective process of transformation.[33] Mutual transformation, on this model, is facilitated by the artist's possession "by something alien."[34] The viewer enters into a shared space with the artist and the work.[35] "Melting" the relationship between work and audience, art of the disturbatory type seeks to achieve a connection with "dark impulses" that have come to be repressed in the course of art's history.[36] As such, this genre of art regresses to what Nietzsche called the Dionysian era, during which art approximated magic in its attempt to make "dark possibilities" real, invoking "alien forces from a space other than the one we occupy."[37] Disturbatory art exercises magic as it purports to render the subject of representation present in the representation itself, hoping to overcome the rift between image and reality. Paradoxically working against its own condition as art, the aim is to break the detachment art ordinarily makes possible, in order to expose both the artist and the viewer to the danger of an unguarded encounter with the real. In this fashion, disturbational art carries the disturbing realities it embodies into the artist's and spectators' lives. Transgressing art's boundaries, this mode of artistic production, in Danto's words, "colonizes, as it were, the west bank of life by art."[38] At stake in this project is a reactivation of our contact with a "subrational constituent" of our psyches.[39] This makes for a special kind of disturbance, to be distinguished from the merely shocking or outrageous:

> It is the kind of disturbance that comes from the dim subperception that a dimension of our being is being signaled at a level below even the deepest levels of civilization. Greek civilization, if Nietzsche was right, owed itself to putting this all at a distance. We don't know what we are capable of, what we might do in response to the beckoning of the disturbatory artist: it is that sense of danger she insinuates which one might have felt as one crossed the terrifying boundaries of the precincts of Dionysus.[40]

Disturbatory art, for Danto, addresses opaque and arational strata of subjectivity that elude the influence of civilization. The disturbance inherent in the experience of this art arises as a result of the spectator's confrontation with these unknown parts of the self. If this is the generic modus operandi of the arts of disturbation, what specific disturbatory dynamics does Botero put to work in his Abu Ghraib series, as read by Danto?

"The Body in Pain" postdates by over twenty years the philosopher's original discussions of disturbation.[41] This recent review slightly shifts the definition of disturbatory art to those works "whose point and purpose [it] is to make vivid and objective our most frightening subjective thoughts."[42]

So conceived, the category includes works of art earlier formulations had labeled "simply" or "conventionally" disturbing. Art of the latter type, which Danto sees exemplified, for instance, in Leon Golub's paintings, represents a disturbing subject matter and may or may not do this in disturbing ways.[43] Disturbatory art differs from mere artistic disturbance in the challenge it poses for the boundaries that, as we have seen, are assumed to keep real life apart from art. But to attempt to bridge this divide is to engage in an illusion, in Danto's theory. On that count, he finds disturbatory art "pathetic and futile."[44] This signals that we have returned full circle to the limitations of Botero's suspect general style.

Stopping short of this, however, the question arises as to what precise borderline(s), among the many distinctions that are taken to separate the realm of art from the sphere of the real, Danto takes Botero's Abu Ghraib paintings to be breaching. The most obvious candidate is the gap between felt and represented suffering, in other words, the distance separating the viewer's affect from that of the depicted figures. Indeed, Danto suggests that key to an understanding of the paintings' particular mode of disturbance is their privileging of feeling over and above perception: "The mystery of painting, almost forgotten since the Counter-Reformation, lies in its power to generate a kind of illusion that has less to do with pictorial perception than it does with feeling."[45] At this point, Danto links Botero's series with depictions of Christ's martyrdom produced during the epoch of the Latin American Baroque. Within this genre, "graphic, even lurid" depictions of Christ's damaged body serve to elicit the spectator's sympathetic identification.[46] Accordingly, the empathetic gallery visitor who, by way of Botero's work, draws the Iraqi subjects of violence close, participates in an affective ritual Danto takes the Abu Ghraib pieces to have been designed to initiate. Merging represented with felt affect, and abandoning distance between self and other, the spectator who takes on the victims' suffering as if it were hers enables the paintings to realize their transformative disturbatory effects.

How does Danto's interpretation of the Abu Ghraib series reflect on the paintings, drawings and sculptures produced in the course of the artist's extended career prior to the 2004 torture scandal? The critic observes a continuity of style between the earlier and the new work: "Although the prisoners are painted in his signature style, his much-maligned mannerism intensifies our engagement with the pictures."[47] Notwithstanding the alleged ineptness of the artist's iconography, Botero's uninterrupted stylistic approach makes a powerful artistic effect in the torture scenes, according to Danto. The finding of this turnabout, if not inconsistency, within Botero's otherwise supposedly stable aesthetic vocabulary fails to provoke a revision of Danto's judgment of the preceding oeuvre. Instead, he resorts to a bipartite conception of Botero's aesthetic repertoire. This construction comes at a price, however.

Danto refuses to read the Abu Ghraib series for its political indictment of U.S. military policies in precisely the way in which both he and Krauss decline assessing the artist's prior oeuvre for its visual critique of power and its irony. Both critics reproduce the worn-out racializing, feminizing, class-inflected, and ethnically othering vocabulary of the childlike and the naïve. The language of Macy's balloons, Disney cartoons, dough puppets, and dinosaurs voices an absence of individual aesthetic authorship. Conjoined with these figures, Krauss's comment on Botero's artistic nonidentity expresses a perceived effacement of artistic consciousness by an overwhelmingly stultified, scripted populist imaginary, which, transpiring outside the realm of artistic significance, can at best attain marketability. Framed through images signifying a popular, childlike, and commercial appeal, Botero's exuberant preoccupation with pejoratively coded commodified content—prosaic, pedestrian, domestic, mass-produced, material, sensuous, formally unconscious, and aesthetically derivative—arises as a vast abject territory encroaching on the art world. The "dark hole" that, for Krauss, in Botero's case, threatens to engulf contemporary artistic subjectivity and relationality, conjures up Hegel's "dark mantle of night" and Freud's "dark continent" and their associations with the extrahistorical, the formless, and the unrepresentable.[48]

Danto's implicit explication of Botero's supposed disturbance effect in terms of the magical, the mysterious, the miraculous, the archaic, the primitive, the extracivilizational, the dark, and the unknown sidesteps the elaborate intertextuality and representational self-consciousness of Botero's idioms. The aesthetic icons Danto and Krauss draw from the children's corner, the parade, and the marketplace, in association with Botero's figures, likewise circumvent the intricacies of the artist's treatment of the body in three-dimensional space and in the picture plane.[49] In a similar vein, by focusing primarily on content, Danto's descriptions of the Abu Ghraib paintings downplay the works' formal functioning. Looking rapidly *through* the level of representation to the depicted pain and violence, he prepares the ground for an interpretation centered on the empathetic feelings of the individual viewer, interpolating the depicted suffering in an affective economy that enables the American public—even if momentarily—to step away from its structural indifference to the victims of U.S. interventions abroad.

Affective responses certainly require a place in art criticism and interpretation. But the ambitions of the Abu Ghraib series do not find adequate expression in the idea that they make the suffering of Iraqi captives available to a global gallery public. This reading performs an appropriative effacement of a more radical artistic gesture. For the collection offers an aesthetic condemnation of the torture inflicted on the prisoners. It interrogates the power structures and the visual regimes that deploy and legitimize such violence. Subjected to physical damage, sexual humiliation, and psychological torture, the large, feminized Iraqi bodies—Botero's distinctive puffing up of the human figure characteristically demasculinizes the male subject—expose the flip side of the values of freedom and democracy, advanced in defense of an economically motivated war. Botero's paintings document torture to catalyze the public's political consciousness, to condemn this systemic injustice, and to hold the United States accountable for it. In a remark on the collection, Botero notes that it represents "both a broad statement about cruelty and at the same time an *accusation* of U.S. policies."[50] Danto disavows this visual critique and averts the ethical demand underlying it.

Indeed, the works' accusation is displaced. Rather than having the works' aesthetic critique qualify his own reading of the collection, Danto locates this challenge in the actions and reactions, real and anticipated, evinced by other segments of the public. For the reader of *The Nation* is told that, when offered the collection by Botero, a number of American museums turned down the gift. This rejection Danto attributes to the same reason for which visitors to the Marlborough Gallery show were asked to have their bags inspected in order to gain entry to the exhibit, a practice, which, he points out, is unusual for commercial galleries.[51] Danto thus acknowledges the political sting of the collection indirectly, as evinced in the negative impulses, if not aggression, the public, including museum donors, is imagined to experience toward the paintings. This implicit recognition by the critic, and if he is right, also by the boards and directors of art galleries and museums, makes the works out to be a threat to a supposed North American mind-set. The collection is understood to touch a sensitive nerve in the U.S. public. However, this mutual vulnerability of viewers to paintings and paintings to viewers receives no critical elaboration in terms of the works' aesthetic functioning. To erase from the site of aesthetic meaning production the reciprocal vulnerability that characterizes the aesthetic encounter is to flatten the exchange and to prepare the ground for a safe yet sanitized passage through the aesthetic homeland. Danto's reading enacts an appropriative form of political containment.

Visual politics are taken to play a more central role in the famous Abu Ghraib photographs than in the paintings. The photos Danto considers "essentially snapshots, larky postcards of soldiers enjoying their power, as their implied message—'Having a wonderful time . . . Wish you were here'—attests."[52] Turning a scene of violence into one of pleasure, these pictures gained the capacity to generate moral responsiveness upon exposure around the globe: "When the photographs were released, the moral indignation of the West was focused on the grinning soldiers, for whom this appalling spectacle was a form of entertainment."[53] Earlier declared outside the scope of Botero's sculptures, indignation does not now make a surprise appearance in the Marlborough Gallery.[54] Indeed,

Danto's text institutes a sharp division of aesthetic labor. While the paintings offer up the suffering of the victimized body for the spectator's affective consumption, the photographic imprints of theatrically staged power and pleasure perform moral work.

Political effect thus is rendered the prerogative of the international media circuits in concert with the U.S. social and military system. Featuring Iraqi victimhood, the Colombian artist supplies emotional resources "real-world politics" may or may not take up. The Abu Ghraib paintings are barred from being full-fledged participants in the aesthetic production of social power. It is Danto's bipartite construction of Botero's style as generally not worthy of serious scrutiny but forcefully arousing in the case of this particular series that creates room to ignore the work's significance as a political critique.

A glimpse of such a critique may be caught in the review's concluding remark, quoted earlier, to the effect that "[t]he pain of others has seldom felt so close, or so shaming to its perpetrators." Shame is a moral emotion, and like empathetic affect, it can be a political incentive. However, in calling for an end to the torture of prisoners, and in making legible a culture's political proximity to this violence, the works press beyond their implications for people's feelings, regardless of whether such people are "merely" viewers, or at the same time torturers, unseen facilitators, cobeneficiaries of imperialist oil policies, or coparticipants in a world system. Botero considered it of particular importance that the American public see the works "because those who did the atrocities were Americans."[55] Hence, presumably, his offer of these paintings to American museums, just as he had donated his earlier collection on the Colombian drug and guerilla wars to museums in Colombia. Empathy and shame, however, fall drastically short of an aesthetically discerning uptake of an artistic imperative commanding justice, an appeal, moreover, that is targeted at a highly legible and precisely denoted constellation of violations.

What of the works' challenge of sexual and religious humiliation and torture staged as visual spectacle? Danto's review shields the viewer from this charge by observing tidy divisions between the painterly transmission of suffering and the photographic problematization of power; between a victim's pain and an abuser's sexual pulse; between a properly empathizing gallery public and the scenographers in the prison who orchestrated displays of torture for their and their friends' consumption; between the different audiences for genres such as hard-core pornography, for the violated bodies offered up and fantasized on a daily basis in the news media, and for Disney movies, Macy's parades, and Botero's art. In omitting the connections that tie together these polarities, Danto's reading closes down openings crafted through the works for examining the viewer's potential complicity in the sexual settings in which the prisoners are forced to pose, or in officially sanctioned, racist patterns of sadism, voyeurism, and sexual humiliation.[56] The U.S. viewer's upright standing finds protection in the failure to investigate how the erotics of spectacularized terrorization reflect on the distinctive nature of racial and ethnic domination exercised historically and to this date on behalf of the American nation.[57] Botero's series creates conditions for a discourse on the subject, of which we do not know precisely where it may take us, or what refused and irrational desires it may bring to the surface. Lending this work an already understood emotional effect, rather than the status of an inquiry or a call for change, Danto's framework for interpretation shelters both the American neocolonial military-industrial-prison complex and the U.S. viewer's aesthetic homeland from Botero's artistic critique. Removing aggression, racialized sexuality, and risk from the aesthetic confrontation initiated by the works, Danto lays the basis for a proprietary reading. As in Addison, we witness here a one-sided process of abjection that readies the work for incorporation as a visual commodity within an expandable, yet rigorously guarded territory of aesthetic culture.

But if the category of disturbatory art is applicable to the Abu Ghraib paintings and drawings, and if these works, as this label suggests, pose unknown dangers for the viewer, it is surely because as aesthetic restagings of pornographic modes and motifs, and variations on already aestheticized theatrical and photographic articulations of racialized debasement and oppression, they destabilize the viewer's position vis-à-vis the ethical and aesthetic distinctions Danto's reading shores up. The elisions enabling the works' appropriation within the economy of the U.S. aesthetic homeland stand out starkly on a brief examination of Botero's body politics.

Botero's bodies are idealized, yet grotesque. They are deliteralized both by their delicious, anachronistic beauty and their hilarious resistance to bodily norms observed by styles of painting across history and geographical zones, bodily norms that support cultural formations of subjectivity and intersubjectivity, producing and reproducing criteria of sensory, rational, affective, aesthetic, and artistic legibility. The bodies of male figures in power (presidents, generals, priests, horse riders, gunmen, drug barons, gang members, murderers, torturers, kidnappers, partners, lovers) deflate this assumed power, mocking the characters' investment in it. Adorned female or feminized figures (presidents' wives, prostitutes, women reading books or in front of the mirror, nuns, drag queens, picnickers, partners, lovers) invite us to ask whether their beautiful bodies, social positions, subjective presence, instantaneous gestures, or sexiness will enable them to fulfill their longings or to realize their aspirations. The poses of families and couples raise questions about gendered structures of intimacy, authority, sexuality, and dominance, as they offer multiple, often contradictory, clues about the satisfactoriness of the bonds connecting individuals.

Botero models the human figure and pictorial space in dialogue with artists as diverse as Giotto, Piero della Francesca, Da Vinci, Dürer, Caravaggio, Rubens, Velázquez, Goya, Picasso, Orozco, Pollock, and countless others. His iconography draws on Olmec, Mayan, Aztec, and Latin American Baroque forms. Returning to images and themes he associates with the Colombian highlands, which he interleaves with postures and idioms inspired by a brazenly diverse range of art historical vocabularies, he writes himself as a Colombian artist rigorously into a transculturated Latin American and Anglo-European tradition.[58] His art encounters racialized national stylistic norms and distinctions through a strategy of disruptive mimesis. This resistant technique, which refracts already given aesthetic materials to orient them toward new expressions and ideas, is instantly recognizable in compositions that directly cite canonical images, but equally characterizes his oeuvre as a whole, which, in his words, does not feature one brushstroke "unsanctioned by the history of art."[59] Good art, for Botero, creates a world that "contains a truth that can be accepted as an alternative, and that also exists as a poetic possibility."[60] He considers it the artist's function to exalt life by communicating sensuality.[61] Disruptive mimesis, locating abundant bodily potential in an atmosphere of pictorial calm, makes for an uproarious body politic in Botero.

Ironizing varieties of masculinized, feminized, and from time to time explicitly racialized power, through physical comedy, the manipulation of scale, and sardonic inversions, Botero depicts embodiment as a fundamentally pleasurable state of corporeal being (see, for example, figure 9.1). Far from realistic or celebratory evocations of the bulging folds and hanging rolls of the obese, aging human body, his figures come protectively wrapped in soft, nourishing, delectable, usually young, elastic fat. Bodily existence, in Botero's universe, is a potentially joyful state of creaturely being, a readiness for delightful sensations. Distress and pain irresistibly interarticulate with a basic modality of happy corporeality, which the figures share with their surroundings. This is also the case in the many variations on the theme of the crying woman, or in Botero's treatment of mutilated bodies. Botero depicts the skin, the flesh, and the body's volumes as sensing organs desiring, needing, touchable.

Characters, animals, objects, and environments (interior spaces, the streets of Medellín, the rooftops of hill villages) exude an appearance of essential lovability.[62] The material world is animated by the vibrant agency of ordinary details that far exceeds their prosaic functioning much in the way in which the momentous (or sometimes radically diminished) human body transgresses canonical codes of spatiality and normative corporeality. Under the signs of comical idealization and tranquil beauty, grotesque registers of abjection determine the contours of a gorgeous range of

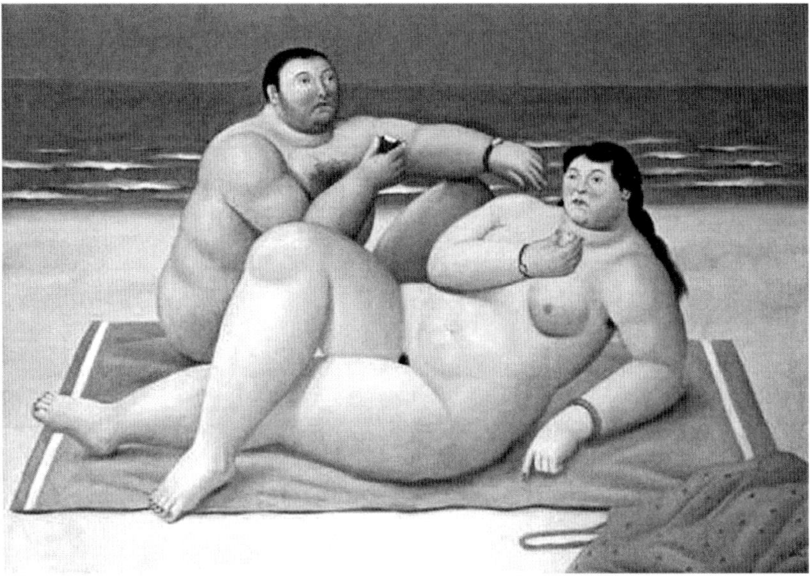

FIGURE 9.1. *The Beach* (2006) by Fernando Botero. Oil on canvas, 131 × 189 cm. © Fernando Botero, courtesy, Marlborough Gallery, New York.

fundamentally adorable human beings, whose lovability is catalyzed by the sensate capacities that disarticulate their positions within established vectors of social power. Botero formulates a critical body politic that challenges normalized regimes of intercorporeal exchange through the expression of the enfleshed pleasures, longings, efforts, and disappointments of minutely particularized bodily postures representing social types rather than individualized psychologies. Inhabiting a temporal register outside everyday historical progression, the body's possibilities for sensuality and desire suspend certain constraints of normative, contemporary sociality, asking for a tenderness, a love, and a generosity beyond the ordinary rule of things, suggesting this "as a poetic possibility."

When these bodies are then shown as being hurt or shot, stunned or humilitated, in mortal fear or agony over the loss of others' lives, as in the series on the violence of Colombia and on Abu Ghraib (see figure 9.2), this belies their generic lovability, challenging the basic, sensory, relational being that constitutes the reality of their embodiment. But this level of bodily being and demand speaks back to the violence. Botero has his desirable and desiring bodies militate against the violence inflicted on them, caricaturing such violence, its tools and agents, and the damage it marks in the body as dissonant with the characters' human life in the flesh. In these paintings, harsh scopophiliac regimes, acts of physical abuse, fences, ropes, dogs, blood, tears, vomit, urine, sticks, explosions, bullets, and the holes left by gunshots in the body take on a schematic, grotesque uncanniness, not altogether unlike the snakes and flies in his earlier paintings.

Botero's works on the violence in Iraq and Colombia inscribe his aesthetic figuration of this violence into a transculturated European and Latin American tradition, indelibly marking the medium of painting with the sensory body's capacity to alienate and protest these atrocities. We encounter here thus an utterly self-conscious, intertextual artistic tactic of disruptive mimesis crossing racialized, national art-historical boundaries, forms, and techniques.[63] It is these levels of signification that Danto's racialized and nationalist conceptual framework ignores. By way of structural

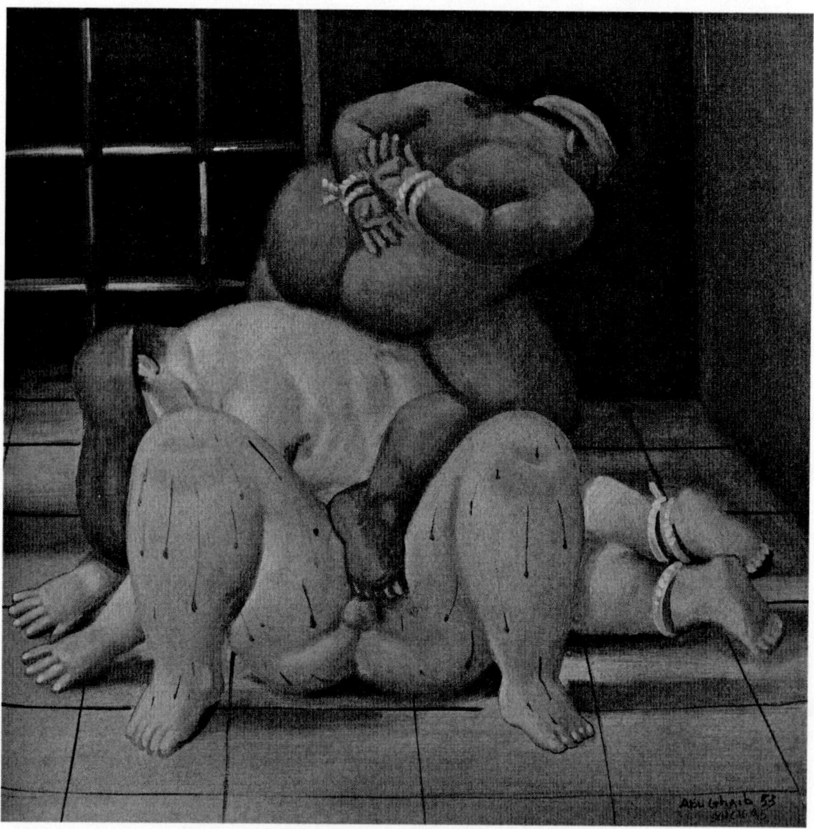

Figure 9.2. *Abu Ghraib 53* (2005) by Fernando Botero. Oil on canvas, 37 × 35 cm. © Fernando Botero, courtesy, Marlborough Gallery, New York.

interpretive omissions, his reading renders the Abu Ghraib oeuvre a proper item for consumption by a proprietary, racialized and nationalist cultural sensibility, a commodity in which the benevolent inhabitant of the U.S. aesthetic homeland can safely, even if not altogether comfortably, encounter her own reflection.

Botero's deliberate anachronisms give the lie to a straightforwardly progressivist understanding of art. Giving rise to a tranquil grotesque, mixing popular and high art, feminizing the masculinized,[64] writing the Latin American into the European and the European into the Colombian, Botero's oeuvre challenges certain gendered, racialized, class-inflected, and nationalist oppositions at the heart of the art world, conceived on the model of an evolving discourse of reasons. Krauss's and Danto's fearful intent to abject Botero's style from the art world transparently posits as the disavowed origin of the history of art a repertoire of familiar and fundamentally unstable cultural distinctions, which his art threatens to shake up. These include oppositions we have considered before, such as those between the modern and the archaic, between the civilized and its dark, primitive prehistory. Constitutionally bound to these binaries, the art world is forever at risk of regression, destructuration, and decentering in its encounters with idioms that dislocate the hierarchies encoded in these dualities. Danto's and Krauss's implicitly racialized critical language subsumes Botero's work under already given normative oppositions in which these critics are invested as participants in the art world, oppositions whose racializing force they reproduce without critical distance. The relevant binaries establish principled analytical barriers that keep art criticism from resonating with the force of Botero's art—its comedy, its mockery of power, its taunting of social respectability and imperial politics. Inhibiting, furthermore, the reciprocal flow between the popular, the vanguard, and the high in art, Danto's and Krauss's methodologies hinder the symbolic transmissibility at which Botero aspires, which finds clear expression, for example, in his comment to the effect that he is "delighted by the idea that a poor person in Colombia, with no cultural background, should have reproductions of my work in the house."[65]

Danto's and Krauss's conceptual frameworks, divergent as they are from one another in language and philosophy, obscure the aesthetic complexity of Botero's oeuvre. Locking the excessive Botero body into prefabricated aesthetic categories, and their coded assurances of differential social propriety, both critics limit what can be heard by way of aesthetic dissent. This amounts to a diminishment of the art world as well as the aesthetics of the ordinary. Notwithstanding the discontinuities between Danto's and Krauss's critical approaches, their protocols of reading, in each instance, project an overly homogeneous understanding of aesthetic and artistic vocabularies and meanings. Thereby Danto and Krauss position themselves as contemporary inheritors of the racialized aesthetically nationalist modes of address practiced by Shaftesbury, Addison, Hume, Kant, and others in more overtly racialized terms.

Proprietary constructions of the aesthetic do their work at the level of quotidian existence, in the institutions of the art world, and at their intersection. The above discussion has explored forms of seduction and surveillance that press artworks and everyday aesthetic practices into entrenched matrixes of race and nation. We have investigated cultural strategies that position the art world and everyday aesthetic collectivity as ethnocentrically defined homeland. Because the art world intermeshes with the everyday, racialized aesthetic nationalism in the institutions of art reverberates in the structures of quotidian existence and vice versa. Thus, this stance must be contested at multiple, interlocking levels.[66] It is then in the name of a vibrant, unattenuated artistic and aesthetic culture that we need to examine how proprietary constructions of the aesthetic and their attendant regimes of racial abjection operate, how they can be undone, and what alternatives may be realized. For the philosophy of art, this poses the task to rethink the workings of race and nation as conditions of pleasure, violence, and power, and to revise those conceptual structures that allow artistic norms and boundaries to draw on or reinforce unacceptable constellations of race and nation.[67]

We have seen that racialized, aesthetically nationalist forms of everyday address (such as the shopping command) can help foreclose political inquiry that pushes beyond the impulses of victimhood and market rationality. Furthermore, as constituents of interpretations of art objects, racialized and nationalist conceptions appear to conceal the political bite of an oeuvre that condemns instances of U.S.-perpetrated violence. Racialized aesthetic nationalism thus shortcuts political existence and truncates cultural life. If we cherish the critical power and vitality of those poignant places where the quotidian and the artistic meet, we need to dismantle racist and nationalist constraints on art and everyday aesthetic life.[68]

Notes

1. See my "Racialization as an Aesthetic Production: What Does the Aesthetic Do for Whiteness and Blackness and Vice Versa?," in *White on White/Black on Black*, ed. George Yancy (Lanham, MD: Rowman and Littlefield, 2005), 83–124.

2. Modes of address are multisensory forms of signification we direct at other humans, animals, objects, and the environment. For an influential approach to address, see Barbara Johnson, "Thresholds of Difference: Structures of Address in Zora Neale Hurston," in *A World of Difference* (Baltimore: Johns Hopkins University Press, 1987), 172–183.

3. See *Portraits: 9/11/01: The Collected "Portraits of Grief" from the New York Times* (New York: New York Times, 2002).

4. Arthur C. Danto, "The Body in Pain," *The Nation*, November 27, 2006, 23–26.

5. For analyses of race, nation, and ethnicity in Shaftesbury, Hume, Kant, and others, see my "Racialization as an Aesthetic Production" and "Beauty's Relational Labor," in *Beauty Revisited*, ed. Peg Zeglin Brand (Bloomington: Indiana University Press, forthcoming). The expansiveness of racialized aesthetic nationalism is in part a function of the ways ethnic and cultural identities signify race and vice versa. See Linda Martín Alcoff, *Visible Identities: Race, Gender, and the Self* (Oxford, UK: Oxford University Press, 2006), 241–243.

6. On perceptual habits conditioning racializing experience, see Martín-Alcoff, *Visible Identities*, 187–194.

7. Joseph Addison, *The Spectator* 411 (June 21, 1712), vol. 3, ed. Gregory Smith (London: J. M. Dent, 1907), 278.

8. See, for example, Jerome Stolnitz, "On the Origins of 'Aesthetic Disinterestedness,'"*Journal of Aesthetics and Art Criticism* 20, no. 2 (1961): 131–143.

9. Ibid.

10. See Winnie Hu, "A Message of Peace on 2 Shirts Touches Off Hostilities at a Mall," *New York Times*, March 6, 2003, B1, B6.

11. To cite a recent instance of this phrase, the *Washington Post* introduces a special report, "September 11, 2001," commemorating the first, second, and fifth anniversaries of the events, as "Post Coverage of the Worst Terrorist Attack on American Soil" (www.washingtonpost.com/wp-dyn/content/nation/special/index.html). This headline then becomes a caption for a photograph showing the burning Twin Towers with the Empire State Building centered massively in front (www.washingtonpost.com/wp-dyn/content/linkset/2006/03/30/LI2006033000769.html).

12. Peter G. Gosselin and Warren Vieth, "As Markets Reopen, U.S. Seeks to Prop Up Economy," *Los Angeles Times*, September 17, 2001, A18.

13. "President Bush's Address on Terrorism before a Joint Meeting of Congress," *New York Times*, September 21, 2001, B4.

14. See Leslie Eaton and Joseph P. Fried, "Already, Grim Statistics for New York Consumer Sales," *New York Times*, September 22, 2001, B9.

15. Along the lines of what Wendy Brown calls "a fully realized neoliberal citizenry" in "Neoliberalism and the End of Liberal Democracy," in *Edgework: Critical Essays on Knowledge and Politics* (Princeton, NJ: Princeton University Press, 2005), 43.

16. See Pierre Bourdieu, *Distinction: A Social Critique of the Judgment of Taste* (Cambridge, MA: Harvard University Press, 1984) and Regenia Gagnier, *The Insatiability of Human Wants: Economics*

and Aesthetics in Market Society (Chicago: University of Chicago Press, 2000).

17. Sheldon S. Wolin argues that Bush's exhortation to "unite, spend, and fly" confirms the equation of American power with corporate power, and that of citizenship with politically dissociated consumerism and media spectatorship in "Brave New World," *Theory and Event* 5, no. 4 (2002), available at http://muse.jhu.edu/journals/theory_and_event. Both sides of these equations implicate aesthetic registers of identification and desire, including a sense of the aesthetic homeland to which citizens *do have* political bonds, in which they *are* complicit and *do* recognize themselves.

18. On the prominence of narratives of economic individualism in Britain and the United States in the 1980s, see Gagnier, *The Insatiability of Human Wants*, 186-196.

19. Nancy K. Miller, "'Portraits of Grief': Telling Details and the Testimony of Trauma," *differences: A Journal of Feminist Cultural Studies* 14, no. 3 (2003): 122.

20. Danto, "The Body in Pain," 23.

21. Ibid.

22. Krauss discusses Botero in an interview with Steve Kroft for the show "Botero," *60 Minutes*, CBS Broadcasting Inc., November 8, 1998.

23. Such tropes appear also in other Botero critiques. Grace Glueck remarks that "when you've seen two or three Boteros, you've seen them all" ("Art in Review: Fernando Botero," *New York Times*, November 8, 1996, C23). Roberta Smith distinguishes Botero's "usual pneumatic inflatables," from figures in the Abu Ghraib series, in which she observes him to have modified his "daffy style" for the better ("Botero Restores the Dignity of Prisoners at Abu Ghraib," *New York Times*, November 15, 2006, E5).

24. Arthur C. Danto, "The Art World Revisited: Comedies of Similarity," in *Beyond the Brillo Box: The Visual Arts in Post-Historical Perspective* (New York: Farrar, Straus and Giroux, 1992), 46.

25. Danto's notion of reasons, though primarily pertaining to art historical explanations ("The Art World Revisited," 33–53, 42, 47, 48, 52) is not so precisely delineated as to preclude this fundamentally unstoppable yet contingent discursive swelling of the realm of reasons, which undercuts any effort to stabilize the boundaries of the art world, conceived as an atmosphere of reasons or theory ("The Artworld," *Journal of Philosophy* 61, no. 19 (1964): 580).

26. As I reconstruct the scene from the transcript of the show.

27. Danto, "The Body in Pain," 25.

28. Ibid., 26.

29. Danto uses the terms "disturbational" and "disturbatory" as equivalents. See his "Art and Disturbation," in *The Philosophical Disenfranchisement of Art* (New York: Columbia University Press, 1986),

131–133. This demonstrates that, for him, Botero's so-called disturbatory series displays the special logic of the disturbational.

30. Danto, "Art and Disturbation," 131; Arthur C. Danto, "Richard Serra," *The State of the Art* (New York: Prentice Hall, 1987), 180.

31. Danto, "Richard Serra," 180.

32. Danto, "Art and Disturbation," 126.

33. Ibid., 129, 133.

34. Ibid., 131.

35. As Serra and Vito Acconci suggest in relation to their work. See Danto, "Richard Serra," 181.

36. Danto, "Art and Disturbation," 122, 126.

37. Ibid., 126.

38. Ibid., 119.

39. Ibid., 131.

40. Ibid., 132.

41. Danto, "Art and Disturbation" and "Richard Serra," which was originally published in *The Nation*, April 19, 1986, 561–565.

42. Danto, "The Body in Pain," 23.

43. Danto, "Art and Disturbation," 119–121; "Richard Serra," 180.

44. Danto, "Art and Disturbation," 133.

45. Danto, "The Body in Pain," 24.

46. Danto attributes his own understanding of the *European* Baroque to Rudolph Wittkower but traces Botero's awareness of Baroque modes and images to the artist's knowledge of the *Latin American* Baroque (ibid., 24), despite the artist's elaborate engagement with the European Baroque. Danto thereby projects national boundary lines onto far more complexly layered, transculturated artistic interactions. He facilitates a racially and nationally partitioned conception of the contemporary art world, one that he denies elsewhere. See Danto, "American Self-Consciousness in Politics and Art," *Artforum International* 43 (September 2004): 206 and (implicitly) 208.

47. Danto, "The Body in Pain," 26.

48. G. W. F. Hegel, *The Philosophy of History*, trans. J. Sibree (New York: Dover, 1956), 91. Sigmund Freud, "The Question of Lay Analysis: Conversation with an Impartial Person," in *The Standard Edition of the Complete Psychological Works of Sigmund Freud*, vol. 20, trans. and ed. James Strachey (London: Hogarth, 1953), 212.

49. Krauss's and Danto's readiness to *interpret* Botero's work as unworthy of *interpretation* and their readings-without-reading of this artist as a formulaic populist who lacks genuine artistic standing, demonstrate a reluctance to rigorously engage with his oeuvre. This refusal must be read as a manifestation of racialized aesthetic nationalism if only because it is exceedingly unlikely that these two seasoned critics would have

disregarded the self-conscious intertextuality of an oeuvre so rapidly in the case of a white artist of European or Anglo-American descent. Oriana Baddeley and Valerie Fraser register the differential ethnic standards underlying critical distinctions between derivativeness and the reworking of predecessors' ideas in *Drawing the Line: Art and Cultural Identity in Contemporary Latin America* (London: Verso, 1989), 61.

50. David Ebony, "Botero Abu Ghraib," in Fernando Botero, *Botero Abu Ghraib* (New York: Prestel, 2006), 12; emphasis added. In an interview, Botero indicates that "he became incensed because he expected better of the American government" (Juan Forero, "'Great Crime' at Abu Ghraib Enrages and Inspires an Artist," *New York Times*, May 8, 2005, sec. 1, 10). He also announces that "his indignation over war and brutality may turn up increasingly in his work." Botero aligns the Abu Ghraib collection with his earlier series on the guerrilla war and the drug-related violence in Colombia, the mission of which it was to show "the absurdity of the violence" (Forero, "The Colombian Artist Fernando Botero Captures the Agony and Absurdity of a Drug-Fueled Conflict," *New York Times*, May 3, 2004, E1). Connecting the two series in a comment on the Abu Ghraib works, he states, "I rethought my idea of what to paint and that permitted me to do the war in Colombia, and now there's this" (Forero, "'Great Crime'").

51. Danto, "The Body in Pain," 26.

52. Ibid., 24.

53. Ibid.

54. This in spite of the fact that the works, as Botero has said, "are a result of the indignation that the violations in Iraq produced in me and the rest of the world," and in spite of the fact that he takes this indignation to be embodied in the work (Forero, "'Great Crime,'" see n. 51).

55. Ebony, "Botero Abu Ghraib," 12. See also Forero, "'Great Crime.'"

56. Hazel Carby situates the Abu Ghraib photographs in the context of the postcards of lynchings, the Rodney King video, and other spectacles of torture that highlight the central reliance of American fantasies of freedom on the (sexualized) violence and intimidation inflicted on brown and black bodies throughout the history of colonialism, slavery, the deployment of U.S.-trained death squads in Latin America, and U.S. incarceration practices, in "A Strange and Bitter Crop: The Spectacle of Torture," October 11, 2004, available at http://www.openDemocracy.net/media-abu_ghraib/article_2149.jsp. In Slavoj Zizek's reading, the Abu Ghraib photographs bring out the obscene underside sustaining "U.S. popular culture" and, more generally, "the American way of life." See his "What Rumsfeld Doesn't Know that He Knows about Abu Ghraib," *In These Times*, June 21, 2004: back cover and 31. Susan Sontag points to

the policy and leadership crimes exposed by the photographs, which she also links to pornographic and lynching images, in "Regarding the Torture of Others," *New York Times Magazine*, May 23, 2004, 24–29, 42, though without recognizing the full implications of the photograph's continuity with spectacles of racist violence. For a critique of Sontag on this point, see Carby, "A Strange and Bitter Crop."

57. Even if mostly as a matter of image management and a general concern about pornography, Danto does address this question in relation to the photographs, which he lends a paradigmatic status as political artifacts, in relation to which contemporary art's political efficacy is to be measured ("American Self-Consciousness in Politics and Art," 209).

58. On Botero's affinities with the "American Neobaroque," understood as a postmodern decolonizing strategy that displaces European codes and recenters representation in America, see Wendy B. Faris, "Larger Than Life: The Hyperbolic Realities of Gabriel García Marquez and Fernando Botero," *Word and Image* 17, no. 4 (2001): 339–359. Lois Parkinson Zamora analyzes the Neobaroque as a postcolonial transculturated form in *The Inordinate Eye: New World Baroque and Latin American Fiction* (Chicago: University of Chicago Press, 2006), xv–xix, a style that revises texts and traditions through a recuperative reworking (79, 262).

59. Ana María Escallón, "From the Inside Out: An Interview with Fernando Botero," in Fernando Botero, *Botero: New Works on Canvas*, trans. Asa Zatz (New York: Rizzoli, 1997), 30.

60. Ibid., 32.

61. Ibid., 33.

62. This lovability is of a different order than that of Barney, the dinosaur, the Pillsbury Dough Boy, and the paradigmatic Macy's balloon or Disney character.

63. Botero's body politics warrants further discussion, among other things, on account of its dynamic between tranquil beauty, lovable sensuousness, and comical and uncanny registers of the grotesque. Crucial is also the functioning of transmissibility, anachronism, limitless intertextuality, caricature, and stereotyping in the service of a critical mode of transculturation.

64. And possibly also, but to a lesser extent, masculinizing the feminized, as in the paintings representing magnified females in the company of miniaturized males.

65. Escallón, "From the Inside Out," 22.

66. It must be challenged on intermeshing moral, political, and aesthetic grounds. This does not entail that a racially and nationally neutral aesthetic is possible or desirable. On the unacceptability of race neutral, color-blind stances, and the importance to antiracist agendas of altering sensory practices, see Martín-Alcoff, *Visible Identities*, 179–204, and 215.

Aesthetic transformations, at numerous levels of aesthetic embodiment and agency, must be included among the changing perceptual dispositions that are to initiate and support new modes of perception.

67. We must study, for example, the racial functioning of the distinctions between art and magic, appearance and reality, reality and representation that inform Danto's account of art's historical emergence in *The Transfiguration of the Commonplace: A Philosophy of Art* (Cambridge MA: Harvard University Press, 1981), 76–83. His Botero critique echoes the "pathetic frills" he encounters in "the effeminate mimesis of the transvestite," which, in his view, "has no semantic character whatever" (68). The allegedly "pathetic" and "ludicrous" in Botero, the supposed lack of sexiness and the failure to demand interpretation, resonate with Danto's denial of the meanings of disruptive mimesis when practiced as a dimension of transgendered performance. What normative and normalizing conceptions of art follow from the sexually wholesome, masculinized mimesis, and gender binarism that Danto produces by contrast with transgendered pathos? How do such conceptions impact constructions of race and nation in the aesthetic field?

68. My thanks to Norman S. Holland, Mariana Ortega, Carmen Ana Pont, Mary Russo, and Elizabeth V. Spelman for comments and discussion.

Contributors

Alia Al-Saji is associate professor of philosophy at McGill University. Her research interrogates the ways in which race and gender are at play in Western representations of Muslim women, specifically regarding the Muslim head scarf or "veil." She is also currently investigating the relation of affectivity, embodiment, and memory from feminist and phenomenological perspectives. She has recently published on Bergson's theory of memory ("The Memory of Another Past: Bergson, Deleuze and a New Theory of Time" in *Continental Philosophy Review*) and on Bergsonian influences in Sartre's work ("Bergson'sche Spuren in Sartres Philosophie," in *Über Sartre: Perspektiven und Kritiken*). She has also published on Husserl's theory of sensation and on Merleau-Ponty's aesthetics.

Namita Goswami is assistant professor of philosophy at DePaul University. Her areas of interest include nineteenth and twentieth century continental philosophy, postcolonial theory, critical race theory, and feminist theory. She has published in *SIGNS: Journal of Women in Culture and Society* and *South Asian Review: A Journal of South Asian Literary and Cultural Studies*. Her article "Existence Authoritarian: Compulsion, Facticity, and the Philosophy of Identity" will be published in 2009 in *Rethinking Facticity*, edited by François Raffoul and Eric Sean Nelson.

Elizabeth Suzanne Kassab is currently research fellow at the German Orient-Institute in Beirut, with a project on cultural critique and sociopolitical change in the Arab world. She has taught philosophy and cultural studies at the American University of Beirut and at Balamand University in Lebanon, as well as at Yale and Columbia. Her work is mainly in the philosophy of culture, both Western and postcolonial. Her latest book is on contemporary Arab debates on culture in a comparative perspective. It is due to appear in the fall of 2009 under the title *Contemporary Arab Thought: Cultural Critique in Comparative Perspective*. In her teaching she has been developing new syllabi that convey this comparative approach. For a presentation of one of her sources, see "Integrating Modern Arab Thought in Postcolonial Philosophies of Culture," in the fall 2004 edition of *American Philosophical Association Newsletter*. She is the cochair of the Society for Arab, Persian and Islamic Philosophy at the American Philosophical Association.

Kyoo Lee is assistant professor of philosophy at John Jay College of Criminal Justice, CUNY. Her areas of interest include continental philosophy and literary theory. Her academic publications have appeared in *Angelaki*, the *Comparatist*, *Encyclopedia of Nineteenth-Century Thought*, *How to Talk to Photography*, *Mythos and Logos*, *Parallax*, *Philosophical Writings*, *Philosophy in Review*, *Poetry Review*, *SOAS Literary Review*, and *Social Identities*. For more information, visit *http://www.kyoolee.net/*.

María Lugones is a popular educator and philosopher. She teaches at the Escuela Popular Norteña, a popular education center, and at Binghamton University in the Philosophy, Interpretation, and Culture Graduate Program and at the Comparative Literature Department. She directs the Center for Research in Philosophy, Interpretation, and Culture. She is the author of *Pilgrimages/Peregrinajes: Theorizing Resistance against Multiple Oppressions*. She is currently working on finishing two books: *Intimate Interdependencies: Theorizing Collectivism* and *Radical Multiculturalism*.

Linda Martín Alcoff is professor of philosophy and women's studies at Hunter College. Her most recent books include *Visible Identities: Race, Gender and the Self* (2006), *The Blackwell Guide to Feminist Philosophy* (coedited with Eva Kittay, 2006), *Identity Politics Reconsidered* (coedited with Hames-Garcia, Mohanty, and Moya, 2006), and *Singing in the Fire: Tales of Women in Philosophy* (2003). For more information, visit www.alcoff.com.

Eduardo Mendieta is professor of philosophy and director of the Center for Latin American and Caribbean Studies at the State University of New York–Stony Brook. He is the author of *The Adventures of Transcendental Philosophy* (2002) and *Global Fragments: Globalizations, Latinamericanisms, and Critical Theory* (2007). He is presently at work on another book entitled *Philosophy's War: Logos, Polemos, Topos*. His edited books include *Take Care of Freedom, and Truth Will Take Care of Itself* (2006), a volume of interviews with Richard Rorty. Mendieta is the executive editor of *Radical Philosophy Review* and serves on the advisory board of the American Philosophical Association.

Mariana Ortega is professor of philosophy at John Carroll University. Her research focuses on the question of self and sociality in existential phenomenology, specifically Heideggerian phenomenology. She also works on race theory and Latina and Latin American feminism. Her publications have appeared in the *International Philosophical Quarterly*, *Hypatia*, *The Journal of International Philosophical Studies*, and *Radical Philosophy Review*. She is currently working on a book project on multiplicitous subjectivity.

Mindy Peden is associate professor of political science at John Carroll University. She writes on nationalism, race, and the role of science in political inquiry. She has published in *The Journal of Economics and Politics* and *Political Concepts*. She is currently working on the role of chance and luck in theorizing the political.

Joshua M. Price is director of the Broome County Jail Health Project (NAACP) and director of research and education for the Southern Tier Social Justice Project in Binghamton, New York. In 2004, he was awarded the title of "Citizen of the Year" (Broome/Tioga NAACP) and was noted for "Outstanding Contribution to Civil Rights of New Yorkers" (New York State Assembly). Josh also teaches at State University of New York–Binghamton where he is director of the Philosophy, Interpretation, and Culture Program. His current writings are on structural violence, prisons, and reproductive justice for women of color.

Monique Roelofs is associate professor of philosophy at Hampshire College. She teaches and writes at the intersection of European, analytical, and postcolonial philosophies with a special focus on aesthetics, the philosophy of art and culture, feminist philosophy, and critical race theory. Her articles on structures of address, race, detail, and antiessentialisms have appeared in journals such as *differences*, and anthologies including *White on White/Black on Black* (edited by George Yancy, 2005). She is at work on a book, presently entitled *The Cultural Promise of the Aesthetic*. She is also coauthoring *Reclaiming the Aesthetic in Latin America*, and is the editor of *Aesthetics and Race: New Philosophical Perspectives*, a special volume of *Contemporary Aesthetics* (available at www.contempaesthetics.org, 2009).

Falguni A. Sheth teaches philosophy, feminist, legal, and critical race theory at Hampshire College. Her book, *Towards a Political Philosophy of Race: Technologies and Logics of Exclusion* (2009), draws on several figures in continental philosophy, and from political theory and critical race theory. She has also published articles on the technologies of race, racial dynamics in the U.S. political imaginary, on the feminism of Charlotte Perkins Gilman, and ethics of various public policy issues.

Name Index

Subject Index